Game
Development
with
ActionScript

Lewis Moronta

PREMIER PRESS

GAME DEVELOPMENT

Premier
p
Press

Premier

The Premier Press logo and related trade dress are trademarks of Premier Press and may not be used without written permission.

Press

SVP, Professional, Trade, and Reference Group: Andy Shafran
Publisher: Stacy L. Hiquet
Senior Marketing Manager: Sarah O'Donnell
Marketing Manager: Heather Hurley
Manager of Editorial Services: Heather Talbot
Acquisitions Editor: Mitzi Koontz
Associate Marketing Manager: Kristin Eisenzopf
Project Editor/Copy Editor: Estelle Manticas
Technical Reviewer: André LaMothe
Retail Market Coordinator: Sarah Dubois
Interior Layout: Susan Honeywell
Cover Designer: Mike Tanamachi
CD-ROM Producer: Brandon Penticuff
Indexer: Sharon Shock
Proofreader: Cathleen Snyder

ISBN: 1-59299-110-6
Library of Congress Catalog Card Number: 2003109349
Printed in the United States of America
04 05 06 07 08 BH 10 9 8 7 6 5 4 3 2 1

Premier Press, a division of Course Technology
25 Thomson Place
Boston, MA 02210

To my wonderful family

Acknowledgments

There are many people to thank, but from this long list, I would like especially to acknowledge my family for their endless support. Thank you Mom and Dad—and, of course, my sister Stephanie.

This book couldn't have been written without the great copy and project editor, Estelle Manticas—thank you. Your expertise made me realize how much I love writing.

Thank you Mitzi Koontz, my acquisitions editor, for your patience and for helping me to maintain my sanity during that rough start.

And to the great André LaMothe, a sincere thank you for everything. I still can't believe I got to work with you. Thank you once again for every other goal you have helped me to achieve. I don't know what this industry would be without you.

Thank you, Joe, for endless motivation and for that extra push-to-the-limit on every project I work on. I'll also thank your daughter, Mia Nicole, for being so cute and intelligent. She will soon be teaching me the new wave of technology.

Jerron: I thank you for your support. I appreciate all the game and demo ideas that you gave me.

Samantha Ellswick: A special thank you for all your support.

And finally, thanks to Dave and Eddie for their hum.

About the Author

Lewis Moronta, of Queens, New York, has been programming and working with computer graphics for over six years. Lewis has been freelancing as a graphic designer for the past four years through his virtual studio, www.m80produxions.com. Here he also hosts many articles on math, programming, and computer graphics (including 3D animation). You can reach Lewis at lewis@m80produxions.com.

Contents

Chapter 5
Arrays and Objects 103

Part Two
The Intermediate Info 123

Chapter 6
Dynamic Movie Clips 125

Chapter 7
Drawing with a Script 151

Part Three
Interactivity and Sound 175

Chapter 8
User Interactivity: The Keyboard 177

Chapter 9
More Interaction: The Mouse. 193

Chapter 10
Sound Effects and Music 221

Part Five
Advanced Topics 293

Chapter 16
Debugging and Avoiding Common
Programming Pitfalls 339

Chapter 17
Matridia II: The Project 351

Appendix A
Keyboard Keys and Key Code Values 381

LETTER FROM THE SERIES EDITOR

If there's one thing that's on the minds of every Web programmer, designer, and surfer these days, it's Macromedia's Flash! Flash has quickly become the preeminent Web technology, blending ultra-high-speed vector graphics with sound, animation, and other elements to finally take the graphical look of the Internet from static tables and images to an explosion of fast-paced multimedia.

Naturally, it didn't take long for game developers to catch on! Aside from the incredible graphics and sound engine that Flash runs on, there's another major feature that's getting a lot of attention lately: ActionScript. That's right, Flash is squarely based on a powerful, flexible scripting language with a C-like syntax and an emphasis on to-the-point, no-nonsense programming. Now game programmers of all skill levels can take their abilities and imaginations to a new platform—one that isn't tied to any specific operating system like Windows or Linux, and one with built-in support for high-performance multimedia. In short, ActionScript allows you to write incredible games that run in Web browsers or as stand-alone applications with graphics and sound APIs that are truly a breeze to use. And best of all, an ActionScript game written on Windows will immediately run on Mac or Linux, or any other platform that Flash itself has been ported to!

If you think Flash sounds complex, you're right. It's a hugely powerful application with a ton of features and a lot of potential. But luckily for you, the book in your hands was written from the ground up as a concise, highly accessible introduction to the incredible world of game programming with ActionScript. Lewis Moronta isn't here to waste your time with endless pages of theory and proofs—he's here to deliver the goods. You'll quickly pick up speed and familiarity as you progress through the chapters, and, before you know it, you'll be pumping out games and animations of your own!

Sincerely,

André LaMothe

Series Editor, Premier *Game Development* Series

Introduction

In this book, I have tried to take programmers, graphic designers, Web developers, and animators to a place of pure fantasy—painlessly. I have, in these pages, done my best to turn the inexperienced programmer from any field into a well-rounded ActionScript game programmer.

If you've encountered any type of programming before, you know it isn't always easy. For this reason, I have tried to keep the text as friendly and as non-technical as possible. This way, you can quickly get a solid foundation in programming as you experiment with the source code in the book. As soon as you're confident enough—which should be relatively soon if you practice—you will begin to make your own creative games.

Why games? If you are like me, you've sat in front of your game console or computer and wondered, "How did they do that?" Most of these secrets will be unveiled in this book. You will pick up solid concepts that will help your game-programming career using ActionScript.

You'll be using Macromedia Flash to create these games. Flash has become so powerful that it is now heavily used for Web development as well as an animation package. You'll explore many possibilities within the Flash environment and discover what it can do for you. I will start off at an easy pace, assuming no knowledge of Flash on your part, and then will build on my lessons.

I won't discuss operating-system specifics in this book, as that discussion could take up a few books itself. Flash is on cross-platforms, meaning it's on virtually every known system out there. But, just because I'm a nice guy, I will post shortcut keys for both Windows and Mac OS environments in the text. These shortcuts will greatly improve your productivity.

What's in This Book?

This book will cover a lot of ground—enough for you to take off on your own. There will also be a few (advanced) chapters that will open new doors and lead you to continue expanding your knowledge of ActionScript. This section briefly outlines what's to be found in each chapter.

Part One: The Essentials

Everybody needs to start at the beginning—this first part of the book will ensure that you gain a solid foundation and that you're on the right track. These first five chapters will introduce you to the world of Flash and will prepare you for further advancement.

- **Chapter 1, The Flash Interface: Getting Acquainted**. This chapter will start off with some Flash history, and then discuss what Flash is today. All major Flash components and shortcuts will be discussed and you will learn enough start comfortably using the application.

- **Chapter 2, Programming and Design: Concept to Production**. This chapter starts off by explaining what ActionScript is and how it came to be. I'll answer common questions regarding interpreted, scripted and compiled languages. Also this chapter will also introduce the concepts of ActionScript game design and explain the steps necessary for building any project in ActionScript.

- **Chapter 3, The Fundamentals: Variables, Conditionals and Loops**. This chapter will introduce the concept of variables, conditionals and loops. The chapter will begin by showing you how to create variables and introduce the operators that change a variable's contents, and then you'll move on to conditional statements that affect the program flow.

- **Chapter 4, Movie Clips and Buttons: Methods and Properties**. I'll introduce movie clips and buttons in this chapter, as well as the concept of *scope*. I will also talk about methods and properties of movie clips and show you how to add custom properties to movie clips.

- **Chapter 5, Arrays and Objects.** In this chapter, I will introduce arrays and show how they are used in practical situations. Once you understand arrays, you will move onto custom objects.

Part Two: The Intermediate

Things get a little trickier here—you will learn how to prepare special types of movie clips that will allow you to have complete control from within your scripts. You will also explore possibilities that will help the players of your games enjoy their game playing experiences!

- **Chapter 6, Dynamic Movie Clips**. ActionScript has the capability to reproduce objects that you have created in the project's library—this is where all your symbols are stored. ActionScript can also duplicate an object that is

currently in the scene. I will explain all of these subjects and show you demos that demonstrate how to use them in practical situations.

- **Chapter 7, Drawing with a Script**. Empty Movie Clips will come alive within this chapter. They allow you to draw within them from ActionScript with a special set of commands. I'll show you really cool demos that demonstrate the power of this built-in tool, and will explain all of the drawing commands in detail.

Part Three: Interactivity and Sound

What's a game without any controls or sound? In this section, you will learn how to take keyboard and mouse input and use it to make your games complete. Everything from creating your own mouse cursor to detecting the arrow keys to transforming your own sound effects will be explored.

- **Chapter 8, User Interactivity: The Keyboard**. Everything from button short-cuts to installing keyboard listeners will be discussed in this chapter. This chapter will allow you to make your programs come alive.

- **Chapter 9, More Interaction: The Mouse**. The infamous drag n' drop will be introduced in this chapter. The mouse's cursor position will be detected and the chapter will demonstrate how you can use this to your advantage.

- **Chapter 10, Sound Effects and Music**. In this chapter, we get to the really good stuff. This one will start off by rigging a movie clip in order to forcefully use sound within a script. After you master this, you'll learn how to properly load sounds dynamically. You'll learn tips and tricks to include music within a game. Special effects, such as panning, volume adjusting and other transformations, will also be introduced.

Part Four: The Math

Plain and simple—you need to know your math if you want to get anywhere in the world of game programming. This chapter is a light introduction to advanced topics that will take you to the next level when it comes to realism.

- **Chapter 11, Trigonometry Made Easy**. Trigonometric functions are thoroughly explained in a fun, not-too-scary way in this chapter. The unit circle is introduced, and the demos will show off how cool trigonometry really is.

- **Chapter 12, The Physics: Making It Feel Real**. I'll keep physics relatively simple by explaining the concepts through the use of many demos. You'll learn about speed, velocity, acceleration, gravity, wind and friction forces, as well as an overview of vector and scalar quantities will be explained in this chapter.

Part Five: Advanced Topics

Communicating with the rest of the world has never been easier with Flash. In this section you will learn how to manage your memory and also learn how to send and receive information. Web components will also help you exchange information with your users.

- **Chapter 13, Server and CGI Communications**. This chapter will start off with an explanation of what CGI is and how the browser communicates with the server. In turn, I will end up discussing how Flash communicates with the browser and server and vice versa. High score and save-state concepts will be explained.

- **Chapter 14, Memory and Web Management**. In this chapter, I'll introduce very neat techniques for adding load-bars and organizing memory for optimal Web performance. Demos will be broken down and all the dissected pieces will be thoroughly explained.

- **Chapter 15, Advanced Interaction with Components**. Components really come in handy when you want fancy controls in your movie or game. I'll introduce Flash components and show them in practical situations.

- **Chapter 16, Debugging and Avoiding Common Programming Pitfalls**. You'll use the Flash debugger extensively in this chapter, and all of its panes will be thoroughly dissected. I'll also discuss ways to optimize code.

- **Chapter 17, Matridia II: The Project**. Everything you've learned in this book will be reviewed and seen in action in this full-blown demo. I'll dissect the demo to ensure that you understand how everything is put together. You'll be encouraged to modify and improve the program in the chapter's exercises.

What's on the CD?

The CD contains many goodies that you will enjoy. Besides all the source code and graphics, you will also find a trial version of Flash that you can use with this book!

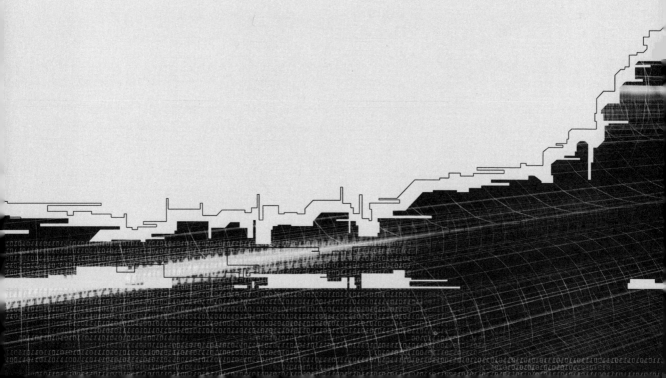

PART ONE

THE
ESSENTIALS

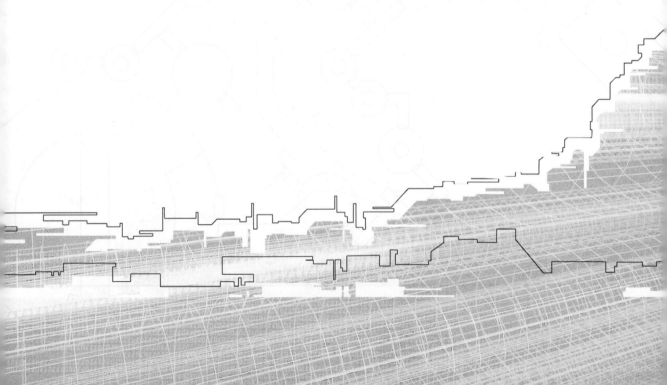

CHAPTER 1

THE FLASH INTERFACE: GETTING ACQUAINTED

Before I jump into the code, you need to be comfortable with the environment that we'll be working with in the rest of the book. This chapter will introduce the Flash platform and keyboard shortcuts that your fingertips should memorize. After you're finished reading this chapter, you'll know what Flash is all about and you'll even know how to create graphics that will aid you in game development. This chapter will cover the following topics:

- Flash history
- The Timeline
- The Toolbar
- The Properties panel
- The Library window
- Button, Movie Clip, and Graphic symbols
- Movie publishing

Flash History

In the beginning, Flash's scripting engine was very primitive, consisting of very short and quick commands. Flash took a few giant steps before it developed the champion we know today as ActionScript. It wasn't until the fifth version of Flash that the program began to display its abilities. Let's dive into the past and check out Flash history, shall we?

First off, Macromedia didn't invent Flash—they bought out a developer because they had a gigantic vision for the software. Before becoming the well-known program it is today, Flash was called FutureSplash. Yes, FutureSplash was its name. Even though it was very primitive, the whole idea behind the interactivity was grounded. Computers were initially meant to be interactive, and HTML was mainly static and not interactive at all. Something flashier was needed to get things moving. A mere GIF animation wasn't doing it anymore.

Flash later became known as Macromedia Flash and made a huge impression on the game development industry with all its applications. Flash and ActionScript have been used for games, business presentations, Web development, scientific demonstrations, and much more. In addition, it runs on every major system known to man! Since Flash apps all run inside the Flash player (and not directly on the native hardware) a Flash app written on Windows will run on other platforms without modification. And so, Macromedia has come a long way with their little application.

ActionScript itself didn't start catching on until Flash 4 came out. At this stage, the only way the programmer was able to enter instructions was through restricted dialog boxes. A drop-down box was the extent of your flexibility. Looking back at it, it sucked! But at that time it was a major breakthrough.

Flash 5 had a gigantic impact and revolution-ized what Flash meant to the world. Tons of commands were added, and a Flash devel-oper was now able to take this nice set of commands and actually type them into a new built-in text editor. This was so much more efficient compared to the past, and games started to sprout everywhere!

Now, Flash 6—which is distributed as Flash MX—contains over 300 commands for you to play with. Every development task you could think of can be done within Flash MX (with ActionScript of course)! You're only limited by your imagination. It's a very pow-erful application and you will be rewarded if you use it professionally.

NOTE

ActionScript follows the ECMAScript (European Computer Manufacturers Association Script) standard. Many other languages also follow this standard, and this is why they are similar in structure. JavaScript (Netscape) and JScript (Microsoft) are both examples of ActionScript relatives.

Flash Today

Many people are not aware of this, but Flash has a powerful big brother. His name is Macromedia Director. Director is a fully integrated 3D programming and animation system which is also much more expensive. Usually bigger commercial corporations use this pro-gram. Even though this big guy has been around longer than Flash, Flash is far more popu-lar and, in some ways, superior. Why? For reasons that you will learn firsthand very soon.

As a game development platform, there seems to be no limit to what Flash can do. There is one major complication though. The issue is this: Games require immediate feedback, and Flash is slow! There, I said it. If you have a fast computer, then you won't have to worry about this issue (only of course, if you're going to distribute your game). The truth is that most people don't have fast computers so this will be a major consideration.

You have to constantly keep Flash's lack of speed in mind when producing any type of pro-ject in it. There is nothing more annoying than awesome graphics and animation moving in stuttering slow motion!

The best thing about Flash is that it is a vector-art program. This means that everything is drawn on-the-fly, mathematically. (Yes, you can import images and modify them, but we'll go over that later.) What this all means is that, using lines and colors, you can create really complex scenes that would otherwise take megabytes to load. It's easy to stay within a rea-sonable size-limit in Flash and you should use this fact to your advantage.

Sound processing is wonderful in Flash. It accepts MP3 technology, and can even load sounds on-the-fly to help keep the source-file size small. The only drawback is that your file size will be huge if you embed your sounds in your Flash movie. If you are developing for the Web, keep in mind that *no one likes to wait*. If, after optimizing your movie, you end up with a 3MB file, you can load smaller games to entertain the user while he or she is downloading the huge file. Besides awesome scripted animations and presentations in games, Flash can also communicate with the server through certain protocols. Don't get alarmed by the word *protocol*. All it means is that applications have a standard to communicate over the Internet. Flash has easily adapted to these protocols and can communicate with XML, Macromedia's Communications server, and even through CGI (Common Gateway Interface), which in turn communicates with other scripts on the server (most commonly those written in Perl).

I know that most of this is probably a foreign language to you right now, but it will fall into place pretty soon. To keep up with the technology, I would suggest using Flash for a certain amount of time each day. Your curiosity and skill will grow if you spend enough time with the program.

Of course it all starts with inspiration. What inspires you?

The Flash Tour

I hope you brought your cameras, because we're about to tour the Flash interface. Take a quick peek at Figure 1.1i

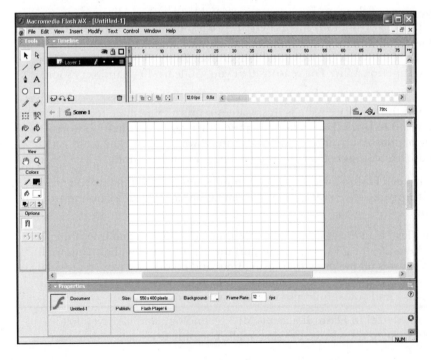

Figure 1.1

*A picture to remember!
Here's the Flash
Interface.*

It looks like a neat workspace. I know you probably went ahead and started clicking around before arriving at this chapter. If you haven't even installed the program because you don't have it, go ahead and install the one provided on the CD at the back of this book. Follow the onscreen instructions and come back. I promise I won't go anywhere.

In the following sections, we'll be taking a closer look into the picture you see in Figure 1.1. As the tour guide in me says, "You can see the Toolbar to your left, while approaching your Timeline at the top: This is where all the action is coordinated and produced. If you look south, you can see the Properties panel. Dead-center is the stage. This is where the graphics are composed and modified."

TIP

You should try some of the built-in lessons that come in the Flash Help system; these will help you acquaint yourself with the graphics portion of Flash. The Help system is a great complement to this book. To access these lessons, go to Help, Lessons. A dialog box that will guide you through the whole system will open. The system doesn't go into anything complex, but the basics are all you need for this book. This exercise is optional, and I don't require that you learn the lessons in order to follow along with this book. You can literally lock yourself in your room (for a month) with this book and your computer and you will learn how to program games in Flash. If you are crazy enough to do that, go get some food before locking the door.

The Toolbar

Becoming familiar with the Toolbar can greatly improve your productivity. Check out the screen shot of the Toolbar in Figure 1.2.

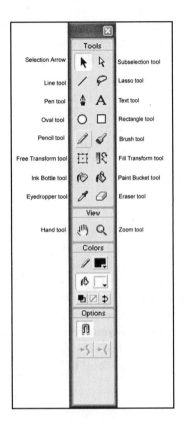

Figure 1.2

Our utility belt, the Toolbar

The Toolbar is a nice set of tools that you will use and keep using. They will be there when you need them and when you don't. The Arrow tool to the top left will be your most commonly used tool. Right now, it doesn't seem too powerful, but you'll realize how important the tool is as you progress through the book. With it, you can click on an object to select it. You can also drag out a rectangular marquee to select portions of an object.

The white arrow next to the Arrow tool is a bit complex, but people who use Adobe Illustrator will definitely find it useful. This is a Subselection tool, which is similar to the Direct Selection tool in Illustrator; it can manipulate points and segments of a line. Again, this doesn't seem useful now, but it's crucial to know the Subselection tool is there when tweaking graphics to perfection.

If you look under the Arrow tool in Figure 1.2, you'll see that there is a Line tool there. Open Flash if it's not already open and select the Line tool. Go to the workspace and drag-and-click some lines. Check out my line work in Figure 1.3. I got a little carried away and tried drawing text, but forgive me, I have a passion for Flash. I hope you develop the same passion.

There is actually a better way to write text in Flash. Flash has a very efficient Text tool that can do wonders with typography. That's definitely a plus if you are a graphic designer. I'll talk more about the Text tool in a minute.

Figure 1.3

Line work on the workspace

The next tool we'll look at is the Lasso tool. As you can see in Figure 1.2, the Lasso tool is right next to the Line tool. The Lasso tool comes in handy when you want to select something that the square marquee (the result of using the Arrow tool) can't select. You can thus get into tight areas of a selection and even cut it away.

Try selecting parts of the line work that you made with the Line tool and then select the Arrow tool. Hover over the partial selection and drag the selection away. Check out Figure 1.4 to see what I'm talking about.

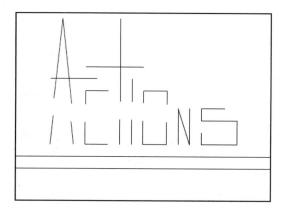

Figure 1.4

Lasso tool selection pulled apart with the Arrow tool

The next tool that we'll examine is the Text tool, which I mentioned previously. If you go ahead and click once on the workspace, you will get a cursor that looks like that in Figure 1.5.

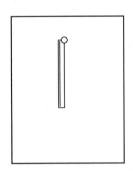

Figure 1.5

The Text tool is ready for you to input text.

Once you're ready, you can go ahead and type in your message. It can be formatted in any way that you want through the Properties panel, which we will go over next. Select the Arrow tool once you're done typing your message. Figure 1.6 shows what I typed in.

Game Development
with
ActionScript

Figure 1.6

Select the Arrow tool after you have finished typing and formatting your message.

NOTE

I also went ahead and "published the movie." What this means is that I outputted the Flash Player file with the extension .swf. Find the GDA_PROG1.1.swf file on the CD in the GDA_CH01 folder, then go ahead and click on it. You will see the movie "play" in the Flash Player. There is only one frame in it, so it will look exactly like Figure 1.6, except that it's in a window. You will learn how to publish your movie later in this chapter.

Under the Text tool you will see a small, white square. You can draw rectangles of any size with this tool. To the left of that, there will be a small white circle. You can draw circles and ellipses with this tool. You can choose a border color and a fill color by clicking on the small bucket in the Color panel in the Toolbar. You can then click-and-drag these shapes to draw them. Go ahead and take a minute to get acquainted with these tools. You'll see it doesn't take a rocket scientist to use them, but it does take a bit of practice to get familiar with them.

TIP

You can always change the color of your vector shapes after you make them.
All you have to do is select the Arrow tool and then click on the part of the shape
that you want colored. If you want the whole shape selected, either use the
square marquee (by dragging a square selection out) or by double-clicking on the
whole shape. Once you have what you want selected, you can go ahead and use
the Color panel on the Toolbar to change the color of the fill and/or stroke.

The Pencil tool is a freehand tool that is very easy to use—you can click it and just start
drawing lines. The tool is right under the white circle on the Toolbar. You can select the
type of line you want to draw from the small options panel at the bottom of the Toolbar.
The Pen tool can do the same plus more. It's positioned right over the white square and it
is generally an advanced tool and will not be covered in this book, but that shouldn't stop
you from learning about it. If you really want to learn how to use it, I would suggest using
the Flash Help file.

The next tool we will cover is the Free Transform tool. This tool, located under the Pencil
tool, will create a box around the currently selected object. Take a look at Figure 1.7.

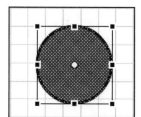

Figure 1.7

A shape being modified by the Free Transform tool

You'll notice tiny filled boxes around the edges of the marquee. These boxes are called
handles. You can drag these handles to shape the selected object in various ways. Go ahead
and experiment. You'll notice that you can scale, skew, and rotate the shape. You'll find
yourself using the Free Transform tool often if you're picky with your composition.

The Ink Bottle tool, Paint Bucket tool, and Fill Transform tool will only be briefly covered
here. The Ink Bottle tool allows you to change the line style of any shape. It also allows you
to add an outline to any fill. The Paint Bucket tool, as I mentioned previously, allows you to
fill solid and gradient colors into closed shapes. The Fill Transform tool will actually allow
you to adjust gradient fills after they are applied to objects.

NOTE

The reason I'm spending more time on certain tools than others is that I want you to focus on the tools that you will need to use in order to test your scripts. Remember that you bought this book to learn ActionScript, not computer illustration. Either way, the Flash Help file is great for this kind of stuff. You can find extensive help on the tools that I covered only briefly. If you really want to get deep into things, go ahead and master the Pen tool. You will fall in love with it. Never mind Valentine's Day.

The last two tools that are left from the group are the Eraser tool and the Eyedropper tool. The Eraser tool will allow you to erase parts of a graphic (duh). It will not let you erase grouped objects or symbols. Keep this in mind when the damn tool seems to be broken. The Eyedropper tool will actually sample any color on your stage and change the color of the currently selected object to the color you picked. This comes in handy when you want to make a quick color shift.

That's pretty much it for the Toolbar. In the next section, you'll learn about another vital part of the Flash environment that will allow you to adjust tool properties to get exactly what you want. And you should get what you want; after all, you're the developer, aren't you?

Properties Panel

The Properties panel will allow you extensive flexibility throughout your Flash life. It will enable you to do things that can usually only be done with very expensive packages. Everything from color transformations to adjusting object behaviors can be accomplished with the Properties panel. Take a look at the Properties panel in Figure 1.8.

Figure 1.8

The Properties panel

Keep in mind that the Properties panel options will change depending on what you have selected.

Go ahead and select the Arrow tool and then select the gray area on the stage. Your panel should look like that in Figure 1.8. From here, you can actually get some practice using the Properties panel by changing some settings. You should be able to see the Background label on the panel. When you select it, the little pop-up shown in Figure 1.9 will appear.

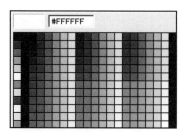

Figure 1.9

The Color pop-up panel

Notice that your mouse arrow has become an eyedropper. This will allow you to change the color of the background of the stage to any color you pick onscreen. This is only one of the many ways to customize your movie. By default, the background color will be white. Figure 1.10 shows my background color changed (to a dark blue, which of course will appear as black in your book).

Figure 1.10

Background color changed to blue (no, really!)

On that same Properties panel, you can also change the frame rate (you don't need to worry about that now, we will come back to it). You will also find a button labeled Size with the dimensions of the viewable movie within its caption.

Go ahead and click on the Size button on the Properties panel. A dialog box called Document Properties will open. Then take a look at Figure 1.11.

NOTE

The gray area of the movie stage can be treated as a working area. This area is generally not seen when published in the HTML page, so you can use it as a work table while you put together your puzzle on the actual stage.

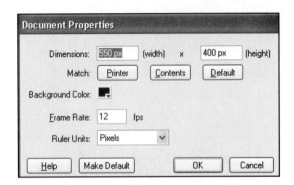

Figure 1.11

The Document Properties dialog box

From here you will be able to change very important settings. It is a good idea to settle on one setup before you continue through with your project. If you don't plan your setup ahead of time, you'll find yourself spending more time on the project than you expected or wanted to.

Now that you're somewhat familiar with the Properties panel, let's put this knowledge to (real) work. Go ahead and click on the Text tool and access your Properties panel. You should get something like Figure 1.12.

TIP

You can also access the Properties panel by keyboard shortcut Ctrl+F3 for Windows users and Command+F3 for Mac OS users.

Figure 1.12

Text tool

properties

Did you ever think that typing in text would have such complicated properties? Don't be intimidated because, though it is a lot of stuff, it's all relatively simple. You can change the font, font size, font position, text box position, and a few other things too, just like in your favorite word processor. Where I really want to focus is on the first drop-down box you see to the left of the Properties panel, the Text Type drop-down box. Take a look at the other options within this drop-down box in Figure 1.13.

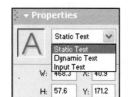

Figure 1.13

Text Type drop-down box

For displaying text that will show information that won't be manipulated at all by ActionScript, the Static Text setting will suffice. The other two settings, Dynamic Text and Input Text, are actually the settings we will be using more often. The effect that they produce isn't as sharp static text, but the things you can do with the Dynamic and Input textboxes are great. If you go ahead and click on Dynamic Text in the Text Type drop-down box, the new panel layout will look like that in Figure 1.14.

Figure 1.14

The Dynamic Text settings

There are two things here worth noticing—new text boxes in the panel, one called Instance Name and the other one called Var. Once we jump into the ActionScript of things, you'll find yourself using these properties very often. I introduced them now so they won't come as a surprise later on.

Go ahead and click around on the text box Properties panel and change the text box type from Static to Dynamic to Input until you feel comfortable with these options. Try using different tools and modifying the different options that you get in the Properties panel. It's really the only way to learn—the practical hands-on experience.

The Timeline

The Timeline is one of the most complex and vital components in Flash. You will need to be completely comfortable working with it because the entire movie organization of the project is managed here. If you don't know how to use the Timeline well, your movie will suffer.

NOTE

I keep referring to the current project as the "movie." This is the terminology used to reference the file that is output by Flash. Don't be intimidated by the terminology. I'll introduce the vocabulary subtly enough so that you will begin speaking Flash in no time.

Before we continue, check out Figure 1.15.

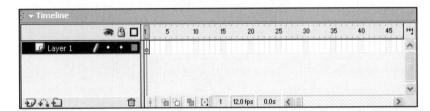

Figure 1.15

Your new friend, the Timeline!

The left pane in Figure 1.15 contains the layers that are in the current movie. A *layer* is a set of frames that can hold graphics and other information independently from other layers. They can be stacked upon each other, and the graphics on a higher layer will always be displayed over the graphics that are on a lower layer. Moreover, layers can be added, deleted, and moved around. There are also special kinds of layers that we won't cover in this chapter. The right pane contains keyframes (a major frame within a sequence of animation), empty keyframes, motion tweens, and shape tweens. In addition, you can also embed code within these frames. We'll get more into that as you progress through the book.

NOTE

The word tween originated from the term "in-between." It is a term used to refer to the frames of animation that are played within keyframes. In other words, these tweens fill frames that lead from one keyframe to another. These help streamline animation while keeping the animation smooth and the file light.

In order to get a basic understanding of how layers work, let's dive into some exercises. Let's create some layers, delete them, and then make a simple tween that can be played back.

In Figure 1.16, you can see that the layer management controls reside at the bottom right and left side of the right-hand pane on the Timeline.

Figure 1.16

The layer management controls

The Insert Layer—the first control on the left—of course creates layers. Let's create a layer right now. Figure 1.17 shows the layer I created. It will be highlighted in black; what the highlighting means is that this is the current layer we're working on. It's always a good idea to keep track of the layer that you are in. This is especially true if you work in groups.

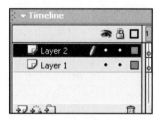

Figure 1.17

Creating a new layer

Now I'll name the layer I just created. Doing so is a bit redundant for these examples but it's good practice to name your layers in practical situations, after using or creating them. How do you do this? Just double-click on the layer name and Flash will allow you to edit the current layer name. You can see what I did in Figure 1.18.

Figure 1.18

Renaming a layer

The next button that you'll need to know about is the one that looks like a small trash can, at bottom-right of the layer pane. Click on the trash can with the new renamed layer selected. You will see it disappear along with its timeline (see Figure 1.19).

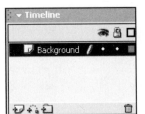

Figure 1.19

Deleting a layer

I have prepared a file called GDA_PROG1.2.fla; it can be found on the CD under the folder for Chapter 1. Figure 1.20 shows the Timeline. Let's examine it and let's see what these keyframes and tweens are all about.

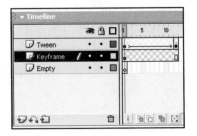

Figure 1.20

Examining a project's timeline

One important thing that you should know about layers is that graphics on one layer can block the graphics of a layer under it. If you double-click on the file GDA_PROG1.2.swf you will see a scaling box that stretches over a circle. The circle is on the second layer while the box animation or *tween* is on the third. Is the picture starting to come together for you now? Make sure you understand the puzzle before moving on. See the screen shot of this .swf file in Figure 1.21.

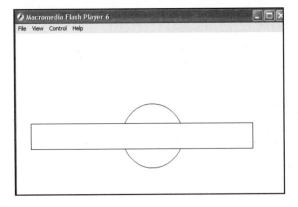

Figure 1.21

GDA_PROG1.2.swf in action!

If you refer back to Figure 1.20, you will notice that I labeled the first layer Empty. I wanted to simply show you what an empty keyframe looks like. Besides not having any content on the stage, it looks like a hollow circle on the Timeline. To create empty frames after this keyframe, select the frame you would like to convert to a keyframe and then press F5. This

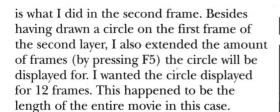

is what I did in the second frame. Besides having drawn a circle on the first frame of the second layer, I also extended the amount of frames (by pressing F5) the circle will be displayed for. I wanted the circle displayed for 12 frames. This happened to be the length of the entire movie in this case.

The third layer was a slightly more complicated case but can be mastered easily if you pay close attention to what I'm about to show you. It is a good idea, right about now,

TIP

Layers can be moved up and down the stack by dragging them to their new position. This comes in handy when you want a certain animation to play over a background or other animations.

to create a blank project in Flash. Rename your layer Graphics and draw a square in the middle of the stage. When you're done, it should look like that in Figure 1.22.

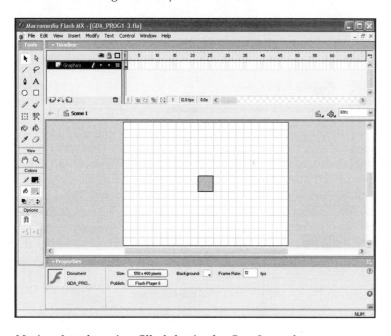

Figure 1.22

Setting up a tween

Notice that there is a filled dot in the first frame because you created a graphic there. Now choose Frame12 on the layer and press F6. Notice that a gap is formed in between both Frames (1 and 12). What this actually did was copy the previous frame, which was Frame1, and paste it to Frame12.

Choose the Free Transform tool from the Toolbar while still on Frame12. Remember those little handles? Drag some of them in order to make Frame12 look different from Frame1.

Go back and select Frame1 and press Ctrl+F3 to open your Properties panel (press Command+F3 if you have a Mac). There is a little drop-down box on the Properties panel labeled Tween. You can use this to select the type of tween that you want. As we modified the graphic's shape, let's select Shape Tween (see Figure 1.23).

Figure 1.23

Selecting a Shape Tween

As soon as you select Shape Tween (and I hope you were on the first frame), you should immediately see the Timeline change. The gap turned from gray to green, and there is now an arrow pointing from Frame 1 to Frame 12 (see Figure 1.24).

Figure 1.24

Experiencing a tween before your eyes

Your file is actually ready to be published, but we'll settle for playback right now. Press Enter (or Return if you are on a Mac) when you're done setting up. You will see your first animation play before your eyes. You can see what I produced in the file GDA_PROG1.3.swf.

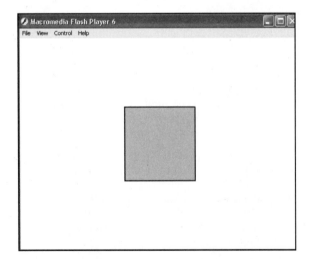

Figure 1.25

My scaled box animation!

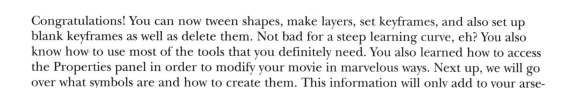

Congratulations! You can now tween shapes, make layers, set keyframes, and also set up blank keyframes as well as delete them. Not bad for a steep learning curve, eh? You also know how to use most of the tools that you definitely need. You also learned how to access the Properties panel in order to modify your movie in marvelous ways. Next up, we will go over what symbols are and how to create them. This information will only add to your arsenal. Let's keep rolling.

Symbols

The term *symbol* in Flash can represent a Movie Clip, button, or graphic. You will use these special symbols quite often. They all have their advantages and time and place when they need to be used. Within the next sections, I will break these symbols down in plain English.

Movie Clips

Without Movie Clips, ActionScript wouldn't be what it is today. By simple definition, Movie Clips are smaller timelines within the main Timeline that can be animated independently from the rest of the project. They can also be controlled by ActionScript and even have scripts written within the Movie Clip's timeline. Other Movie Clips can be embedded within the currently embedded Movie Clip's timeline, and so on. Thus, we can also treat our main timeline as the "parent" or "root" Movie Clip, and the embedded timelines as the "children." See Figure 1.26 to visually understand this somewhat complex relationship.

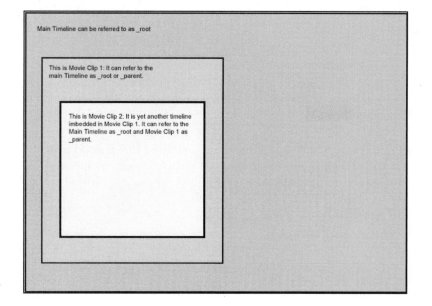

Figure 1.26

Movie Clip relationships

Movie clips are versatile because they allow you to change certain properties about them. We will definitely see this in action during Chapter 4, "Movie Clips and Buttons: Methods and Properties."

Open up Macromedia Flash, if not already open, and start a new project. Create a simple graphic on the stage with either the Square or Circle tool. Use the Arrow tool to drag a marquee over the new graphic. That's exactly what I did in Figure 1.27.

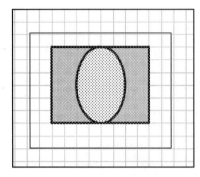

Figure 1.27

Selecting your new graphic

Either press F8 or go to Insert, Convert to Symbol up on the menu. The Convert to Symbol Dialog dialog box shown in Figure 1.28 will open.

Figure 1.28

The Convert to Symbol dialog box

Where is says Name, type in something friendly. I abbreviated the term Movie Clip and added a 1 at the end. The next thing to do is to check the proper behavior. Select Movie Clip and then click OK.

The next thing you should notice is that you now have a blue bounding box around your graphic and you also have a center registration (assuming you didn't change the settings). See Figure 1.29 to make sure we are on the same page.

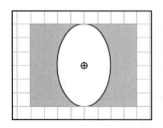

Figure 1.29

After converting to a Movie Clip

To edit the new Movie Clip's timeline, double-click the Movie Clip object, then go to Edit, Edit Symbol. At this point you should see a fresh timeline like in Figure 1.30. Notice that the stage tells you how far in you are in the hierarchy.

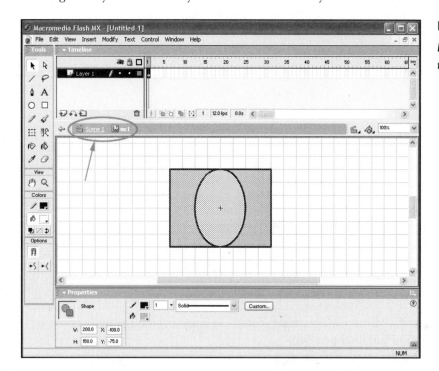

Figure 1.30

Exploring a Movie Clip's timeline

Just to give things a little twist (and to expand your knowledge about tweens), let's group the object. (Please note that you should be working within the new Movie Clip's timeline.) To group your graphic, select it with the Arrow tool. Select Modify, Group—you should now have a grouped object. Why group an object? Because I want to show you how to do a motion tween that can't be readily done with shapes (simple graphics). Once you group a shape, it becomes an object that you can then motion tween. What this means is that you can move and scale this baby without the morphing or distortion that would otherwise happen if it were a shape.

Select Frame12 in the Movie Clip's timeline. Press F6 to set a keyframe. You will notice that a copy of the first frame is placed into Frame12. Go ahead and click on any frame before Frame12 on that layer and right-click that frame (Ctrl+Click if you are on a Mac). Select Create Motion Tween. You will see the gap turn blue and an arrow will appear. You won't see any change in the animation because you haven't modified any of the frames. You can verify this by pressing Enter; the frames will cycle through and nothing will happen on the stage.

To make things more interesting, let's click on Frame12 on the first layer and move our new grouped graphic. I moved mine to the left, as you can see in Figure 1.31.

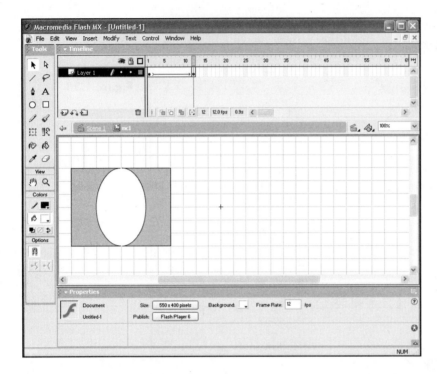

Figure 1.31

Adjusting a motion tween

If you press Enter to see the Movie Clip playback, you'll see your grouped graphic move from its original position to the final position.

Now click on the blue arrow pointing left (which is on the stage controls). See Figure 1.32. I have highlighted the arrow for you.

Figure 1.32

Maneuvering back to the main Timeline

Now that now you have prepared your file, go ahead and save it wherever you want. Pick a place where you can access it easily.

Notice that you only have one keyframe on the main Timeline. All your animation is neatly embedded within your Movie Clip. Now that you are aware of all these things, go ahead and select the Control, Test Movie menu item. You will see your animation previewed and played back repeatedly. You can check out what I did in the file GDA_PROG1.4.fla.

Buttons

Buttons are a very useful part of Flash. They will be our first encounter with user interaction in your applications. I will not go into any ActionScript in this chapter, but I will explain a button's nomenclature.

Let's start off by creating a button from scratch. From the Insert menu, select New Symbol. From the Behavior option, select "Button" from the New Symbol dialog box and press OK. A special timeline that looks like Figure 1.33 should appear.

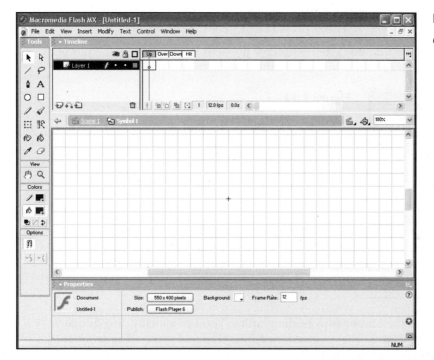

Figure 1.33

Creating a button

This is a good time to discuss a button's timeline. It has a special format that contains only four frame states. These are the Up, Over, Down, and Hit states. Any graphics within the Up frame will be displayed while the button is left alone. Anything in the Over frame will be shown when the mouse hovers over the button. When the mouse is clicked and held, the Down state will be displayed. Once the user releases the mouse button, it is considered a Hit and that frame then plays.

Now that you understand how a button is put together, let's go ahead and finish this exercise so you can see this button in action!

Select the Up frame and draw a circle over the center registration (the crosshairs in the middle of the screen). Once done, select the Over frame and draw a square. Remember that you need to press F6 to create a keyframe (that copies the previous frame, which is Over). In order to draw the square, you will need to delete the current copied keyframe and draw in the new graphic (which in this case is the square). Now go ahead and select the Down frame and draw another square in a different color. Leave the Hit frame alone. This is to show you how flexible creating and configuring a button can be.

Go back up to the main Timeline by clicking on the blue arrow on the stage controls. Notice that there is no button on stage on the main Timeline. This is because you created a new symbol in the library, not directly on the stage as you did before. If you remember correctly, we took the contents already on the stage and converted them to get our symbol. In this case, we created a new symbol that must be accessed through the Library window.

What's this mysterious Library window? It's a very important symbol management system that's built into Flash. To access it, either press F11 or Ctrl+L/Command+L.

In Figure 1.34 you can see that this Library window previews the symbols in the movie. It also displays the behavior and what you named the symbol. Seems very convenient, no?

Figure 1.34

Exploring the Library window

You can consider this as the master copy of the graphic. You can actually drag as many copies to the stage as you want. These copies are considered and referred to as *instances*. Go ahead and drag an instance to the stage.

Now that you have set up the button and also dragged an instance onto the stage, go ahead and save the movie so you can test it. Test it by pressing Ctrl+Enter or Command+Enter.

During the test, you can see your button's Up frame. In this case, it's the circle you drew. Once you hover over it, it becomes a square because it responds to the Over stage. I dare you to click on it! When you do, it turns into a square of a different color. This is exactly what you wanted—the Down stage that you drew in.

Congratulations! You've just created your very first button! I'm aware that it has no other functionality other than to sit there and respond to your mouse moves, but hold tight because we haven't gotten to any ActionScript yet. We will soon though. (Evil laughter.)

You can check out the file that I made during this section in the GDA_PROG1.5.fla file in the GDA_CH01 folder.

Graphics

The Graphic symbols will be the least popular option you have when it comes to symbols. Graphic symbols give you some advanced advantages when using them. I won't cover these advantages in depth because they don't directly relate to ActionScript, but here are a few things you can do with Graphic behaviors: perform motion tweens, motion guides, tint shifts, and alpha blending. These are cool effects, but there is nothing a Graphic can do that a Movie Clip can't. Graphic symbols are simply watered-down versions of Movie Clips.

Publishing

Flash allows you to publish your movies with a click of a button. Don't get too excited, though, because what this really means is that you get to output a file (or files) in various formats. The most popular format for a Flash Player is the SWF format. An HTML file is usually outputted along with the swf file if you are publishing to the Web.

Open up any of the FLA project files that are included in the Chapter 1 folder on the CD. Select File, Publish Settings. The Publish Settings dialog box shown in Figure 1.35 will open.

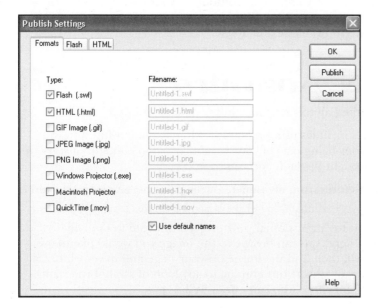

Figure 1.35

The Publish Settings dialog box

Here, you can see a list of file formats that you can output. By default, HTML and SWF are selected. The default file names follow the naming convention derived from the name you gave to your file when you saved it. That sounds complicated, but all it means is that if you named your file project1.fla, your SWF file will be named project1.swf.

To publish, click on the Publish button below the OK button and that's it! You will see a progress bar if it's a big project, but otherwise, the files will be immediately outputted to the folder where you saved the original project.

If you left the HTML check box checked before pressing the Publish button, you will be able to find an HTML file that you will be able to view in your browser and see the SWF file being played through the built-in plug-in in your Web browser. This prepares your file for the Web and allows it to be published as is. All you have to do is upload your SWF and HTML file to your Web server and you're in business. I'll discuss more Web-related stuff towards the end of the book. You have to master ActionScript first, don't you think?

Summary

Quite a bit of information for the first chapter, eh? Lucky for you, the sections are neatly divided so you can just jump back at any time and review the info.

We went over some Flash history and learned what Flash is. After that, we went over the Flash environment in detail. You learned all about the Timeline, Toolbar and Properties panel. After using and learning about those tools and panels, you learned all about symbols and how to create and use them. As a very important addition to your career, you briefly went over how to publish your movie project files. With this under your belt, you are ready to learn some programming concepts in the next chapter.

Questions & Answers

Q. I'm having trouble understanding all this new vocabulary. What can I do?

A. One of my teaching techniques includes using repetition while making it fun. You will end up with all the new terminology being part of your vocabulary soon enough. Just try to read and understand the book straight through and you should be fine.

Q. I would like to import some pictures from my camera or my paint program. How would I do it?

A. This is actually nothing difficult to do. Just open your project, navigate to the File menu and click on Import. From here, you can browse to the image you would like to use, double-click it and that's it. You will then find the image on your stage and in your Library window. For more flexibility, you can convert this graphic to any kind of symbol you want. This will definitely come in useful for those who can't draw well.

CHAPTER 2

PROGRAMMING AND DESIGN: CONCEPT TO PRODUCTION

Can't you just feel the excitement in the air? The excitement comes from knowing that you will soon master many important programming concepts. Most of these concepts will seem a bit abstract at first, but they are essential to forming a solid foundation in your programming career. This is what you want, so let's proceed.

When I first started out, I used to skim chapters like these—I always thought they were a waste of time. After a much trial and much error, I can now honestly recommend that you put up with, read, and absorb the information in this chapter. I can assure you one thing: I have made the concepts in this chapter as reader-friendly as possible, as opposed to other conceptual programming books. I have cleaned up all of the complex "techie-talk" so that you can easily pick up the crucial ideas.

Among the concepts you will learn in this chapter are the following:

- Programming definition
- ActionScript definition and description
- Pseudo code overview
- Programming methods

What Is Programming?

To ease you in, I'll first describe what a computer program actually is. Simply put, a computer program is a file that contains a list of instructions for the computer to follow. Now that I've thrown that general statement at you, let's talk about generic system architecture. This will help you better understand the concepts that will be explored throughout this book.

When you click on a button, or select an option from a menu, or give your computer any other task to carry out, your computer fetches the instructions from its RAM. RAM stands for *Random Access Memory*. This is where all the running (and sometimes dormant) programs are stored while the computer is on. RAM is also the place where your scripts will be interpreted and where the computer will fetch the code.

Once the computer finds the instructions for carrying out the task you've ordered, the CPU executes the task. The CPU, or *Central Processing Unit*, is the brain of the computer.

> **NOTE**
>
> *Hertz* is a measure of cycles per second. Computers nowadays are measured in gigahertz, which clock in at a billion cycles per second. Older computers are measured in megahertz, which clock in at a million cycles per second.

The speed at which the CPU can fetch instructions is measured in cycles per second, or hertz. Check out Figure 2.1 for an easy-to-swallow visual.

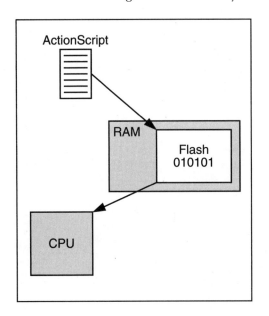

Figure 2.1

Simplified generic system architecture

As you get more experienced, you will learn how to optimize your code so that your program can run much faster overall. But there's no need to get ahead of ourselves. As I said before, a computer program is simply a file that contains a list of instructions for the computer to follow.

What instructions does the computer understand? A computer language is nothing like a spoken language. It's more like an instruction set that can and should be written out in a certain way. This certain way is referred to as the language's *syntax*. The computer will complain if it doesn't understand the instruction that you give it—if you don't use the correct syntax.

A few examples of computer languages include C, C++, BASIC, Assembly Language, and ActionScript. These languages are all different, but once you understand the fundamental programming concepts behind them, it won't be difficult to understand them all. Most of the learning curve comes while learning your first computer language. Our language in this book, of course, is ActionScript.

Computer languages were designed to be understood by humans, not by machines. In order for the machines to understand the code that humans write with these languages, special pieces of software called compilers and interpreters are designed to "explain" what these languages are saying in a form that a computer can understand. This being so, some languages are compiled and others are interpreted. What this means is that compiled languages are compiled through compilers and interpreted languages become understandable to the CPU through interpreters.

NOTE

Compiled languages are translated into machine code, which the CPU directly understands. This is why a compiled program is said to run "on the CPU." Some examples of compiled programs include Macromedia Flash MX and Adobe Photoshop; you can run these programs by simply double-clicking on their icons. An interpreted language it not designed to run directly on the CPU, but rather "inside" another software program, called an interpreter. An example of such a language would be ActionScript's cousin, JavaScript. A Web browser takes this code and performs the actions the scripts specifies, thus performing an interpreted task. ActionScript is always interpreted because it needs Flash to be executed.

Compiled languages have some advantages over interpreted languages, some of which are vital when it comes to games. One of these advantages is speed. As compiled languages are converted to the computer's native machine code at an earlier stage, there is no translating necessary when the program is being run. Interpreted languages like ActionScript are generally slower because they must be translated while the script is being executed. This overhead causes a significant slowdown.

NOTE

Internet Explorer is an excellent example of a compiled stand-alone executable program. It was built with another language, such as C++.

One thing you must know about interpreters is that when you give your code to someone else to run, he or she must also have that darn interpreter. A nice thing about Flash is that millions of Internet users on cross-platforms have the Flash Player installed. The Flash Player not only plays Flash movies but also interprets our wonderful ActionScript language. But Macromedia didn't stop there. Their Flash Player can actually compile the Flash movie into a stand-alone projector file. This will allow anyone without a Flash Player to view the movie. As virtually everyone with a computer has the Flash Player installed, the only time I would use the projector is an instance in which a user doesn't have an updated player.

Now that you have a basic idea of what programming is, let's move on and expand your knowledge of what ActionScripts are. ActionScripts fall into the category of computer programs but their execution process is completely different from a stand-alone compiled program. As we move through the chapter and pick up these essential concepts, I will get more ActionScript-specific with my text. Before you know it, you will be writing and showing off your own ActionScript games.

What Is ActionScript?

ActionScript is a powerful, full-featured language that is built into Flash. Believe it or not, ActionScript has really evolved since the earlier versions of Flash. It's now quite similar to other programming languages like JavaScript, Java, C, and C++.

ActionScript, for our purposes, is the best thing that has happened to Flash. Ever since the birth of full-blown scripts in Flash 5, the interactive industry hasn't been the same. These scripts can control Flash and basically make it do anything you want it to do. And the best part of writing scripts in Flash is that you can make Flash interactive. Without it, animations would be static and simply there for show, but with scripts, you can write code that can be used to make fully interactive games.

What are ActionScripts? ActionScripts are instruction code that control animations and program flow from inside Flash. And as of Flash 6, which is now known as Flash MX, ActionScript was made very flexible and more powerful than ever before. It can do almost anything your imagination can conceive. You do need to be a little speed-conscious, but I'll speak more about that later.

Let's go back to the architecture and see ActionScript's relationship to the rest of a Flash program. Check out Figure 2.2 for a visual.

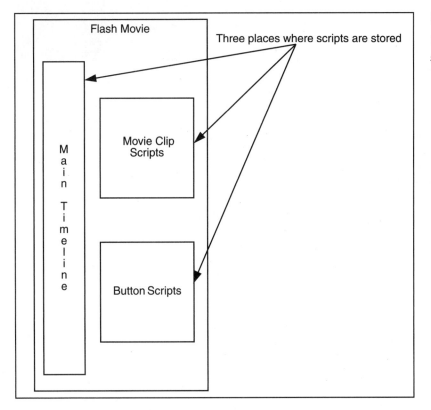

Figure 2.2

Three places where scripts are stored

In Figure 2.2, you can see the familiar parts of every Flash movie. You learned about these in Chapter 1, but just as a refresher, the three parts are: the main Timeline, a Movie Clip and a button symbol. All these can contain ActionScripts and control the interactivity from within.

If you remember correctly, the main Timeline is where all of your keyframes and tweening occurs. A Movie Clip is a type of symbol that contains another timeline within it. The button symbol is a special type of symbol that is completely interactive and has four frames on its timeline. All of these elements can be scripted.

So where do programmers type their scripts? Well, back in the old days, many separate programs were necessary to write and execute code and it was a hassle at times. Nowadays, these programs have been integrated to make a programmer's job much easier and keep all of their tools in one place, and Flash has been designed this way as well to make ActionScript easy to program with.

> **NOTE**
> Learning ActionScript terminology is very important because if you can't speak like a Flash expert, you will never be one. As I go along, I will shout out important terms for you to memorize. But don't worry—after this book, you will speak ActionScript like an expert. Have paper and a pencil ready, though. It's a good idea to take notes throughout the book.

> **NOTE**
> For our purposes, the words script and program can be used interchangeably.

To sum up, ActionScript is used to control Flash animations and Flash program flow. As you already know, ActionScripts cannot run without the Flash player and it is the language that you will be using to program your games in. Let's move on.

Production Pipeline

I think it's time for a demo, don't you? On the CD, you will find a folder called GDA_CH02, and in that folder you will find a file named GDA_PROG2.1.swf. Go ahead and double-click on it. A splash screen similar to that in Figure 2.3 will open.

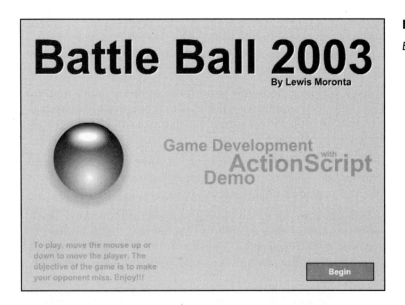

You can play the game by moving your mouse up or down to move the paddle. Try to make the ball bounce back to the computer player. The objective of the game is to make the computer opponent miss. Once you get 30 points, you win. On the other hand, if the computer gets 30 points, you lose.

I chose to make a simple game like this one so you wouldn't be distracted playing the game while you should be reading the chapter! Actually, the real reason is that I can easily strip this game down to its bare design bones. This way, I can demonstrate the production pipeline to you with parts of the game that you can relate to.

What went on in my head before I produced *Battle Ball 2003*? Well, like any project, it all started out with an idea. Ideas for a game are usually developed from a story, but I decided to skip the details of the story for this demo. The story, in this case, isn't the most important thing. So what is? The fun factor! It can't be considered a good game if it's boring!

> **TIP**
>
> No matter what crazy ideas you have for your games, always consider the fun factor. No matter how many pretty graphics and awesome sounds effects you may have, you won't have a great game if you don't also make it fun to play. Otherwise, it's just another Flash movie.

The Idea

Before I go on and talk about how I prepared my idea for the demo in this section, I would like to talk about how you can conceive an idea for your game.

Assuming that you're a game player, you have definitely seen things in other games that you like. I suggest you start a checklist of effects and/or functionality that you would like to program into your own game. From this list, other ideas spring out that you can also jot down until you have a well-rounded idea for a complete game.

No idea that you think of in the beginning is to be etched in stone. Most of the best ideas in this industry occur during production, so don't reject anything that sounds good—the idea you thought sucked can turn your game into a bestseller.

As for the demo in this section, I decided to dig up an oldie that was a hit in its time. This game has a simple computer opponent that tracks the position of the ball, and when it makes contact, the ball bounces back to you. Your job is then to hit the ball back and not let it get past you. If you miss the ball, then the opponent scores. Whichever player gets 30 points first wins the game.

As it's basically a sports game, a story wasn't really necessary. So I went ahead on to the next stage after I figured out all the details. These details consisted of how the opponent is supposed to act, how the player's input would be processed, and how the ball will react to all this battling.

Throughout this stage, you shouldn't think of touching the computer until you have a solid idea for your game. Many novice programmers have the bad habit of going straight to the computer and coding away. These are also the people that end up spending most of their time fixing errors in their programs. If you are not careful, the ideas stage can take up more time than actually coding the game. If you're organized, coding is a breeze.

The Approach

How would you approach a program like this? Well, think of your options. You *could* go ahead and work on the superficial stuff like the graphics, or you could work on an area of code that you think will be the hardest. These two methods of approaching the program are called the *top-down* approach and the *bottom-up* approach, respectively. The top-down approach means starting with the basic idea and refining it and adding details, while the bottom-up approach means starting with individual details and then expanding them and connecting them with each other until they form the big picture. In other words, "top" means the general, basic idea, while "bottom" means the nitty-gritty details. Makes sense, doesn't it? Which approach you choose will depend on the project at hand.

I didn't feel *Battle Ball 2003* should be graphics-intensive, so I left the art for last. I actually went and ironed out my idea on paper. It's always a good idea to make some preliminary sketches on paper in order to have a better idea of what your game would look like in the end. More importantly, it will give you a guideline for how you should approach and design the visuals later on.

Pseudo Code

Besides all the chicken scratch all over my notepad, I got a few important things out of my sketches: I decided that the opponent will have a very simple AI, or artificial intelligence.

But before I present the AI, I would like to introduce what is called *pseudo code*. Pseudo code is an English representation of computer code. It usually helps to write, or sketch out, your stuff in pseudo code before you hit the computer because it helps you nail down the logic (for your program) as you originally planned it in the idea phase of the game. There are no rules when writing pseudo code and people tend to have their own style when writing it. The point of it is for you to gain a clear vision of what you are about to code in ActionScript and it's also a way you can work out logic on paper. Take a look at the following listing.

> **NOTE**
>
> Whole books have been written on AI, but this book doesn't concentrate on making opponents too smart for two reasons. One: I wouldn't want computers taking over the world. Two: You need to concentrate on your solid programming foundation!

```
IF Ball is coming Towards me THEN

  IF Ball's Y-Position is Greater Than mine THEN
    Move towards the ball's Y-Position
  END IF

  IF Ball's Y-Position is Less Than mine THEN
    Move towards the ball's Y-Position
  END IF

END IF
```

If you try to read through this pseudo code, you will see that there are a few comparisons happening here. Let's step through the code, shall we?

The first IF statement checks to see if the ball is coming towards me. In this case, me represents the computer opponent. If it is, it then executes anything inside the IF block.

> **NOTE**
>
> An IF block is generally anything inside the IF...THEN...END IF statements. We will see what ActionScript blocks look like in the next chapter. For now, we'll be happy playing with pseudo code.

The next line checks to see if the ball's Y-position, or vertical position, is greater than mine. If it is, then I'll try to match the ball's position. Stop right there a second! It seems as if I'm just restating the pseudo code. And guess what? I am. The logic is so close to English that you can almost understand it right off the first read. Computers happen to use similar logic, so it's a good practice to "think" like the computer by using pseudo code.

The next block checks to see if the ball is lower than the computer's position. If so, the computer opponent then goes and tries to match the ball's position. Keep in mind that neither of these two inner IF statements will execute if the outer IF isn't true. In order words, Player 2 won't do anything if the ball is going away from him (or "it," in this case).

And that is the extent of the opponent's AI. Did you ever think it would be this easy? I recommend you go to the game one more time and examine the way Player 2 behaves. Isn't it freaky? It sometimes seems to "think." Check out Figure 2.4.

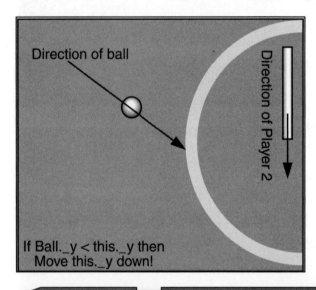

Figure 2.4

We see our logic in action!

> **NOTE**
>
> I know that some concepts that I'm explaining may be unclear at this point, but I just want you to get the overall feel for this. We get to the real stuff in the next chapter and the chapters after that. You will benefit more from this book if you read it straight through while doing the exercises all throughout.

Notice that in Figure 2.4 I slightly changed the pseudo code. My objective is to introduce you to ActionScript slowly in a non-intimidating way so that you can feel comfortable and take over the world if you like. I prefer if you use these powers for good, but who's stopping you? Anyway, the pseudo code you see in Figure 2.4 goes like this:

```
If Ball._y < this._y then
  Move this._y down!
```

This is still not ActionScript. It's just a tease. It is very similar, especially in the dot notation. For instance, Ball._y means that _y is a property of Ball and none other. So what this code is saying is: "If the property _y, or vertical position, of Ball is less than the property y, or the vertical position, of this, then move this._y property down in order to match the ball's position."

The code for Player 1 is the simplest of all. It basically matches the cursor's vertical position. Check out the following listing and see how similar it is to the computer's AI.

```
IF Mouse's Cursor Vertical Position is Different than mine THEN
   Match Mouse's Cursor Vertical Position
END IF
```

Simple enough, but let's go through it anyway. Notice that we aren't restricted from moving at any time. The computer was allowed to move only when the ball was moving towards it. In the preceding listing, you can see that

```
IF Mouse's Cursor Vertical Position is Different than mine THEN

   Match the Mouse's Cursor Vertical Position
```

This basically makes the graphic that represents Player 1 jumping to where the mouse is located. Since you are tracking only the Mouse's Cursor Vertical Position, the cursor's position only allows us to move up and down.

And now for the ball's AI. The following listing shows you just that.

```
IF Ball hits top wall THEN
   Reflect Position
IF Ball hits bottom wall THEN
   Reflect Position
IF Ball hits either player THEN
   Reflect Position

IF Ball reaches left side of screen THEN
   Add 10 points to Player 2's score
IF Ball reaches right side of the screen THEN
   Add 10 points to Player 1's score
```

There's a little more code here but it's a bit repetitive. This repetition allows us to break it down and understand it completely. When the ball hits the top wall, its vertical position will be reflected, making it appear as though the ball is bouncing. (All this math will be explained later, so sit tight.) You see something similar when the ball hits the bottom wall: it also reflects. If the ball goes by either player, it will bounce off that player.

The next section is the juicy stuff. This is where all the scoring takes place. The game is governed by the scores when it comes to winning or losing.

```
IF the ball reaches the left side of the screen THEN
   Add 10 points to Player 2's score.
```

The score is also updated on the screen in this block but no need to worry about that now. You will be an expert on that when the times comes.

```
IF the ball reaches right side of the screen, which means the computer misses, THEN
   Add 10 points to Player 1's score.
```

The score is also updated on the screen in this block.

There is a section in the pseudo code that will analyze the scores and change the flow of the game as the game progresses. This will also be covered later.

Now that it seems that you have a complete game with a purpose, you can begin putting together the FLA file. That's exactly what you'll see in the next section.

Setting Up the Source

What elements does a game need? Questions like this are what you should think of when preparing the source FLA file.

For one thing, the game needs a splash screen. This is the first screen that you see in any complete game. You also need the stage where the game is played. You also need the appropriate screens for winners and losers. Instructions should also be included, for people who have never played your game before.

Before touching the computer, I recommend tracing this setup out on paper. Make a simple checklist of what you need and then incorporate all the elements. Check out Figure 2.5 and try to follow it before reading on.

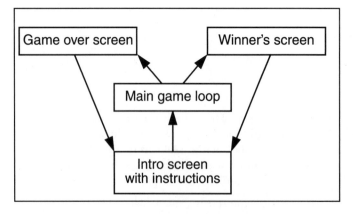

Figure 2.5

Game logic layout

Here I put together what my overall game logic should look like. Doing this on paper can usually solidify your idea, and more advanced concepts can be applied from there. For the purpose of this chapter, I kept it simple enough so that anyone could understand what's going on.

I originally wanted the splash screen to have instructions, so I posted it that way. From the splash screen, a game will usually branch out and give the player various options for how to play, but this game is so simple that no options are given. The user will be able to go right from the Intro screen to what is called *the main loop*. This basically means that the program will keep doing what it's doing until something changes it. In *Battle Ball 2003*, one of two things can happen: the player can lose or the player can win. If the player loses, a Game Over screen is displayed and the player is given the option to go back to the main menu, where everything starts all over again. If the player wins, he is taken to a winning screen and given the option to go back to the beginning and play again.

Now that you have mapped out exactly what's going to happen, you can go to the computer and start clicking and typing away. Everything should be a simple application of all this setup planning. This should be the fun part.

If you don't perform any of these setup procedures, you will probably live to regret it. I want you to like programming—that's why I stress preparation and organization so much.

Writing the Code

If you followed all of my suggestions in this chapter up to this point, you should have diagrams of your overall game logic, pseudo code for all your game functions, and an idea or sketches for each of your screens. All this preparation will aid you in the code writing process even though I haven't gone over how to sketch out ideas for your screen design yet, so don't freak out. I understand that most people are not artists, but sketching on the computer is also possible, and I recommend it because many other ideas usually sprout out from a simple brainstorming computer-sketch session. Try saying that three times fast.

NOTE

We will mainly focus on writing code in the rest of the book. You will actually do exercises that will get you used to the process of writing code. As you progress through the book, I will start assuming that you know how to do very simple tasks like opening windows.

There are a few things that are worth mentioning again and again to the novice programmer. Here's one: you should test your code throughout the whole coding process. Don't wait until you've written 500 lines of code to test your program. The errors will drive you crazy. It's a good idea to keep your program sections about one screen length. This way you can easily trace errors and concentrate on solid code. Once that section is nice and complete, you can then move on to the next block.

One harsh reality when it comes to programming: You will always make mistakes. Don't think that after reading this book you will be an expert. You have to practice, practice, and guess what? Practice some more! The only way to become an expert is by practicing all the time, not by simply reading really good books like this one.

Bugs, Bugs, and More Bugs

This is the time when you roll up your sleeves and start hunting.

Bugs can lurk in your code even though all your code was read in correctly. For example, let's say you wrote up a set of instructions to move your little character across the screen. He's basically supposed to walk forward and at the end of his journey, pick up a prize. Instead, when you run the program, you catch the character doing the moonwalk! You do not want this, because this is a nasty walk...I mean *bug*.

Why can't we just call the debug-inator? Oh wait—you *are* the debug-inator! So when did you officially get this position and title? You earned it when you started to learn how to program. Now how do you put this title to use?

Well, before anything else, you should work to prevent bugs from occurring in the first place. I've set you on the path already by explaining good programming habits.

The next step is to find the bug. When you run your program, you have to push it to its limits and assume that the user will try to break your program. You have to make it break-proof. You'll encounter various examples of making a program break-proof throughout the book and book demos.

If you've been dedicating yourself to fixing up *Battle Ball 2003*, you've probably found a few annoying bugs. I will leave them for you to figure out. Try letting your opponent beat you. Then try beating your opponent.

NOTE

Errors in your programs are commonly called *bugs*. The process of finding and fixing these errors is called *debugging*. This is a very critical stage when you are doing commercial work. *Run-time errors* is another term for bugs.

TIP

It is a good idea and practice to test parts of your code to make sure the pieces work. This way, if all the smaller pieces are intact, then you know the whole program will be a solid composition!

NOTE

Okay, to satisfy curious minds, an example of bug-preventive programming would be how Player 1, in *Battle Ball 2003*, doesn't go past the upper or lower bounds of the screen when the mouse is pushed to the extremes. The implementation will become second nature to you soon enough. If the code wasn't written for this situation, you would actually be able to see Player 1 go off the screen when the player (the human one) got overly excited using the mouse. That would definitely not be good.

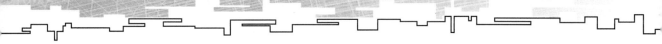

See if all that is working correctly. Then play some more and try to crash the program. This is part of the great debugging stage.

As a matter of fact, a lot of the big-time game programmers started out as game testers. This job entails essentially playing the unreleased game for hours on end and helping the producer to find bugs, in order to make it ready for public distribution.

And those steps, coming up with an idea, figuring out an approach, setting up the source and fixing bugs are what you should focus on for your future productions. Make sure you understand everything in this chapter before moving on.

Summary

I can see you climbing that ladder already—you're absorbing all the information like a pro. You even learned generic system architecture here. You learned what RAM is and how the CPU uses this piece of hardware to run programs. After learning what computer programs and computer languages are, you learned the differences between scripted and compiled languages.

Once you got the basic execution concepts down, you dove into a demo that helped you better visualize the production pipeline. You went through all the required steps, including the idea stage, approach stage, setting up the source, coding the logic, and finally ironing out the code for clean execution.

Now that you have all of this down, you can graduate to the code. After these exercises, go ahead and flip the page. Enjoy.

Question & Answer

Q. The information in this chapter was kind of hard to swallow without being able to program. Was it meant this way?

A. Everything will fall into place. A lot of the concepts are hard to grasp because they are circular in nature—you can't learn one thing without learning the other. Keep on reading and practice everything, and maybe return and read this chapter again later. I probably am repeating myself, but you do not want any knowledge gaps when learning how to program.

CHAPTER 3

THE FUNDAMENTALS: VARIABLES, CONDITIONALS, AND LOOPS

You're going to be using the left side of your brain in this chapter. Those with a curious mind, prepare to lose sleep. I'm going to show you how to write your very first program within a few minutes. But remember, this is only Chapter 3. No *Quake*-style games in this chapter—just the basics that will soon help you get up to that level.

This chapter covers:

- Where scripts go
- The `trace` command and syntax
- Your first program
- Commenting your code
- Variables, operators, and conditionals
- Loops and iteration

Where Do Scripts Go?

There are three places where scripts can be placed and written. If you remember the symbols we went over in Chapter 1, you'll recall that Movie Clips and buttons can contain ActionScript.

Buttons can contain attached scripts and do whatever helps your user navigate or control other parts of your program. Movie Clips can also contain scripts and more—they are one of the most flexible parts of the Flash program. What I mean by this is that you can attach scripts to Movie Clips and even attach scripts to its Timeline. You'll bump into each of these uses as we move on through the book.

In order to program components like buttons and Movie Clips, you must have somewhere to type. Flash has a nice built-in editor, called the Actions Panel, that you can use to type in your scripts. You can access this panel by selecting Actions from the Window menu, or by simply pressing F9.

Before you continue on to the next section, customize your Actions Panel for maximum flexibility. Start up Flash if it's not already open. Click on File, New, then press F9 to open the Actions Panel. It should look like Figure 3.1.

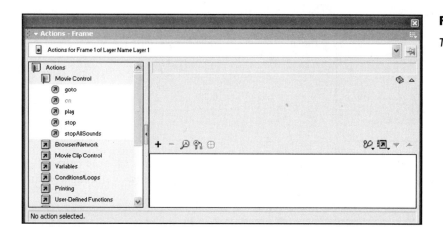

Figure 3.1

The Actions Panel

The panel in Figure 3.1 is set up in a quite antiquated style. What I mean by this is that the only way you can type in commands in the Timeline is by clicking on the commands that are listed in the pane on the left.

We won't be working in this mode for long, as it's extremely restrictive, but let's feel it out for a moment. Use the pane on the left to navigate to Actions, Movie Control, stop. Go ahead and double-click stop. The editor will add this action to the source pane on the right. Take a look at Figure 3.2 to see what your window should look like.

I have circled the elements in Figure 3.2 that you should notice in this exercise. First, the description of the command is briefly stated toward the top of the right side. Next, the command you clicked on is listed on the right. There are no options for the stop command, so it is one of the easiest commands that you will learn.

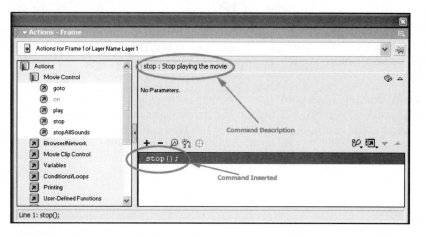

Figure 3.2

Insertion of the stop *command*

Meanwhile, in your main Timeline, you can see that you've made your mark (check out Figure 3.3). If you look closely at the first frame of the only layer there, you'll notice a little "a" over the hollow circle.

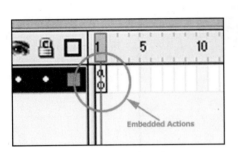

Figure 3.3

The "a" above the keyframe tells you there is a script in there.

Now, let's look at how to access commands another way. Right over your new stop command, you'll see a plus sign. Click on it and you should get a pop-up window similar to that in Figure 3.4.

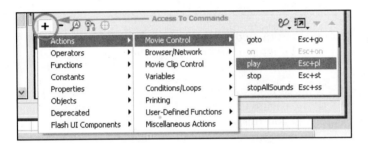

Figure 3.4

A new way to access commands

After you click on the plus sign, you can navigate to the stop command in the same way you navigated with the command pane on the left. Just to catch a feel for it, go ahead and use it to navigate to the play command. It's under Actions, Movie Control, play.

You'll notice that the play command was added after your stop command. You'll also notice that they both end with opening and closing parentheses and a semi-colon. We'll go over this syntax shortly.

> **TIP**
>
> **Syntax is a programming language's formatting rules. Think of it as the "grammar" of the language.**

As I have just showed you, that left command pane is redundant; go ahead and remove it. Click on the arrow right on the divider within the Actions Panel (it's circled for you in Figure 3.5). The left command pane will close. Now you've got more room to work!

Figure 3.5

Collapsing the command pane

You have more room but you still don't have all the freedom that Flash can offer. The window is set up right now in Normal Mode, but you don't want to be merely normal—you want to be an expert. And to become an expert, you have to start thinking as such. You also need to be in Expert Mode.

So how do you switch to Expert Mode? Click on the View Options button over to the right side of your Actions Panel. You will get a pop-up that will have Normal Mode checked. Go ahead and click on Expert Mode. Use Figure 3.6 to locate the View Options button.

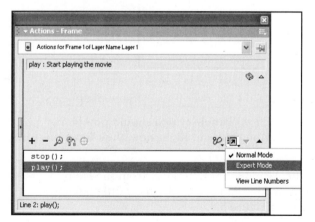

Figure 3.6

Switching to Expert Mode

The designers at Macromedia didn't think that one way to switch modes was enough, so they included a main pop-up menu on the Actions Panel that can allow you to switch modes and more. The button to access this menu is located on the top right. Check out Figure 3.7 to see where it is located.

NOTE

Future versions of Flash will only allow you to work in Expert Mode. There will be no such thing as "Normal Mode." In other words, the Expert Mode will be the normal mode.

In Figure 3.7, you can also see what Expert Mode allows you to do. It allows you to convert your click-and-insert window to a full-blown code editor. You can actually edit our two previously entered commands. But go ahead and delete them both. We won't need them at this time.

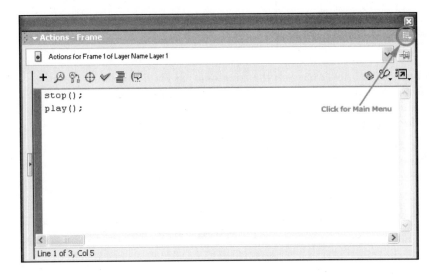

Figure 3.7

The Actions Panel in Expert Mode

Notice that when you do delete these commands, the "a" over the keyframe disappears.

As far as the other mysterious buttons on the Actions Panel—which should now be in Expert Mode—I will be covering them when you need them. Right now, their functions will be useless to you.

The one thing you should keep handy is the ActionScript Reference from the Help file. There is a shortcut to the Reference on the Actions Panel. It looks like a little book with a question mark on it. I have circled it for you in Figure 3.8.

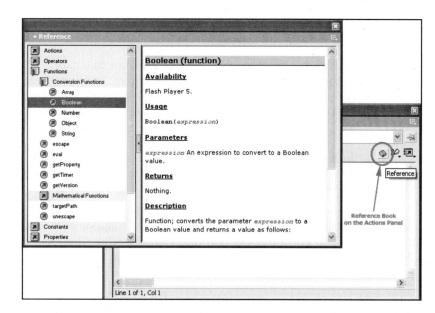

Figure 3.8

Accessing the ActionScript Reference

Once you have the Reference window open, you can find information and examples on any command that exists for the ActionScript language. Use it wisely. It's there for a very good reason—to help you write great code.

The trace Command and Syntax

I'm about to introduce a command that will be your close friend throughout your Flash development career. It is called the `trace` command. Don't worry—it has nothing to do with drawing or tracing paper. What the command does is simply output information into a special window called the Output Window.

Remember the debugging stage I discussed in the last chapter? The `trace` command will be one of the many tools that you will be using to find bugs in your programs.

Now is actually a perfect time to introduce the proper syntax for the commands that you will be using so often. Remember the opening and closing parentheses with the ending semi-colon at the end of the command line? Let's talk about these.

> **TIP**
>
> Always use a semi-colon to separate commands. Even though Flash is sometimes lenient with this rule, there is no excuse for sloppy programming. As a rule of thumb, always end a command with a semi-colon.

First off, all commands are separated by semi-colons. There is usually a command per line, so you'll usually see the semi-colons at the end of each line.

Most built-in actions and commands end in a function call. Executing a command can sometimes be referred to as "calling the command" or "calling the function." This function call is denoted by parentheses(). This tells Flash to execute the built-in command. Later on, I will show you how to build your own command set. Let's look at an example:

```
trace();
```

You can see above that I typed in the name of the command, the function call notation (the parentheses), and the semi-colon. Once this command is typed into the main Timeline in the Actions Panel (in Expert Mode), you will be telling Flash to output something to your Output Window.

Back up a second. I stated previously that the trace command outputs information to the Output Window. What will it display? The answer is: nothing. That's because there is a syntax error. So where's the error? In order for Flash to display some result, the command must include a *parameter*. A parameter is simply additional information within the parentheses.

So how do we format this parameter information so Flash doesn't complain? What's the complete syntax for the trace command?

```
trace("Text to be displayed!");
```

The line above is written correctly and Flash will have no problem interpreting this code and displaying "Text to be displayed!" This is an example of proper usage of this command. You can easily make it display something else by replacing the text in between the quotation marks like this:

```
trace("Hello world!!!");
```

Your First Program

You've waited a long time for this moment—and here it is. You're about to set up and produce your very first program.

Open up Flash and create a new movie project by going to File, New. You should now have a blank stage ready. Along with the blank stage, notice the blank keyframe on the first (and only) layer.

Right-click on the first frame that's on the first layer; the pop-up menu shown in Figure 3.9 will open. Select Actions from the menu. If you don't have a right mouse button (as on Mac OS systems), you can select the frame and press F9 to access the Actions Panel.

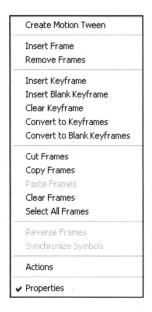

Figure 3.9

The Timeline's pop-up menu

Type in the trace command as so:

```
trace("My first ActionScript program!");
```

Close the Actions Panel. Save the file as something friendly like Exercise3-1.fla. Access the Control, Test Movie menu item and you should get an Output window like the one in Figure 3.10.

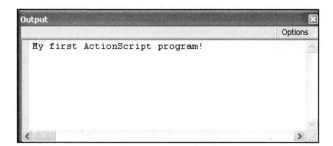

Figure 3.10

Your first output

NOTE

You should be aware of one thing. The contents of the Output window can only be viewed from inside the Flash development environment. It cannot be viewed from the Flash Player.

Now that you have your first program up and running, let's get more acquainted with the Actions Panel. I'm going to show you how to check your syntax so that Flash doesn't complain when you try to run the program.

Go back to your main Timeline by closing out the Output Window. Make sure you're back at the Actions Panel. If you are not there, press F9 to access the panel. You're going to mess up your program, on purpose, just to get familiar with the way in which Flash complains.

Type in the following line—notice that it is the same line as the program you typed in before, except that it's missing a closing parenthesis:

```
trace("My first ActionScript program!";
```

Go to Control, Test Movie and watch Flash complain in that same Output Window. You should get a message similar to Figure 3.11.

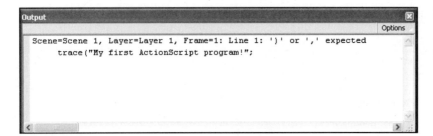

Figure 3.11

Syntax errors were found

Before you go on and decipher what Flash is trying to communicate to you, let me show you how to check your syntax before running the program. Go ahead and click on the Check Syntax button on the Actions Panel. Check out Figure 3.12 to see right where it's located.

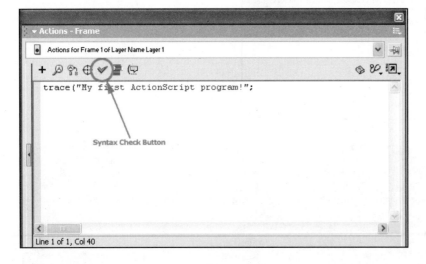

Figure 3.12

The Check Syntax button

Once you press the Check Syntax button, you'll get the message box shown in Figure 3.13.

Figure 3.13

Flash has found an error.

You will also find that the Output Window pop-up contains the same information you saw in Figure 3.11. In the Output Window, the first part of the message tells you exactly where Flash encountered the problem. In this situation, it goes like this:

```
Scene=Scene 1, Layer=Layer 1, Frame=1: Line 1:
```

Flash can have many scenes in a movie project, so first it tells you the name of the scene you are working in. By default, Scene 1 is the name of the only scene in the file.

Flash also tells you what layer the script was on. Our only layer—named Layer 1 by default—is where our script lies.

Our great program gets even more specific and tells us what frame the error was encountered on. It was Frame 1.

The problem was with the first line of the script—as the error told us. The piece that comes after this tells us what Flash expected to be or not to be there. Let's see what it said:

```
')' or ',' expected
```

Here, you can see that Flash is complaining about a missing closing parenthesis or a comma. Check the line you typed—you'll notice that a comma isn't needed anywhere. You're missing a closing parenthesis. Put it back in where it should go—right before the semi-colon.

```
trace("My first ActionScript program!");
```

Press the Check Syntax button now. You should get the pleasant message box shown in Figure 3.14.

Figure 3.14

No errors found in the script.

You can now go ahead and run the program with confidence.

You've just created your first program *and* debugged it. It's true that the program you created in this section is not visually stimulating, but hey, you did it! Make sure you understand the whole process before moving on to the next section.

Commenting Your Code

ActionScript allows you to type in reminders, notes, and comments for yourself right in the program. Why do this? Well, imagine yourself working on a game project for a client for six months. All of a sudden, your client calls on you to make some revisions on the game. That's great and all but, unless it's a small game, you won't remember a lot of the code that you wrote. Even though it's right in front of you, you won't be able to decipher it without spending hours fiddling with it, re-learning how the logic you wrote works. You'll spend more time figuring out how to update and work with your code than actually updating the game like the client originally wanted!

The solution? Comment your code! Comments are like little notes to yourself—or to whomever has to read your code six months down the line. They can help explain complex pieces of code, and they often help you remember what you were trying to do with that logic. The syntax to a comment is actually similar to other languages. When you start a line with a double forward slash (//), you're allowed to write anything you want on the same line. Try to comment anything that you couldn't simply write out. If you had to think before writing the block of code, then comment it! There are no real rules to commenting.

Comments are completely ignored by Flash. They are strictly there for you to read, nothing else. This is why you can type anything you want in a comment without getting a syntax error.

Commenting your code can actually become a valuable skill if you start to work in groups. This cuts down the time that you'll have to explain the code to your team members.

You will see me use a lot of comments in the demo programs to come. Most of the listings in this chapter are not commented because I'm explaining the code directly in the text. Programs so simple that you can guess what they do off the screen generally don't require commenting even though it's great practice.

Introducing Variables

Here's where all the processing of information takes place. Variables are the very core of any programming language. The commands of the language manipulate the data and this data happens to be stored in these variables.

It helps to understand what a variable really is in order to visualize it. A variable is a way to store data that an ActionScript uses. If you were to write a simple script that asked for the user's name, that name would be stored in a variable. You can put information into a variable, which is called *writing* to the variable, or you can read information from a variable, which is called *reading* from a variable. In the last chapter, the location of the ball and the player paddles in our example game were all stored in variables. Your script must *declare* these variables so that Flash will know what you mean when you refer to them later on in the script. When a variable is declared, it is given a name. This name is what you use to refer to a variable. A variable represents a memory location where information is stored. This memory location can have an alias that can virtually be any name.

There are some restrictions to naming variables, though. They cannot contain hyphens, spaces, or funny characters. They also should not start with a number. They could, though, contain any other combination of letters and numbers. ActionScript is case-sensitive, and for easier readability, you should be consistent when typing out the cases in your variable names. This means that if you named your symbol instance "Ship," and you refer to it from ActionScript as "ship," you won't ever make a connection because Flash distinguishes between upper and lower case letters.

When declaring a variable in ActionScript, you must use the keyword `var`. Right after the `var` keyword, you type the name of the variable you want to use. You could end the statement by putting a semi-colon after that, but why not assign a value while we're at it?

One of the operators that you will learn about in more detail in the next section is called the *assignment operator*. It looks like the familiar equals sign. It merely assigns whatever is on the right side of the operator to the variable on the left.

Here are some examples of legal local variables:

```
var myVariable;
var numOf_Apples =  4;
var guestName = "John";
var badGuy04;
var Ammo = 80;
```

And here are some examples of illegal local variables:

```
var Illegal-Variable;
var 8members;
var Contains Spaces;
var 12345;
var @here;
```

NOTE

You can probably get away with using mixed cases with function and variable names but it's not a good idea. Newer version of Flash will not tolerate this and the flat-out truth is that this is very sloppy programming. Try to stay consistent.

TIP

It is good practice to name the variable something you can easily recognize when skimming the code later on. By this I mean naming it something related to the program logic. For instance, if you are counting the amount of space ships attacking you at one time, you could create a variable named `numOfShips`. You could even use the underscore character (which is common practice) like this: `num_Ships`.

In the set of legal variables, you can see a few of them at work with the assignment operator. The value of 4 was stored in the variable numOf_Apples, "John" was stored in guestName, and 80 was assigned to Ammo.

We'll talk more about the assignments shortly, but for now, I'll explain why the illegal variable names are illegal. The first case of the illegal variables, Illegal-Variable;, contains a hyphen—that's a no-no. The second one, 8members;, begins with a number. That definitely breaks the rules. The third case, Contains Spaces;, contains a space—illegal. This can actually be fixed by replacing the space with an underscore.

So now that you know how to create a properly-named variable, let's go back to the program. Do the usual—open up a fresh document by going to File, New. Go ahead and open the Actions Panel by pressing F9. Type in the following listing:

```
var myVar = "This is my first variable!";
trace(myVar);
```

Save the project, then go to Control, Test Movie. Before you study the output, first examine the code. You are already familiar with the first line. It assigns the sentence "This is my first variable!" as the value of myVar.

On the second line, we see our friend, the trace command. It's being used in a slightly different way. Instead of writing in a string value as a parameter, we are passing on a variable as its parameter. And instead of outputting the variable's name, the trace command outputs its value.

Go ahead and run the program. You should get the same output you see in Figure 3.15.

CAUTION

When assigning a value to a variable that is surrounded by quotes, this value is called a *string*. What this means is that the quotes themselves won't be assigned, only the stuff in between the quotes. In this case, "John" is the information being assigned but John alone is the value. Only *numeric* values like 5, 7, or 3.14159 can be assigned without using quotes.

CAUTION

Remember: The quotes aren't assigned—they are only there to tell ActionScript that we are assigning a value of type string.

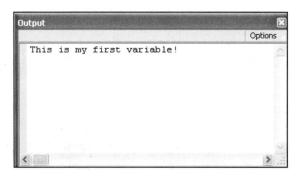

Figure 3.15

Verifying program output

> **NOTE**
>
> Some of the steps that you're going through might seem redundant and a lot of work—especially to get the program to produce close to nothing. But it's better to drill it into your head now than to try to unlearn bad habits later. Trust me on this one.

Now that you understand how to create variables and assign and display their values, let's move on to special operators that you can use to manipulate the contents of variables.

The Operators

In this section, I am going to go over ActionScript's operators in detail. Operators are special symbols that modify and operate the contents of variables—some of these operations include addition, subtraction, multiplication, and division. There are a lot of these guys floating around, and every one of them is just as useful as the next. These operators can do quite a few things for you—they can do arithmetic, assign values, and if that wasn't enough, they can also compare values. Pay close attention to the assignment operator. Try not to confuse it with the comparison operator. I find that many novice programmers usually make the mistake of using one for the other.

Assignment Operators

We already met our friend the assignment operator. Let's see another example using the assignment operator:

```
var anotherVar = 50.5;
```

Here we see a new data type being assigned from the left. It's another number, you might say—albeit a special type of number—called a *floating point* number. If that decimal point weren't there, the number would be considered an integer. You saw examples of those integers earlier. As for this example, anotherVar now has the value of 50.5. Notice that I avoided saying, "anotherVar is equal to 50.5." Even though this is true, the statement is *not* an equation. You will understand the difference when we go over the incrementing operators.

> **NOTE**
>
> Just to review: you have already learned three kinds of data types. These are the string, the integer and the floating point type. I believe the use of data types cannot be learned in one section of a chapter—they must be used throughout the book in order to really get the hang of them. You will learn more complicated data types as you advance through the chapters.

The Comparison Operators

Among the operators there are a few operators that help you compare values; these will be heavily used later in the chapter (and in the book) and are called *comparison operators*. These operators are ==, <, >, <=, >= and !=.

The == Operator

I'm going to speak about the equality comparison operator first. That's ==. Before I show you an example, allow me to introduce another data type. It is called the *Boolean* data type. This data type is only one of two values that can be represented by the keywords true and or false. A Boolean data type can also accept any non-zero number as a true value and zero number as a false value. Now that you have an idea of what a Boolean value is, allow me to finish defining the function of the comparison operator. The comparison is written as two assignment operators butted up against each other. Let's see it in action in the following listing.

```
var temp1 = 5;
var temp2 = 10;
trace(temp1 == temp2);
```

So what is happening here? The program creates two variables. One has the value of 5 and the other has the value of 10. The trace command is being treated differently yet again. It is set up to output the results from the comparison—between its parentheses.

You already know that this statement is false—5 is not equal to ten. So what is the output? It's "false." If you were to type this listing in, save the project, and then run it, you will find the word false in the Output Window.

> **CAUTION**
>
> Remember the difference between = and ==. One assigns a value to a variable and the other compares two values and/or variables to each other. It is a huge difference that can cause many hidden bugs within your program. If you find me repeating this caution again, it's because it's for your own good.

You might not find this operator immediately useful now, but just wait until I get to conditional statements.

For the sake of clarity, let's produce a true condition by modifying the previous listing.

```
var temp1 = 7;
var temp2 = 7;
trace(temp1 == temp2);
```

Type this listing in and test it for yourself. Once you verify this script, you should get the output shown in Figure 3.16.

Figure 3.16

The verified output

Okay, great. So now you know how to use the equality comparison operator. But I mentioned others, didn't I?

The != Operator

Introducing the not-equal-to operator, !=. This operator checks for the opposite of what the comparison operator checks for. It checks to see if the left and right values are *not* equal to each other.

Check out the next listing. See if you can guess the output before even touching the computer.

> **NOTE**
>
> It is common in the industry to refer to whatever is on the left side of an assignment operator as the *L-value* and whatever is on the right side as the *R-value*. I'll keep my text simple but this is good for you to know.

```
var temp1 = 7;
var temp2 = 7;
var temp3 = 8;

trace(temp1 != temp2);
trace(temp1 != temp3);
```

The program creates three variables: temp1, temp2 and temp3. temp1 and temp2 are both equal to 7. temp3 is equal to 8. I have included two trace commands to verify our operator's function.

Step into the program. What is the first `trace` command doing? Read it out loud. It asks, "Is temp1 not equal to `temp2`?"

Replace the variables in this sentence with their values. You'll see it makes more sense this way—the same way that your computer sees it. "Is 7 not equal to 7?" We know this is false because 7 *is* equal to 7. Thus, "false" should be the first `trace` output.

What is the second line saying? "Is temp1 not equal to temp3?" After you replace these with their values you get: "Is 7 not equal to 8?" You know that this statement is true because you know that 7 has never been equal to 8. Therefore, you know that the second output should be the Boolean value of "true".

Go ahead and type in the listing, save it, and run it as usual. You should get a window similar to that in Figure 3.17.

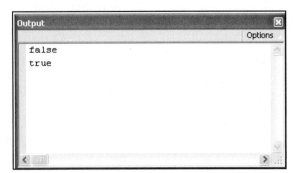

Figure 3.17

Your final output

You're doing well if you understand everything up to this point. It's going to be smooth sailing through the rest of the operators.

The <, <=, > and >= Operators

The next set of operators I want to introduce are the less than (<) and the greater than (>) signs. These operators came back to haunt you from your math class in junior high. But they are here to help you, not harm you. Welcome them.

Start a new project and open up the Actions Panel. Type in the following listing:

```
var temp1 = 5;
var temp2 = 8;
var temp3 = 5;

trace(temp1 > temp2);
trace(temp1 < temp2);

trace(temp1 >= temp3);
trace(temp1 <= temp3);
```

Notice how I sneaked the greater than or equal to (>=) and the less than or equal to (<=) operators into the program also.

You are familiar with most of this listing because you have been dealing with similar programs in past listings. You should be familiar with creating local variables and initializing them with a numeric value.

After creating three dummy variables for the program, it goes on to compare temp1 and temp2. Notice carefully—it compares them twice. The first time, it asks, "Is temp1 is greater than temp2?" We know that temp1 is 5 and temp2 is 8. This tells us that the answer to our question is false—5 is not greater than 8.

The second comparison asks, "Is temp1 less than temp2?" You know that 5 is less than 8, so this would yield "true." We're halfway through the listing—let's finish assuming the output.

The third trace command uses our greater than or equal to (>=) operator. Reading it out loud, it states, "Is temp1 greater than or equal to temp3?" Rephrased: "Is 5 greater than or equal to 5?" Awkward at first encounter, but think of it logically and it makes sense. 5 is not greater than 5, but the question has another part—it also asks if 5 is equal to 5—this is the true part. This trace command then outputs a "true" value.

The final trace command is not too different from the last. It asks, "Is temp1 less than or equal to temp3?" In other words, "Is 5 less than or equal to 5?" This is true because, again, 5 is equal to 5.

So what is our collected output?

```
false
true
true
true
```

The Arithmetic Operators

Here are a few operators that you might use fairly often. The common ones are the addition (+), subtraction (-), multiplication (×), and division (/) operators. As if you didn't have enough in your arsenal, there are also the incrementing and the decrementing operators. These look like double pluses (++) and double minuses (--), respectively.

These operators are best taught in code, so allow me to throw another listing at you. Notice the commenting. Get used to it.

```
// Game Development with ActionScript
// By Lewis Moronta (c) 2003
// This program demonstrates the use
// of valuable ActionScript operators.
// Feel free to use and modify.

var temp01 = 5;
var temp02 = 3;
var temp03; // Notice: No initial value

// BEWARE: This is not an equation!
// If temp's value is 5, then evaluate
// the R-value of the assignment operator
// first. 5 + 1 = 6. Now that we have 6
// on the right side, assign it to temp01.
// Conclusion? temp01 will be added one
// to itself after this line. temp01 = 6;
temp01 = temp01 + 1;

// This does something similar, but
// it's a shorthand form. If temp02
// is now 3, it will be added one
// after this line.
temp02++;

// Let's verify
trace(temp01);
trace(temp02);

// Subtract one from temp01 and temp02
temp01 = temp01 - 1;
temp02--;

trace(temp01);
trace(temp02);

// You can also calculate variable values
// and assign the final value to another variable.
temp03 = temp01 * temp02;
trace(temp03);
```

```
// The other shorthand operators are
// very useful as well. These are the
// +=, -=, *= and the /= operators.

// This operator adds the R-value to
// current L-value and stores it in
// the variable on the left. Seems
// complicated to explain but it's
// very simply written.
temp03 += 5;

// Since temp03 was 15 and 5 was
// added in the last line, it should
// now be equal to 20--let's verify!
trace(temp03);

// Can you guess what its value will
// be after this series of operations?
temp03 -= 10;
temp03 *= 10;
temp03 /= 2;

// Answer should be 50. Why?
// temp03 was 20 before the series
// of operations. 10 was subtracted
// making it equal to 10. It then
// was multiplied by 10 so it was
// then equal to 100. The line after
// that divided it by 2--so we ended
// up with 50. Let's verify this.
trace(temp03);
```

A program can suddenly look long. This shouldn't intimidate you—a game would definitely be longer than this. I heavily commented this code because a lot of what is going on in there we haven't gone over. Allow me to clarify a lot of it. Take a look at the following line:

```
temp01 = temp01 + 1;
```

For many novice programmers, this line is extremely hard to swallow the first time around. Why? Because your schooling brainwashed you to believe that this statement is an equation and would therefore impossible—how could one variable be equal to the same variable plus one?

Remember that this isn't an equation. It is an assignment operation. Remember order of operations in school? This falls into a simple case of evaluating the right side of the operator before the left side. R-value before L-value. If anything were inside parentheses, it would be evaluated first. Multiplication and division are evaluated first, and then addition and subtraction. You must pay close attention to the unary incrementing and decrementing operators. Their execution depends on which side of the variable they are on. I'll discuss that in more detail when we go over conditionals and loops.

As for our expression, the addition operation is the only thing happening, and since it's on the right side, it gets executed first. temp01 started out as 5. 1 is being added to 5—the answer is 6. This value is then pushed into the variable on the left side. temp01 is now equal to 6. The trace command soon after that verifies this. Remember to verify everything!

temp02 is being modified in a similar way. This time, we are using the unary incrementing operator. It adds 1 to its value. The trace command soon after that also verifies its new value, which should be 4.

Soon after, you see the following statements:

```
temp01 = temp01 - 1;
temp02--;
```

TIP

The Help file has a nice table that you can use to learn the operator precedence for all operators in ActionScript. Open the Help file and do a quick search on Operator List. It's a very neat table breaking down the relationship between all the operators used in ActionScript. See how helpful Help can be?

They are very similar to the last additive operators, but there's one difference. 1 is being subtracted from both of these statements.

In the first statement, you'll notice that 1 is being subtracted from temp01's current value. This difference is 5. 5 is then assigned to temp01.

temp02 is being operated on by the decrementing operator. All this operator does is subtract 1 from the variable. Easy, eh?

The following statement…

```
temp03 = temp01 * temp02;
```

…demonstrates the ability to multiply the values of two different variables.

The next four important statements, excluding the trace commands, are all similar—they take the R-value and add it to the L-value and then they store that value in the variable sitting on the left side of the operator. Let's see four examples that I extracted from the listing:

```
temp03 += 5;
temp03 -= 10;
temp03 *= 10;
temp03 /= 2;
```

Allow me to run through the example. temp03 is 15 before hitting that line. Since it's an addition operation, we can see that 5 is being added to 15. temp03 becomes 20. Simple enough, no? 10 is then subtracted in the next line because of the subtraction operation. temp03 then becomes 10. The following line then multiplies 10 to the current value, which is 10. This leaves temp03 at 100. The final line divides temp03 by 2 and its final answer is left at 50.

And the final output?

```
6
4
5
3
15
20
50
```

Just like you predicted! I think you're getting good at this. Let's move on.

> **NOTE**
>
> Notice how I keep stressing what seems to be obvious. The reasoning behind this madness is because when starting out, it will take you a few tries to get it right, unless you have experience with these types of expressions—like in a similar language like C++.

> **NOTE**
>
> You can put together very complex formulas and expressions on one line. For the sake of clarity, I will break down expressions over a few lines just for educational purposes. Once you feel confident enough, go ahead and code as you wish. An example would be: Dist = Math.sqrt ((x*x)+(y*y));. That's actually the distance formula—see how different it looks in ActionScript?

Conditional Statements

What are conditional statements? You already encountered them when you went over pseudo code in the last chapter. Remember that? Remember the if statements that you used to control the program's logic? Those are considered conditional statements. They govern the flow of the program depending on certain variable conditions. These are very powerful structures; pay close attention to them here.

The if statement is a conditional statement that does a comparison. If this comparison results in a true Boolean value, then the if code block is executed. If the result is false, the whole block is ignored.

That's great, but what do I mean by a *code block?* A block of code is any code segment that is surrounded by curly brackets. Let's look at a simple if statement.

```
if (a > 5)
{
  trace("a is greater than 5");
  trace("Now Exiting…");
}
```

So what's going on here? The first line reads, "If a is greater than 5, execute the following block." Note that the parentheses must go around the comparisons. Assuming that "a" was initialized and manipulated prior to this conditional statement, let's say "a" had a value of 6. Just to restate: "If 6 is greater than 5, then output 'a is greater than 5' on one line and 'Now Exiting…' on another line." Notice how I always replace the variable with its value when I'm double-checking. This way, I can clarify what the computer is seeing.

There is more to this if statement than you think. Most of the most complex logic you will ever find is built around if statements. The if statement also has an else clause. The else clause catches everything the first block didn't catch. Look at the following example so you can better understand what I am talking about:

```
if (a > 5) {
  trace("a is greater than 5");
} else {
  trace("a is less than or equal to 5");
}
```

Allow me to restate the logic. The program tells the computer to output the result. If a is greater than 5, then it outputs "a is greater than 5." In any other case, it will output "a is less than or equal to 5."

You can also embed the if statements and also combine them and use else if clauses for precise logic. Let's jump into another example.

> **NOTE**
>
> Notice that the brackets are placed around the single trace statements in each clause. This syntax convention is not needed when you have a block consisting of one statement—it is just good practice. You'll be surprised how many bugs you'll bump into just because of a missing curly bracket.

```
if (a == 5)
  trace ("a is now 5");
else if (a == 6)
  trace ("a is now 6");
else if (a == 7)
  trace ("a is now 7");
else
  trace("a is unknown");
```

Notice that I did not use curly brackets to denote each of the blocks in the last conditional structure. I left them out for the purpose of demonstration, but I suggest you always use curly brackets after your if statements if you are not sure if you should use them or not—you will soon get the hang of creating your own code blocks. Soon enough, I will show you a better way to construct a long conditional structure with the switch statement.

There are four tests in this structure. If any of them are true, they end up doing the same thing—outputting what a is equal to. The first one tests to see if a is equal to 5. If it is, Flash outputs 5. If a is not equal to 5, the code then tests to see if a is equal to 6. If a is 6, Flash lets you know by outputting; if not, Flash goes on to test if a is equal to 7. If a is not equal to 7, the program flows to the final else statement. This statement is executed if the answer was none of the above. Follow me so far?

Aside from mixing and matching, you're also allowed to combine comparisons with logical operators. These are the and (&&) and or (||) operators. They don't make too much sense in text, so let's see them in action.

```
if ( (temp01 == 1) && (temp02 == 5))
{
  trace("temp01 is equal to 1 and temp02 is equal to 5.");
}
if ( (temp01==1) || (temp02 == 5))
{
  trace("Either temp01 is equal to 1 or temp02 is equal to 5");
}
```

If you understand these without my explaining them, you are close to becoming an expert. If not, don't worry.

Notice the wording of the output. I gave you clues to as to *when* the if statements evaluate to true. The and conditional statement won't execute its block unless both parts of the conditions are true. The or conditional statement will execute its block if either one of the statements is true. You'll create a need for these once you start letting your imagination run wild.

The switch Statement

The switch statement is a good alternative when it comes to long conditional structures. It is not as popular as the if statement, but it will come in handy when you need it. Let's look at an example.

```
switch (tempVar) {
  case 6:
    trace("tempVar is 6.");
    break;
  case 7:
    trace("tempVar is 7.");
    break;
  case 8:
    trace("tempVar is 8.");
    break;
  default:
    trace("tempVar is unknown.");
}
```

Don't be alarmed. The switch statement is just as simple as the if statement, though it looks more complex. Once you understand its anatomy, you will be comfortable using it. Allow me to break it down for you.

In order to set up the structure, you must type out the keyword switch and within its parentheses you must type in the variable that is going to be tested. A special block follows the keyword and variable—it is a case block that uses special keywords that work together with the rest of the statement.

The break statement you see in the code forces the code to jump out of the current structure—in this case, the switch statement. If the break statement wasn't used, Flash would keep executing the consecutive commands that follow.

TIP

Don't leave out the break statement at the end of each case unless you know what you are doing. If you forget it, it will execute all the cases after the one it matched. Be careful!

The case keyword is followed by the value that we are testing against. In our example, tempVar is tested to see if it is equal to 6 in the first case statement. If it is, it executes everything after the case statement until it reaches the break statement. Once it does, it exits the structure and continues with the rest of the program. If it's not the current case, it goes on to the next case until it finds a match. If it doesn't find a match, it jumps to the default segment. This is the "catch-all" statement that handles all the values that weren't covered.

NOTE

Notice that all cases in the switch statement end in a colon.

Now that you have a good solid foundation with conditional statements, you can move on to loop structures. Don't worry about the switch statement too much. It doesn't get any more complicated than what you saw here. Most statements require exposure in order for you to become completely comfortable with them.

Loops and Iteration

Loops can be very difficult to understand if you don't pay attention to what they're made out of—conditional statements. Loops are general statements that repeat a block of code if the specified condition is true. If the condition is always true, you'll end up with an infinite loop and your program will never end.

ActionScript has three major kinds of built-in loops (there are others, but they do not concern us now). There is the `for` loop, which executes a block for a certain number of iterations; the `while` loop, which executes until a certain condition is met; and a modified version of the `while` loop, the `do while` loop, which executes at least once and then terminates when a certain condition is met.

Let's go over a `for` loop example first. It is the most complicated of all loops because it combines many smaller statements in one place. Let's see the example.

```
for (var index = 0; index < 10; index++) {
  trace (index);
}
```

Before breaking into this loop, take a look at the output:

```
0
1
2
3
4
5
6
7
8
9
```

Interesting no? Quite automated if you ask me. You achieved this output with two to three lines of code instead of printing out each number individually. Not bad. So what's really going on here?

The `for` loop, as I said before, repeats its code block a certain number of times or until a condition is met. Between its parentheses, it contains three statements. The first one initializes a variable, the second one defines the condition that has to be met in order to end the loop, and the third one modifies the variable—usually incrementing or decrementing it by the respective operators. Look at the following prototype:

```
for (initialize variable; condition; variable modification){ blockOfCode; }
```

We followed it exactly in the previous example. In the first part of the `for` loop, the program initializes the `index` variable. The second one states, "Execute the block of code while `index` is less than 10." Meanwhile, the third piece is incrementing `index` by 1 after every iteration. This causes `index` to eventually be greater than or equal to 10, making the condition false and therefore ending the loop. In our example, I have included a trace command that outputs what index is during the execution of each iteration, so that you can better understand what's going on.

When would you use such a loop? Let's say you wanted to move a car 10 pixels to the right every frame for 100 pixels. What would you do? You would write a loop that moves the car 10 pixels on every iteration 10 times. Is it sinking in?

But what if you don't know how many times you need to loop? What if you need to loop until a condition is met regardless of the number of times you need to loop? This would be a perfect time to use the while loop. Here's an example.

```
var tempVar = 0;
while (tempVar < 10) {
  trace("Look at me!");
  tempVar++;
}
```

It does exactly how it reads: "while tempVar is less than 10, execute the following block." Notice that here we are modifying the variable in the block instead of the parentheses. If we forget to do this, we will have an infinite loop. Just because it's infinite doesn't mean we can't break out of it—all it means is that if we want to get out, we need to use the break command.

```
while (1) {
  if (1) break;
}
```

The last example is kind of awkward, isn't it? There are no conditions in any of the parentheses. What I effectively did here is introduce how to use the break command in a loop and demonstrated another way to use a "true" condition to create an infinite state.

Let's step through it. If you remember back when I spoke about Boolean values, I also mentioned that any non-zero value is equivalent to a "true" Boolean value. So guess what? Since this while statement is forever true, it will forever execute.

But wait! There's more! If a condition is always 1, it means it's always true. That means that in this example, that break command will always execute, thus exiting us from that while loop—how cool is that?

Now what if you needed the loop to execute at least once before testing any conditions? ActionScript is more than prepared. It has the do while loop at your disposal!

```
do {
  trace("Print this out");
} while (b < 10);
```

So what does this loop do? It enters and executes the block and *then* tests for a condition. In this case, we will loop while b is less than 10. If you look closely, it will always be 10, because we are not modifying b in any way. Therefore, this will also be an infinite loop.

I gave you some tricky examples in this section, for the sole purpose of developing that sixth sense for programming and error-finding. As we wrap up this looping section, go ahead and loop through it just once more. Doing so will help solidify your knowledge of these wonderful structures. Once you're done, finish up and take a break. You deserve it.

Summary

Doesn't that learning sensation feel good? You picked up quite a few things in this chapter. You learned all about where scripts go. You made a friend, the trace command. You know now how to comment code. You even put together your first program!

Aside from the basics, you started learning the programming fundamentals that most every computer language is made out of. You learned the concepts of variables, conditions, conditional statements, and loops. This knowledge has given you new powers that will help you advance your career as an ActionScript game programmer (or any other variation of that title).

Questions & Answers

Q. This stuff is hard. I understand the concepts but I keep getting errors when I try to write my own programs. What can you suggest?

A. Don't worry about it. Every programmer gets good by learning from his or her own mistakes. You will become very detail-oriented as you spend more time programming in the environment. Most things snap into comfort only after fixing small mistakes. Make sure you re-read this chapter until you understand where every colon, semi-colon, curly bracket, and assignment operator goes and how they are used. I know it's initially overwhelming, but exposure and repetition is the only way to go. And that's the hard truth.

Q. I've been stuck on this chapter because I can't get anything to work. Help!

A. Most of the examples in this chapter are for demonstration purposes only. The truth is that you haven't seen any *real* game code yet, but you have encountered a real game. *Take Battle Ball 2003* and look at the code in this project. In here, you will find working code that you can relate to this chapter. See if you can modify some of it and create your own version of the game with what you have learned in this chapter. This will help you reinforce what you have learned here while giving you real world experience working with a real game.

CHAPTER 4

MOVIE CLIPS AND BUTTONS: METHODS AND PROPERTIES

You've already been introduced to Movie Clips and buttons, but guess what? There's more! I hate to sound like a cheap salesman, but the truth is that you must buy everything in this chapter or else you will be lost for the rest of the book. I'm about to explain the bare bones of any real Flash ActionScript program. Here's what's in store in this chapter:

- Programmable buttons
- All about Movie Clips
- Custom functions
- Movie clip navigation

Programmable Buttons

As early as Chapter 1, you created your very first button. You learned all about the Up, Over, Down and Hit states. The button you created even reacted to your mouse position—if you were over it, it displayed the Over state;—if you clicked it, it displayed the Down state; and so on. We had one issue though: That was the extent of the button's functionality. In this section, I will explain how to program any button that you might need.

Flash has a Common Library that contains many stock symbols such as buttons, graphics and sound effects and they allow you to save time and get to your programming right away. This stored-away Common Library can be accessed through the Windows menu.

Click on Windows, Common Library, Buttons. The Library window, shown in Figure 4.1, will open.

Figure 4.1

Common button library

Remember that to use something from the library, you have to drag it to your workspace. From the Library window menu, select Arcade buttons, arcade button – orange. Go ahead and drag it to the stage. This little shortcut just allowed you to skip the whole process of making a button yourself; now let's move on to the programming process.

Select the button on the stage with the Selection tool. Either right-click it and select Actions or just press F9. Now that you have a blank screen in front of you, go ahead and set it up so that every time you click on the button, you load an external Movie Clip while streaming audio in the background—just kidding. We'll do that later. For now, make sure you have the Actions Panel open with your button selected and just check out the following listing.

```
on (release) {
  trace("You have clicked the button!");
}
```

You're looking at a new type of code block. This code block is called an *on handler*—partly because it begins with the on keyword (duh!). The on handler can be tricky to understand at first, but it's fairly easy once you get the hang of it. This on handler makes the button execute the code within this block every time the user releases the mouse button (from a click). Makes sense so far?

In other words, the button looks for code that's handling these events. If they are not there, nothing happens. In this case, we defined the on release event. The only time the on release event can happen is right after the user releases the mouse button after initially clicking on your Flash button.

We all know what the trace command does—outputs information to the Output Window. In this case, when the user releases from his mouse click, a message will be sent to the Output Window. Let's test this out. After typing the listing above into the button's Actions Panel, go ahead and save the file. Remember to name it something friendly and also put it where you can access it easily—like on your desktop.

Test the movie by pressing Ctrl+Enter (or Command+Return). You should get a blank white screen with an orange button in the middle. Click and hold on that button. Notice that nothing happens. Once you release the button, you should get a message in your Output Window. Click and experiment a few times. You should have a screen similar to that in Figure 4.2 once you're done.

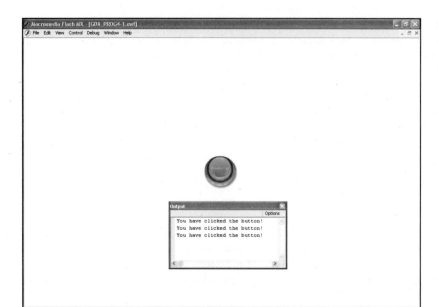

Figure 4.2

Testing the on release
handler

I have saved the project file as GDA_PROG4.1.fla on the CD. If you don't feel like typing in the long listing in this section, go ahead and play with the project file I named above.

Let's change this on release handler into an on press handler so that you can get a feel for the different events to which you can assign code. See the following listing for the modifications. This program has been saved as GDA_PROG4.2.fla on the CD. Again, try pressing and holding the button and then releasing it while observing all the stages of the code execution.

```
on (release) {
  trace("You have released the button!");
}

on (press) {
  trace("You have pressed the button!");
}
```

So a block is executed once you press the button and another block is executed one you release the button—what's the big deal? Flexibility! Flexibility is everything when it comes to a computer language and ActionScript is very flexible. Remember that the more control you have, the more you will be able to tell the computer to do.

We'll revisit buttons after the next section on Movie Clips. As I said before, most of this knowledge is circular—you won't completely understand one thing unless you understand the next. There's no need to worry too much about this because I knocked all the difficult stuff out of the way for you.

In the next section you'll see how you can easily control a Movie Clip from a button's handler. It's simple yet powerful functionality. Think of the possibilities when you can assign any functionality you want to your buttons!

All About MCs

I'm going to spend a lot of this chapter discussing MCs (Movie Clips). Movie Clips have special built-in variables—I'll refer to them as *properties*. MCs also have built-in definable code blocks—we'll call these *methods*.

Mastering the manipulation of properties and methods is the key to understanding Movie Clips thoroughly. Before moving on to any demos, let's revisit MC structure while discussing the concept of *scope. Scope,* in Flash, refers to what can be "seen" from a symbol or timeline. It can also refer to area where the variable is known and can be referenced. The definition of scope isn't any clearer than that in the Flash documentation, and the truth is that you won't fully understand scope until you are through with this section. See Figure 4.3.

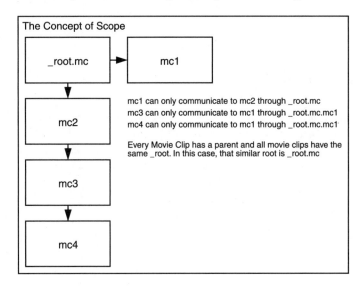

Figure 4.3

Movie Clip scope

As you can see from Figure 4.3, Movie Clips can be embedded within one another. These Movie Clips have special relationships to each other once they are arranged in a hierarchical structure. I'll be referring to this hierarchy as I discuss scope.

What does all this mumbo-jumbo mean? Allow me to offer an example to compliment the visual in Figure 4.3. Let's say you have a master Movie Clip. *This could easily be your main timeline.* Remember that your main Timeline behaves like a giant Movie Clip itself—this is why I can refer to it as a master Movie Clip. Anyway, let's say you created two Movie Clips, MC1 and MC2. Let's also assume that MC2 has another embedded Movie Clip called MC3.

> **TIP**
>
> Sometimes when designing a really complicated hierarchy, you might lose the thread and tangle yourself trying to memorize where everything goes. Use scrap paper if you need to. It will keep you organized and sane. You'll be surprised how much time it can save you.

Now that you understand the basics of scope, you should be comfortable with the fact that if you are within *scope*, you can access built-in variables or properties of any other Movie Clip in your project. This means that one Movie Clip can read and write to variables of another Movie Clip if the Movie Clip knows how to access it through proper scope.

Suppose that you wanted MC1 to reference MC3. MC1 can't do so directly; it has to ask its parent, which is the main Timeline, to reference MC2. From MC2, you can then get to MC3. How would you represent this in code? Instead of using pseudo code, have my comments assist you.

```
// This code is in the MC1 Movie Clip.
// If MC1 were to refer to a Movie Clip not
// within its domain or scope, then it would
// have to use a specific reference to it.
_root.MC2.MC3.someVar = 50;
```

What you just experienced there was *dot notation*. First, allow me to explain what dot notation is. *Dot notation* is when you use an object to refer to another object or property of that object. For example, in the preceding listing, the object that we are using to access is root. root represents the main Timeline, and through this alias, it can be treated like a Movie Clip (as I said before). Anyway, every time you use a dot (a period) after this alias, you can reference another object that is embedded within it. In this example, MC2 is embedded in _root, so it's safe to write _root.MC2 to reference MC2 from anywhere. Since we are looking for a variable (a.k.a. *property* when speaking about objects such as Movie Clips) that belongs to another object that's embedded within MC2, all you have to do is reference the object with another dot just like I did in the listing.

After that nice explanation, you now can see that the listing is taking a variable (or property) declared in another Movie Clip and assigning it a value. This could easily be the number of ammo left in your fighter jet or the number of energy reserved for your shields.

Now, what is really happening here? _root is a special keyword that is used to refer to the main Timeline from anywhere, or whatever scope. MC2 was built on _root, so to refer to MC2, we can say _root.MC2. To refer to MC3 that was built on MC2, refer to MC2 as _root.MC2.MC3. Get it? This is dot notation.

MC Properties

As I mentioned before, Movie Clips have built-in *properties*—variables that you can modify to change the appearance of the Movie Clip.

Let's set up a small scene. Start a new Flash project. Create three layers and name them Background, Buttons, and Labels, respectively. As the background, draw a square and decorate it if you want to, but don't waste too much time with this.

For the Buttons layer, open up the stock button Library window—select Window, Common Libraries, Buttons. Drag out four buttons and place them wherever you think is nice. Use your artistic senses for that one. On the third layer, the Labels layer, use the Text tool to label the buttons. I labeled them Left, Right, + and -. Make sure the text boxes are in Static Text mode in the Properties panel.

I saved what I did as file GDA_PROG4.3a.fla on the CD. Work with that file if you want to continue with what I put together for you.

Create a new layer and name it Movie Clip. I saved this file as GDA_PROG4.3b.fla before taking the screenshot in Figure 4.4.

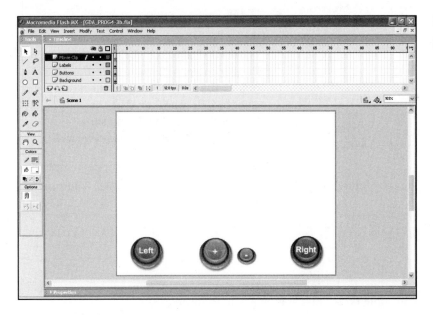

Figure 4.4

Setting up a scene

Create a small graphic, like a circle, in the Movie Clip layer. Select it with the Arrow tool and then press F8 to convert it to a Movie Clip. As you can see from Figure 4.5, I have named it Circle. Make sure to select Movie Clip from the Behavior option.

Figure 4.5

Converting to an MC

Once you have converted your graphic to a Movie Clip, make sure it's selected. Access your Properties panel by pressing Ctrl+F3 or Command+F3. You should have a screen similar to that in Figure 4.6.

Figure 4.6

Properties of your new MC

In order to be able to control this MC from ActionScript, it must have a name—let's name it circle01. Type this name in where it says Instance Name in the Properties panel. Remember that every symbol that is on your stage and main Timeline is only an instance of whatever is in the Library. Every instance is independent from every other, and you have to reference them individually from ActionScript. This is why we have to name this instance.

TIP

If you find that I am talking about properties that are not on your Properties panel, make sure the object that I'm talking about is selected. Remember that the Properties panel will only show properties for whatever is selected.

Here's the fun part. Ready for some interaction? Access the Actions Panel for the button that you labeled Left.

Write in the on handler in the following way:

```
on (release) {
}
```

Now that we finished preparing the button so it can execute anything inside the on release block, we can then type in some code. Take a look at the following listing.

```
on (release) {
  circle01._x -= 10;
}
```

Ignoring the fact that you are using dot notation to access a property in your Movie Clip (circle01), you can assume that 10 is being subtracted from this variable every time the button is released.

You already know that the symbol `circle01` is on the `_root` (the main Timeline) because you created it there. You also created this button—the one you are coding in—on the main Timeline. As this is true, you don't have to refer to `_root` because you're already there. This also being true, you can directly access `circle01` by merely calling out its instance name.

So where did this `_x` variable come from? It's one of many special built-in properties that Movie Clips include. If these properties are modified, you can change color, position and or orientation, therefore changing the Movie Clip's appearance.

As `_x` governs the x position of the Movie Clip, subtracting 10 from it will move it 10 pixels to the left. See Figure 4.7 for how the generic coordinate system works on the stage in Flash.

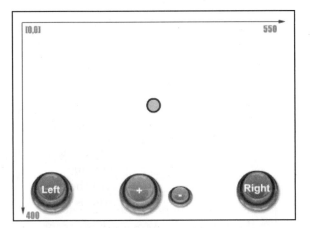

Figure 4.7

Flash's coordinate system structure

The main stage begins at [0, 0]. This is the upper left-hand side. The size of my movie is 550x400 so my highest displayable coordinates are 550x400, but of course, you can go past these.

Go to the button you labeled Right. Right-click or Command+click the button and type in the following listing:

```
on (release) {
  circle01._x += 10;
}
```

I think it's a good time for you to check out how much progress you have made. Go to Control, Test Movie after saving it. Try clicking the Left and Right buttons. You'll see your symbol, circle01, being manipulated. How cool is that?

Now I'm going to show you how to scale the instance on the stage. Find the button you labeled + and type the following listing in it. This is now the button's script that scales the instance by 10 percent.

```
on (release) {
  circle01._xscale += 10;
  circle01._yscale += 10;
}
```

Access the Actions Panel for the button you labeled—and type in the following listing in it.

```
on (release) {
  circle01._xscale -= 10;
  circle01._yscale -= 10;
}
```

If you would like to see what I did, check out the file GDA_PROG4.3b.fla on the CD.

You have just compiled a fully interactive program that responds to your commands. Starting to sound good, doesn't it?

As for the two new properties that I asked you to type in, _xscale and _yscale, they scale the Movie Clip independently. They accept a percent value. A normal uniform scale would be 100 percent. You can set the _xscale property to 50 percent to make the object narrow. If you were to set the _yscale to 200 percent, you would make the object twice as tall. Mess around with the code and with the values and make sure you understand what's going on.

There are two more properties that accept a pixel value. These are _height and _width. As opposed to the scale properties, these properties contain the current width and height of the current Movie Clip. Any other values that are assigned to these properties will modify the MC to fit those new values.

TIP

You can scale your object using different properties. Replace the _xscale and _yscale properties with _height and _width in our last example. You can scale your object through these properties as well but there is one difference—they accept pixel values instead of a percent value. Experiment and make new buttons. Don't forget to try everything that I have introduced up to this point.

The _rotation property is an interesting case. It accepts values in degrees and it rotates your MC for some cool effects. For instance, if you were to assign your Movie Clip _rotation property a value of 45, it would tilt the visual to a 45-degree angle.

Another Movie Clip property that I would like to touch upon is the _alpha property. This one also takes a percent value from 0–100. It allows you to make an MC transparent. A value of 100 percent makes the Movie Clip completely opaque and a value of 0 makes the clip completely disappear. Once you get the hang of ActionScript, you'll be able to fade and cross-fade objects—how cool is that?

onClipEvent Handlers

Movie Clips contain special event handlers similar to the on event handler in buttons—they execute their block of code right after an event happens. I will go through the most common cases of these handlers in the following subsections and I will also explain how to set them up and use them through a few cool demos.

The Rotating Propellers Demo

Let's check out another example. This one is called GDA_PROG4.4.fla. I will be modifying some of the properties of MCs while introducing onClipEvent handlers. See Figure 4.8 for a shot of the demo.

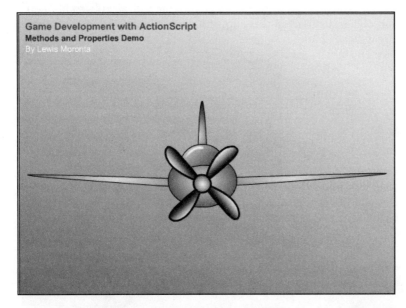

Game Development with ActionScript
Methods and Properties Demo
By Lewis Moronta

Figure 4.8

Moving propellers

This demo might look a little more complicated than the ones before, but don't be fooled. You can dig into it yourself and see that it's a bunch of neatly stacked layers and grouped objects. You'll also notice that the only symbol there is the propellers. This Movie Clip is the only part of the project that contains any code whatsoever. Check out the followin listing for the code.

```
onClipEvent(load) {
   degrees = 0;
}

onClipEvent(enterFrame) {

   degrees -= 20;
   this._rotation = degrees;
}
```

You can view this listing in the project yourself by right-clicking or Command-clicking on the propeller and selecting Actions from the pop-up menu. This will open the Actions Panel, and you'll notice two code blocks. Each code block denotes a `onClipEvent` handler. Let's look at the first handler.

```
onClipEvent(load) {
  degrees = 0;
}
```

As its argument, it has the `load` flag in between its parentheses. This tells Flash to execute the following block after the clip loads. In this case, all that the script is doing (when it loads) is initializing the `degrees` variable. Notice that this `degrees` variable is created on-the-fly. It's not a local variable, as you did not use the `var` keyword. It is a global variable in the scope of the Movie Clip. What this means is that the `degrees` variable will be able to be seen and modified by any function or handler within this clip. If it were a local variable, it would only be seen by the `onClipEvent(load)` handler.

The following block:

```
onClipEvent(enterFrame) {

  degrees -= 20;
  this._rotation = degrees;
}
```

executes the block of code on every frame. As you can see from the variable modification in the block, 20 is being subtracted from `degrees` on every frame. This value (`degrees`) is then assigned to the Movie Clip's `_rotation` property (also executed every frame because it's in the same block).

> **NOTE**
> You'll understand function variable scope better when we go over custom functions later in this chapter.

> **NOTE**
> I want you to notice something that might have slipped by. You already know that this code makes the propeller rotate by subtracting 20 from a current value on each frame and assigning it to the _rotation property. So what's the problem? Actually there is no problem because Flash is so nice.
>
> But what happens when the number is past -360? That's right, the propeller keeps rotating. This means that Flash knows how to translate any amount that is a relative number of degrees when it is being assigned to _rotation, even if it's past -360. This means that if the number is -1080, then the propeller has rotated three times counterclockwise. Any overflow on the number will cause the number to go back to zero and everything will be neatly taken care of.

The Scrolling Street Light Demo

Let's check out another example. This time, let's do a little error preventing. I have put together another project file that scrolls a streetlight and then loops it to the other side of the screen when it is out of view. This creates the illusion of driving up a street. This project can easily be modified to your liking; heck, you can even add buildings in the background and make them scroll, too. It'll be a good exercise. See Figure 4.9 for a visual.

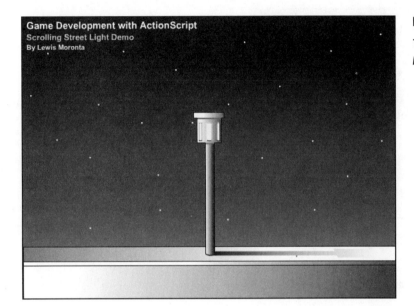

Game Development with ActionScript
Scrolling Street Light Demo
By Lewis Moronta

Figure 4.9

The Scrolling Street Light demo

I added a little twist to the code. Before discussing that, though, check out the demo GDA_PROG4.5.fla on the CD.

After you've finished observing what the program does, let's see where the code is stored. You probably think that the code is stored in the Street Light Movie Clip, but I actually have all the code stored in the main Timeline. If you like, go ahead and check the Action Panel while the light is selected. It's a blank screen.

As you can see from Figure 4.10, I created a layer named Actions with an empty keyframe with an "a" over it. That's our code. Let's check it out in the following listing.

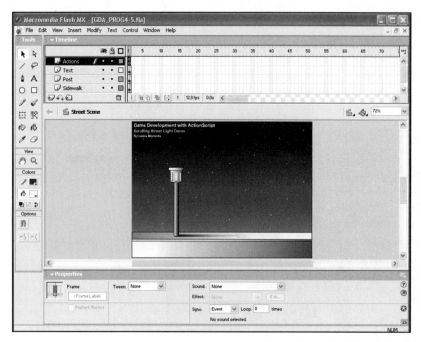

Figure 4.10

The empty Actions layer

```
onEnterFrame = function () {
  post._x -= 10;

  if (post._x < -post._width)
    post._x = 550;
};
```

This small piece of code moves that heavy light post across the screen and then loops it. Allow me to explain the first line before the block begins.

Remember when I said that the main Timeline is really a bigger Movie Clip where everything is stored? Well, the main Timeline happens to have many Movie Clip properties, too. You can also set up an event handler such as the ones we previously used. The declaration of this even handler is written a bit different though. Read on.

As you will learn in the next section, an event handler is really a special case of a function. To declare the function that does the same thing as the onClipEvent(enterFrame) handler in a regular Movie Clip, you have to write the following in the main Timeline:

```
onEnterFrame = function () {

};
```

In the main Timeline, this handler is called onEnterFrame. It executes its block of code on every frame just like its smaller brother, onClipEvent(enterFrame). Don't allow yourself to get confused over the fact that the assignment operator is being used. All this line is doing is defining the built-in method called onEnterFrame with the following block of code.

TIP

A *method* is a special built-in function that is specifically associated with an object such as a Movie Clip. Methods are technically blocks of codes that can be called (or executed) independently. In this case, a handler executes the code after a certain event.

One thing that I did during the setup was assign our street light an instance name. I named it post. This is the name I use to refer to it in ActionScript. (In case you forgot: name your instance in the Properties panel—make sure you have your symbol selected and then enter the name in the Instance Name box.)

You already know that if you modify the _x component of any Movie Clip, you will end up changing its horizontal position. That's exactly what I am doing here in the following line:

```
post._x -= 10;
```

I am specifically referencing post, which is the symbol's instance name. I'm also modifying its _x axis—subtracting 10, on each frame, from it.

That's clear enough, but what is the next piece of the block doing?

```
if (post._x < -post._width)
    post._x = 550;
```

Simply restated it says: "If post's x position is less than its -width, then move the post to 550." The statement is understandable, but what's with this negative width stuff? See the diagram in Figure 4.11.

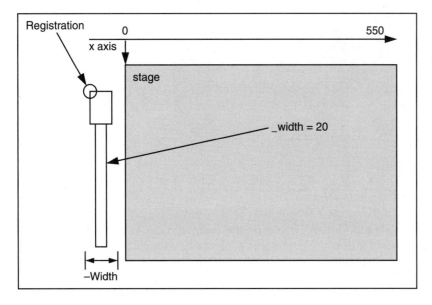

Figure 4.11

The negative width statement

When I created the street light, I drew all the graphics to the lower-right of the Movie Clip's registration point. This was completely intentional. This way, if scrolling left, when the street light hit the 0 position on its x-axis, it would still be completely visible. This would be impossible if the registration was centered.

Now suppose the street light went any negative amount on its x-axis. This would cause all or part of it to be off-screen. I can guarantee that it won't be onscreen if its width is out of the screen. If anything more than `-width` were to be used, you would still be able to see that darn light and our effect would be ruined.

So when the light is completely off the screen, we assign 550 to its x value. This causes the light post to place itself on the right side of the screen. As its registration is still on its upper left, it is not seen on the stage until a few frames pass by as the program continues to subtract 10 to continue the scrolling effect. Yes, there is a whole bunch of detail in this simple program, but like I said before, this will become second nature to you.

The Bouncing and Scaling B-Ball Demo

It's time for yet another demo. They always put a smile on my face when I read a book—what about you?

Check out Figure 4.12. It's a shot of the *Bouncing and Scaling B-Ball* demo.

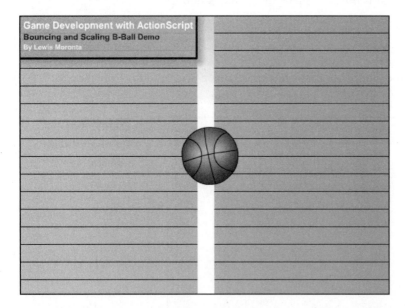

Figure 4.12

Bouncing and Scaling B-Ball demo

Find the file GDA_PROG4.6.fla on the CD and test the movie. You'll find code similar to the last example here. You should already be getting the hang of digging into other people's projects and understanding how the whole thing is put together.

The program basically scales a basketball while looping it left on the screen. You already know how to loop the image. You even know how to scale, but how did I make this one work?

Check out the following listing.

```
onLoad = function() {
  scaleFactor = 10;
};


onEnterFrame = function () {

  // Make the ball move left
  ball._x += -10;

  // Wrap the ball around the screen
  if (ball._x < -ball._width)
    ball._x = 550;

  // Scale the ball evenly
  ball._xscale += scaleFactor;
  ball._yscale += scaleFactor;

  // Reverse the scale direction
  // if certain conditions are met
  if (ball._xscale > 100)
    scaleFactor *= -1;

  if (ball._xscale < 20)
    scaleFactor *= -1;
};
```

This code was found on the main Timeline. (I found it easily because I wrote it!) I put the code on its own layer. I named the layer Actions, just like in the previous example. Then I put all the code on the first frame in the empty keyframe there.

You can see a new function in the code. It's similar to the onClipEvent(load) handler. Check out how I declared it.

```
onLoad = function() {
  scaleFactor = 10;
};
```

In the main Timeline, the handler is called onLoad. The previous block of code was assigned to the onLoad handler but what does this block of code do? It initializes a variable that keeps track of the scale factor. It executes *only* when the whole Flash movie is loaded.

The following onEnterFrame function, which executes at every frame, does quite a few things. I'm going to break it down piece by piece for you.

```
// Make the ball move left
ball._x += -10;

// Wrap the ball around the screen
if (ball._x < -ball._width)
   ball._x = 550;
```

You are familiar with this code. You already learned how to scroll the ball left. In this case, you do so by subtracting 10 on every frame. There is then a conditional testing to see if the ball is out of the screen—if it is, the ball then wraps it around to the right side and continues.

```
// Scale the ball evenly
ball._xscale += scaleFactor;
ball._yscale += scaleFactor;
```

In the following two lines, you are modifying the _xscale and the _yscale properties. This will help you achieve that bouncing effect. My goal was to scale it in and then out enough to create a feeling of perspective. If you ended the code here, you would be infinitely enlarging the ball. Let me show you how to avoid this to complete the effect.

```
// Reverse the scale direction
// if certain conditions are met
if (ball._xscale > 100)
   scaleFactor *= -1;

if (ball._xscale < 20)
   scaleFactor *= -1;
```

The first test compares to see if the _xscale is greater than 100 percent. When this condition becomes true, our scaleFactor variable is inversed. As we initialized it to a value of 10, scaleFactor then becomes -10. What happens when you add a negative value? You are essentially subtracting it. This will cause the ball to scale down—nice trick, eh?

The next conditional statement checks to see if the scale is too small. In this case, I checked to see whether it's smaller than 20 percent. If it is, I then inverse the scaleFactor so that the successive executions of the block will scale the ball back up.

As this is an ongoing thing and becasue the onEnterFrame function executes its block on every frame, you'll find the ball bouncing left—eternally. Got all that? I knew you did—I was just checking.

Custom Functions

You have the ability to define your own commands in ActionScript. You can name your command whatever you want. You can also make Flash do many things. You can even define commands in Flash to control very complicated enemies in whatever game you think of creating. The best part about the ability to create your own commands (a.k.a. functions) is that once you have your command defined, you can *call* it, or execute it, as many times as you want simply by using its name and a pair of parentheses.

To define your own commands, or functions, you can simply create a named block with the keyword function before it, like so:

```
function myFunk()

{

  // Do something...

}
```

So how will you execute such a function? It's not a handler, so it doesn't execute after a certain event; so when does it execute? When you call it, of course. But how do you call a function?

In this case, we named our function myFunk. All we have to do to execute it is shout out its name somewhere else in the project, like this:

```
myFunk();
```

The previous code will execute whatever is inside myFunk. Of course, any genius would realize that there is no real code in myFunk. But, either way, Flash would go into that function and then return where it left off.

Allow me to show you a simple but real example.

```
display();

function display() {
  trace ("My first function!");
}
```

If you were to start a new project and type this into the first frame of the first layer then test the movie, you would get "My first function!" as your output. Why? The defined function cannot execute by itself. It's merely a definition. The only executable code in that listing is the function call, display();.

The function call tells Flash to replace that code with the definition and execute it. What's inside the definition? The trace command, of course. This is why you see this output.

Let's play with variables for a bit. Let's say we had a local variable called temp01; our function won't be able to access the variable unless it is global. How can you expand the variable's scope? By not using the var keyword. This way, every function will be able to see the variable within that frame in the Movie Clip. But what if we don't want that to happen? What if we only want to reveal this variable to a certain function? Lucky for us, there is a way for only that function to access our discrete values.

In the project file GDA_PROG4.7.fla you can find the following listing:

```
var temp01 = 5;
var temp02 = 7;
var temp03;

temp03 = sum(temp01, temp02)
display(temp03);
outputTB = temp03;

function sum(num01, num02){
   return num01+num02;
}

function display(disp01) {
   trace (disp01);
}
```

Towards the end of the code, you can see two function definitions. They were declared in a slightly different way than how I introduced them to you. They have arguments between their parentheses.

If you look at the SWF file, you will see that the output is 12. The reason for this is that I created a dynamic textbox on the stage and assigned the variable outputTB to it. This way, any value that I assign to outputTB will be immediately displayed in the textbox.

TIP

How do you assign a variable to a textbox? All you have to do is create a textbox and access the Properties panel. Make sure it's a dynamic textbox from the drop down on the left. After you have set this setting, you will have a textbox labeled Var: towards the right. This is where you type in the name of the variable by which you want your textbox to be controlled.

After you understand the file's setup, you can start breaking down this program. You are already familiar with creating variables, so let's skim the first three lines. I created three new variables named temp01, temp02, and temp03. temp01 and temp02 I assigned 5 and 7, respectively. temp03 was left un-initialized because we're going to assign a value later, for display purposes.

The main body of the program is as follows:

```
temp03 = sum(temp01, temp02)
display(temp03);
outputTB = temp03;
```

The first line adds our first two variables. It also assigns the result to temp03. The second line then calls another self-defined function that displays the value. And finally, as I told you before, the textbox is also outputting the value because we are assigning temp03 to the variable that was assigned to the textbox.

Check out the sum function and allow me to explain its new style of definition.

```
function sum(num01, num02){
  return num01+num02;
}
```

Here we have the usual function keyword. After that is our alias—in this case I named it sum. There are also two arguments within the parentheses, separated by a comma. These are dummy variables that represent real variables that will be passed along to the function. As our original variables are local, they cannot be seen by this function. The only way their values can be utilized is by passing on the values through these arguments, as you saw up above.

To avoid creating a new dummy variable to store the result inside the sum function, I embedded the addition operator in the same line as the new keyword, return. This keyword returns a value to wherever the function was called, allowing me to use the alias sum as the assigning variable. This is what allowed me to store the result in the temp03 variable.

```
function display(disp01) {
  trace (disp01);
}
```

Now that you've seen that complicated pound cake, let's check out an easier definition. I listed our display function above. Its definition is simple because it only has one argument and because it does not operate on the value except for passing it on to the trace command.

Again, disp01 is only a dummy variable and it only serves the definition. The real variable is passed on from the main code or from another function.

TIP

Try creating your own set of functions just for practice. Try creating subtracting, multiplying, dividing, and other types of functions. How about one that finds the power of a number? Be careful with how you name your functions. If the name is already a keyword, you might get an error. A good way of checking that the alias is not taken is by checking on the syntax highlighting. If it doesn't color to the keyword color, then your name is good.

Movie Clip Navigation

Believe or not, you can stop, play, go to and play, go to and stop, and skip to any frame in a Movie Clip just as you would with your DVD player. It's a great thing.

I setup demo file GDA_PROG4.8.fla for this section. It resembles a main menu; check it out in Figure 4.13.

Figure 4.13

A main menu setup

At first this menu will seem very complicated, so allow me to break it down for you. Once you understand the individual parts, you'll be able to quickly put together a presentation yourself. I'll explain the structure of the main Timeline then all the scattered ActionScript code. The main Timeline appears in Figure 4.14.

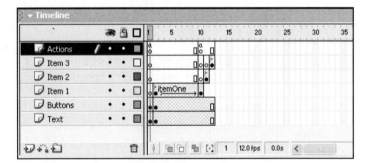

Figure 4.14

Main Timeline structure for a generic presentation

As this is an ActionScript book, let's check out the first frame of the Actions layer. There is a script there; you can view it by selecting that frame and pressing F9.

So what's in the script? A stop command. Without it, the movie would run through all the frames, but this command in particular causes the movie to pause at the frame where the stop command is located. The first frame displays the main menu.

Layers Item 1, Item 2, and Item 3 are empty for the first frame, so let's skip them for now.

The next layer I would like to talk about is the Text layer. It contains a few textboxes that have pertinent (yet generic) information. I have designed a title for this menu, added menu item names, and added the small legal information at the bottom. That's all.

The Buttons layer contains three buttons. Each of these buttons contains scripts. We can safely assume that one or all of these buttons is our only way to the other frames. If we don't find code to advance to other frames, we will be stuck in frame 1 for as long as you can stare at the screen.

Luckily for us, most of the code in the buttons is familiar. Right-click (or Command-click if you are on a Mac) on the button to the left of label Item 1. Select Actions from the menu. You will find the following:

```
on (release) {
  gotoAndPlay("itemOne");
}
```

You are already familiar with the on release handler—it executes anything inside it once the mouse button is clicked and released. This handler happens to have only one command inside it, the gotoAndPlay command. This command tells Flash to go to and play from a certain frame, which is specified within its parentheses.

In this case, I used the itemOne label as a target frame to "goto-and-play." So which frame is this? If you carefully look at the Item 1 layer, you will notice a red little flag over the keyframe of Frame 2. This indicates that this frame was labeled. Go ahead and select this labeled frame and access the Properties panel. It so happens that this is the keyframe that I labeled itemOne. How and where did I label the keyframe? The Properties panel has a special textbox under the Frame label where you can label your frames. See Figure 4.15.

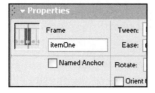

Figure 4.15

Labeling a frame

So now that you know that the gotoAndPlay command can jump to and play from any labeled frame, what happens if you don't have a label on a frame that you want to jump to—do you have to label it? Nope. You can simply use the frame number like this:

```
gotoAndPlay(50);
```

So what happens when the program finally jumps to frame itemOne after the user clicks on the first button? Let's examine that frame.

We have three active frames at this point—three frames with displayable information. The Text layer has keyframed information on Frame 2, and that keyframe is displayed until Frame 12, which is the end of the movie.

The Buttons layer has a completely different Frame 2 keyframe where the original three buttons are nowhere to be found. There is only one button thereafter that is next to the label, Back to main menu. Let's look into this button to see what it does. Select it and press F9.

```
on (release) {
  gotoAndPlay(0);
}
```

That makes sense. This button is our only way back to the main menu. Since our main menu is Frame 0, we can confidently say gotoAndPlay Frame 0—cool, no?

Our Item 1 layer is something we went over before. It's a simple tween. I took the textbox in Frame 2 and keyframed Frame 10. I then created a motion tween by selecting it from the drop-down from the Properties panel.

Look carefully at Frame 10 on the Actions layer. If you look into it, you will also find another stop command there. Why? If I didn't do that, the movie would continue playing the rest of the information on the Timeline. That wouldn't be good.

As long as we understand that much, we can go back to Frame 0 and examine the second button down. Let's look at the following code together:

```
on (release) {
  gotoAndStop("itemTwo");
}
```

Here's a variation of the gotoAndPlay command. Instead of going to and playing from a frame, this one goes to and stops at the specified frame. As the section with the itemTwo label (Frame 11) is only one frame, there is no need for us to use the gotoAndPlay command in this situation.

When the user does click for Item 2, Flash will go to and stop at Frame 11. Since the Buttons and Text layers are being displayed at that frame, the user will have the option of clicking that main menu button if the user wants to navigate back to frame 0.

The third button is a similar case. We covered most of the technicalities already. It is good practice to keep the main Timeline as small as possible with as few tweens as possible. Check out Frame 12—there is no tween there, but it's an animation section of the movie. What's going on?

You guessed correctly. There's a Movie Clip on that frame. If you were to double-click on that textbox, you would be in the Movie Clip's timeline. I had converted it earlier behind your back—don't you just like surprises?

When you view the Movie Clip's timeline, you'll notice a simple keyframe-to-keyframe tween. There is also a stop command at the end of those frames. If that stop command wasn't there, the Movie Clip would loop when viewed from the main Timeline. If you don't believe me, remove that stop command and test the movie.

Open up the SWF in the Flash Player and play with it. See what you can do to modify it.

For my next trick, I have prepared another file with a similar set of commands. This one is more of a slideshow than a main menu. The file is called GDA_PROG4.9.fla and can be found on the CD. See a screen shot of the demo in Figure 4.16.

NOTE

If this is a game development book, why are you being shown how to put together a slideshow? That's a very good question! There are valuable commands that can be easily understood through a project like this. When I prepare a demo for you, I plan for a version that is stripped-down compared to its realistic counterpart. This will allow you to concentrate on what you need to learn. This could have easily been a movie sequence before Stage 1 in your war game. See what I mean?

Figure 4.16

Our slideshow demo

The setup is pretty simple. The first layer only has one frame—our Actions layer. It also only has one action, a simple `stop` command. Once again, we need the command so the movie doesn't advance on its own.

There is nothing on the second layer, the Slideshow layer, so we'll skip it until we get to Frame 2. As for the Navigation layer, there is an oversized button straight in the middle. It contains the following script:

```
on (release) {
  nextFrame();
}
```

First thing you notice is that new command, the `nextFrame` command. This is a special case of the `gotoAndStop` command. It allows the movie to advance and stop one frame forward. This is an excellent command for when you need to display screen after screen to your user.

Let's suppose the user clicks on the huge button in the middle of the stage after running your program. Flash will advance him to the second frame and wait. What's on the second frame? Some graphics and another navigation button. This button also has similar code to the one above.

Now, once the user bumps into Frame 3, he finds that there are Forward and Backward buttons. Let's check out the actions for the button pointing backwards.

```
on (release) {
  prevFrame();
}
```

You can already tell us what this command does—it moves the movie backward one frame and stops there. How interesting.

Test the movie and play around with the buttons. Make sure you understand all of it before moving on.

Summary

You're one chapter away from finishing Part I of this book. You have learned a great deal so far. You learned how to program buttons and even how to detect when the user presses and releases the button. You also learned about and now understand Movie Clip scope. You understand the complex hierarchy that makes MCs tick.

You also started to handle bigger projects. You can open them up with more confidence and know how to locate scripts with ease. You learned how to move Movie Clips from within a script—how exciting was that?

From the built-in Movie Clip methods, you learned how to use the onClipEvent(load) and the onClipEvent(enterFrame) handlers. These handlers helped you modify properties like scale, rotation, and alpha throughout each frame of your movie.

You also went on to more advanced topics—you learned how to create your own commands. You even now understand how to pass on local variables and how to set up their definitions. As a classy touch, you learned how to access the special onLoad and onEnterFrame methods built-in to the main Timeline.

While examining the new commands within the demos in this chapter, you also learned how to label and call upon a frame and play (or pause) the movie from there. Of course, you will put all this knowledge together in the end and make your own creations.

Questions & Answers

Q. Where can I get a list of all the methods and properties that a Movie Clip can have?

A. The Flash Help file, of course. You can find anything you want in there. Don't forget about it.

Q. I'm still kind of fuzzy on the concept of scope. All this local and global stuff makes me hurl. What can I do?

A. Try using local variables wherever possible. Don't use global variables unless you absolutely have a good reason to do so. The reason I am suggesting this is because having 100 global variables in a game can get messy. It's not the best memory-management way to do things either. When you create a local variable, the space for the data is allocated and then deleted once the variable is out of scope. This is not the case with global variables—they stay in memory for the life of the game. Also, make sure you name your global and local variables differently, or else you will have bugs creep up on you.

Q. I'm thinking of setting up a set of functions that I can use and reuse in any project file. Would I have to copy and paste them into every project every time I want to use these functions?

A. No. You can use the #include directive to load in a text file that contains your functions. You can save your code into a regular text file. For self-reference, it is a good idea to add the *. extension so you can be easily understand what's in the file. We will go over this later in the book.

Exercise

1. Create a project file that has a main menu. Create buttons on the menu that can jump to one of five frames. On each of the frames, have a button that can return the user to the main menu at any time. Have other navigational buttons that can move the movie backward and forward after the main menu selection. Make sure that the first slide and the last slide can only go in one direction, as in the demo in this chapter.

CHAPTER 5

ARRAYS AND OBJECTS

Y ou already have a chunk of the ActionScript basics down. This chapter will round out your all-around skills by showing you how to create, set up, and access arrays and objects. They are the very core of what is called *object-oriented programming*, or OOP. This is a concept used in programming to reference parts of the code such as an object, which is a collection of variables and functions that act on those variables. You've already seen a built-in example of an object, the Movie Clip.

In this chapter, you will learn the following:

- What arrays are
- How to reference arrays
- How to create and initialize arrays
- What ActionScript objects are
- How to create and initialize objects
- How to use objects

What Are Arrays?

When you learned how to create variables, what you were essentially doing was creating a storage location for a piece of data. *Arrays* are a collection of variables that can hold individual pieces of data. Most of the time, these pieces of data are related, allowing you to reference them through one alias or name. Each of these elements has a unique position within the array. This is referred to as the *index*. Once you have your array, you can then access your data element by referencing it through your index and you're set.

Arrays can include more than one data type; what this means is that the first element in the array can be of type integer, the second could be type float, and the following type string, and so on. This can allow you to store an address, for instance. Along with this address you can also store the person's name and age as separate elements.

To better visualize this, check out Figure 5.1.

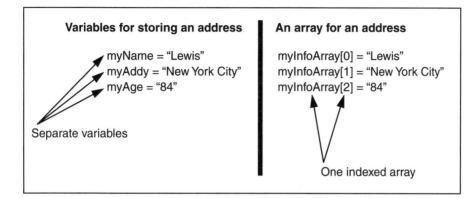

Figure 5.1

The difference between arrays and variables

So what is Figure 5.1 showing? It's demonstrating the fact that you can be more organized by storing your related data into an array variable instead of into many different variables.

You learned how to create your own functions and how to pass variables to those functions in the last chapter. You can actually pass your array variable to a function in one shot instead of passing many arguments at once. This reduces program overhead, thus reducing slowdown. To pass your array variable to a function, just pass on the array's name.

NOTE

You'll see examples of all of these programming techniques in chapters to come. It would be a good idea to create short programs that verify all of what I'm telling you. This is one of the best ways to retain all the information I'm throwing at you.

As another example of using arrays, let's say you had to print a list of names that you have collected over a period of time. This collection of names could be a high-score list. If you collected, say, 50 names in separate variables, imagine the mess you would have!

Let's add an array to the scene. You could easily create an array that will contain 50 elements that will store each of those names. Now what would you do if you wanted to display these names? The best solution would be to create a function that can loop through each element while posting it to the screen, in whatever manner you like.

Now, if you didn't have this array working with you, you would have to forget about that nice little loop. In order to display the information in those 50 variables you created, you would have to actually call the function 50 times—and that wouldn't be fun or practical.

Referencing Arrays

In order to ease into arrays, you should practice using them before learning how to create them. So, to that end, what would the array I described in the last section look like? It could look something like this:

```
scoreNames
```

Looks like a regular variable, eh? That's where the convenience comes in. If you were to "trace" this array with your `trace` command, you would see all of its elements. Take this for instance:

```
trace(scoreNames);
```

Of course, if you were to type this code in, you wouldn't get anything—the array hasn't been created yet. You will see working examples soon, but first let's get the theory out of the way.

If you want to reference a specific element in an array, you would have to use an opening and closing bracket with an index number in between. To reference the first element in the array, you would type something like this in there:

```
trace(scoreNames[0]);
```

This would output the value of the first element in the array, `scoreNames`. If this is true, then why are we indexing the 0 element? All indexing starts at zero—that means that index 1 is element 2, and index 2 is element 3, and so on. This will seem awkward at first, but you will get used to it quick.

> **CAUTION**
>
> Don't forget that indexing starts at zero! I'll remind you where I think it's necessary, but don't even think about sleeping on this fact. Just imagine the bugs that'll creep into your program if you access the wrong information from an array.

It's time to test yourself. Look at the following list of elements.

```
["Cathy", "25", "David", 23, "Eddie", 24]
```

In a program, I would treat these as pairs, but they still have to be referenced individually. They could easily be the person and the person's age, respectively. In this case, to reference Eddie's age, you would have to go through index 5. Get it? It's the sixth element. Try to guess the reference for the following:

```
member[0]
member[4]
member[2]
member[3]
member[1]
member[5]
```

If you answered "Cathy, Eddie, David, 23, 25, 24," then you're on the money! Remember that the only reason you got these answers is because the first index starts at 0.

> **NOTE**
>
> Keep in mind that even though the last element in this array is index 5, its length is still 6 because it has six elements in it. I know this seems obvious, but sometimes careless mistakes are made when you do not pay attention to this fact.

Creating and Initializing Arrays

Okay, you know how to reference an array—so how would you create one? There are a few ways to create arrays. Let's look at the array constructor first.

```
myArray = new Array();
```

Here you see the new command along with the array constructor. The constructor is nothing more than a special built-in function. The statement new Array(), in this case, creates a new array that can be assigned to an alias that can later be initialized and indexed. That's all there is to it.

There is no predefined number of elements in the array just created. This array will actually create the elements as you assign them to the indexed element—this is called a *dynamic array*. Take a look at an example:

```
myArray[0] = 42;
myArray[1] = 63;
myArray[2] = 34;
```

The first three elements to this array were initialized to 42, 63, and 34. You could handle these just like I explained in the last section. You could even use each of the elements as a variable to assign or to manipulate its contents. For instance, you can do this:

```
tempVar = myArray[2];
```

You should do this if you don't want to operate directly on the array's contents because this way, you could work on tempVar without worries. This assignment will definitely come in handy if you're about to enter a section of code that specifically works on this one element—instead of writing the reference out all the time you can simply refer to the second alias.

> **TIP**
>
> If you see a way to simplify your code, don't hesitate to do so. I personally go for code flexibility. What I mean by this is you should try to plan for the future. If I believe that anything might be changed or modified, I then program in such a way that the code is easily upgradeable. As I see it, the code is never finished and can forever be tweaked. I guess that's why there are so many versions of programs out there.

Creating an array like this is fine, but what if you have a predetermined amount of elements you want to work with? Luckily, there is a way you can tell ActionScript to create a certain number of elements that won't immediately be initialized—by stating the number within the constructor's parentheses, like this:

```
myArray = new Array(50);
```

This way, you can automate the initialization of this array with a loop or some other program flow statement. Just to throw some examples of this to you, say you wanted to initialize 25 different enemies in 25 different screen positions. You could easily put this array in a loop that initializes pairs of random x and y values in the array. Doing so will cause your enemies to be in different screen positions just as you intended.

Another quick example would be creating a number list that will be stored and saved for later use—let's say, the numbers from 1 to 365. Once again, the loop can come to the rescue and fill these values into the array with no problem.

It is possible to skip the initialization of elements in between other initialized ones. Allow me to restate that: It is *possible*, but *not recommended*, to skip the initialization of certain elements. This type of array is called a *sparse array*. See Figure 5.2.

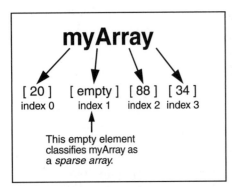

Figure 5.2

Visualizing a sparse array

CAUTION

As I said, it's not a good idea to use sparse arrays. Using an array with gaps in it, or even misreferencing the array can cause unpredicted results in your program. The funny thing about a sparse array is that Flash will not complain. If you are assigning a value to an element that is not initialized, Flash will simply create the element and the program will move on. This isn't good, especially if that wasn't your original intention.

So is there another way to initialize the array if we already know what the values are? Of course there is! There are a couple of ways, actually. Let me show you how to initialize the array using the current notation of our constructor (you'll see what I mean shortly). Check this out:

```
myArray = new Array("Lewis", "Eddie", "David", "Jerron");
```

If you type this line in, you create a new array with four elements. These elements were initialized to four names: Lewis, Eddie, David, and Jerron. This way to initialize an array is fine for a few values, but it would be ridiculous for anything past 30 values—at least you have the choice to initialize them in this way.

Just because you initialize an array through the constructor doesn't mean that you can't add elements to the array. If the fourth element was your last element, you can easily create the fifth element by assigning something to `myArray[4]`. It's that easy.

Here's another, shorter way to rewrite the statement `new Array()`:

```
myArray = [];
```

This also declares an array with an unknown number of elements. The two ways of declaring an array can be used interchangeably.

What would you do if you wanted to assign some values to the array? Easy enough—just write in the values in the brackets—if you have more than one value, separate them with a comma like this:

```
myArray = [25, 24, 35, 18, 58];
```

Cool, now you know how to create and initialize arrays. Don't be surprised when you see both types of notations.

Multi-Dimensional Arrays

In the past sections, you've been dealing with one-dimensional arrays. They are useful for many tasks like storing the last 10 locations of your mouse cursor—this would be useful when creating a mouse trail. In this section, you will explore *multi-dimensional arrays*. These are special arrays that contain other arrays within one or more of their elements. The number of arrays embedded determines how many dimensions the array is considered to be. Two-dimensional arrays can also be used as matrixes, depending on how you look at it.

One use for multi-dimensional arrays is in a situation where you need to store different sets of data into different elements of the array. An example would be an array of spaceship enemies in a game. You can store individual sets of information (of each enemy ship) as an array, and then take all these sets and store them in one bigger array for even easier access—this would then include all the enemies in space. Once you have this multi-dimensional array setup, you'll be able to access all the properties of all the enemies in the world just by using one alias.

NOTE

There are many uses for multi-dimensional arrays, but for the demonstration purposes in this section I will only discuss two-dimensional arrays. This will help you better understand the concepts quicker and more clearly.

So how would you declare a 2D array? There are a couple of ways to do so. Here's one way:

```
Age01 = [23, 25, 27, 29];
Age02 = [20, 15, 17, 18];
ageGroups = [Age01, Age02];
```

This example shows the creation of three arrays. The first two have four elements each. These arrays are used as initialization values when creating `ageGroups`. What this means is that you can now access all those values through one alias, `ageGroups`. Take a look at the following syntactic example:

```
mainArray[whichElement][whichElementInSubAlias]
```

`mainArray` would be `ageGroups`, in this case. The first pair of brackets indexes the element you want to further reference. In other words, by stating `mainArray[1]`, internally, you are indexing `Age02` because it is the second element in `ageGroups`. The second pair of brackets indexes whatever element is in `Age02`.

Just to give you an example, `ageGroups[0][2]` will yield the value 27. Why? The 0 index is referencing `Age01`, and within `Age01`, the 2 index is referencing the third element. Check out Figure 5.3 before moving on.

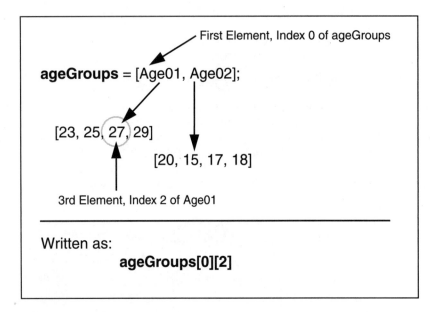

Figure 5.3

Indexing a 2D array

If you understand what we have gone over so far, you should easily understand how more arrays could be embedded into other arrays to create complex structures.

Let's look at other ways that you could declare multi-dimensional arrays. The following example shows you how to declare multi-dimensional arrays with the `array` constructor:

```
multiArray = [50, new Array(50)];
```

Don't let yourself be fooled by the last statement. Look at it closely and then decide what it really does. `multiArray` is a 2×50 2-D array. The first element in it is the value 50 and index 1 is another array of another 50 elements (embedded within `multiArray`).

Of course, as you can see from our example, the 50 elements embedded in the second element are not initialized. You can put this array in a loop, such as the one in my following example, to loop through each element for initialization:

```
for (var index = 0; index < 50; index++) {
  // The value of index is being assigned
  // to the index'th element in multiArray.
  multiArray[1][index] = index;
}
```

Looks a little complex, but it's not. You already know how to loop for 50 iterations, but as a refresher, let's go through it anyway. The for loop initializes the local index variable to 0. It then loops while index is less than 50. After each iteration, the for loop increases index by 1.

If you notice carefully, multiArray's second index is the index relative to the loop's indexing variable during each iteration. What in the world does that mean? It means that when the index variable is 0, multiArray will be indexing like this: multiArray[1][0]. When index is 1, it will be indexing like this: multiArray[1][1], and so on.

At the same time, during each iteration, index is the value being assigned. That means that if you were to list the 50 elements (embedded in the second element of multiArray), you would get a list of numbers from 0 to 49. Why? Because index starts at 0 and ends at 49 because the loop becomes false and exits at that time.

> **TIP**
>
> If you are having trouble visualizing this loop, I suggest breaking it down into smaller pieces. First thing you should do is add a trace command to the block of code to verify what is being put into the array during each iteration of the loop. Also try assigning a different value instead of assigning index. These are just a few tips to help you understand code. It is also a good idea to comment your code.

Using Arrays

You can do much with arrays once they're created and initialized to some value. In this section, you're going to start out by simply finding out the length of an array and then get more advanced by examining array stacks.

Let's start:

```
tempArray = [28, 35, 48, 13, 7];
trace(tempArray.length);
```

This example will display the number 5. Why? Because there are five elements in tempArray and this value can be read through the special built-in variable named length—this goes for any array. The dot notation notates that it is a property of tempArray.

Sometimes it is useful to figure out the length of an array when manipulated on-the-fly. One place where the length of array can be efficiently used would be in a loop. Remember in the previous example when we looped 50 times because the loop condition was set to 50 and also because it was the length of the array? What do you do if you don't know the length of the array? Well, you could do this:

```
for (var index = 0; index < tempArray.length; index++) {
    . . .
}
```

Cool, no? This way, you can have that array be any length and you won't have to worry about creating new elements if the array is too short, or not accessing all of the elements if the array is too long.

The Push and Pop Commands

Now I'll show you two very useful commands, push and pop. Sounds like candy, but they're even sweeter when you need them.

The push command essentially adds an element of the specified value on top of the last element on the array (or stack). For instance, look at the following example:

```
tempArray = new Array();
tempArray.push("USA");
tempArray.push("BMW");
tempArray.push("NYC");
```

The first familiar line declares the array. The following three lines add USA as the first element (index 0), BMW as the second element (index 1), and NYC as the third element (index 2).

If you were to use the push command again, it would add another element after the third element. Try messing around with the code. Use the trace command to help you better understand it. Try figuring out the length of the array before and after you use the push command. You'll see the number of elements affect the length of the array right before your eyes!

Let's work on our previous example. This time though, I'm going to show you how to use the pop command.

```
result01 = tempArray.pop();
result02 = tempArray.pop();
```

Assuming the last element in tempArray contained the value of NYC, result01 would also equal that value. Why? Because the pop command returns the value it is removing from the top of the stack. That's exactly what the pop command was made to do, and it does so fabulously. See Figure 5.4 for a visual of the pop command. See Figure 5.5 for a visual with the push command.

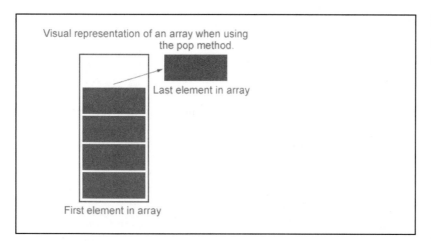

Figure 5.4

Removing the last element in an array

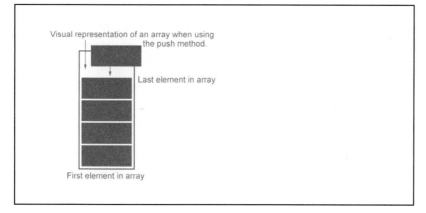

Figure 5.5

Concatenating an element to the end of an array

TIP

When removing a value, the pop command also returns the value. This allows you to use it before throwing it away. Remember that the pop command also reduces the array length by one.

At this point, you can pretty much guess what the following line (in the last example) does—it removes the last element and spits it out into result02. Assuming the value was BMW, result02 will be BMW and the array's length will be one less.

Take a look at the following example; it demonstrates how to remove the first element in an array:

```
myPets = ["cat", "roach", "snail", "kangaroo"];
shifted = myPets.shift();
trace(shifted);
```

If you were to check the length of myPets, you'd see that the modification is reflected here also. I bet you're starting to get the hang of this array thing; you probably already know that if there is a method to remove the first element, there is probably a method to add an element before the first one—and you're right!

The unshift Command

You can use the unshift method of the array object to add new elements in front of an array. In other words, if you needed three new elements in front, you could add them with this command. Let's see it in action:

```
LengthOfarray = myPets.unshift("spiders", "rats", "hamsters");
```

If the myPets array used to contain cat, roach, snail, and kangaroo, it now contains spiders, rats, hamsters, cat, roach, snail, and kangaroo. Yes, in that order.

The unshift method of the array object returns the length of the new array that it constructed. See Figure 5.6.

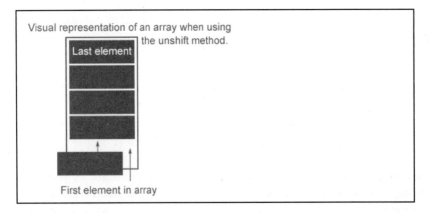

Figure 5.6

Adding an element to the front of an array

The slice and splice Commands

There are a couple of other methods that many novice programmers seem to confuse; the slice and splice commands. They sound as if they are out of an old martial arts flick, and they can inflict just as much damage if not used correctly. I will point out the distinct differences so you can be on your way to reaching your master status.

The `slice` command returns a subsection of an array without modifying the original array. This is great when you want to work on a particular piece of an array without touching the main one.

```
myPets = ["cat", "roach", "snail", "kangaroo"];
subArray = myPets.slice(1, 3);
```

This returns `roach` and `snail` in a two-element array.

Now listen carefully—the first parameter in `slice` indicates the index number where you want to start extracting. The second parameter indicates where you want it to stop. Listen even closer—the element indicated by index 1 will be included in the return array, but only up until the index indicated by the second parameter. In other words, the element indicated by the second parameter will not be included in the sub-array.

> **TIP**
>
> If you omit the second parameter to the `slice` command, the command will return everything from the index indicated to the end of the main array. See the Help file for more examples.

So what does `slice`'s brother `splice` do? In Macromedia's documentation, the command is defined as:

```
myArray.splice(start, deleteCount, value0,value1...valueN)
```

Before discussing the definition I should tell you that the main difference between `slice` and `splice` (besides the spelling) is that `splice` modifies the array it's working on and `slice` doesn't—got that?

The `start` parameter tells `splice` where to start deleting or inserting the values. `deleteCount` decides whether to delete or insert. Insert 0 there if you don't want any elements deleted. After this parameter, the remaining parameters are optional. Any values inserted hereafter will be pushed into the array starting at the position indicated by `start`.

> **NOTE**
>
> Don't think I'm driving away from the fun graphics. Arrays are heavily needed. You will see why soon.

What Are ActionScript Objects?

The generic ActionScript object is at the root of the ActionScript hierarchy. But what is this great object that I'm talking about? An object is an entity in Flash that can have properties and methods, or functions that act upon those properties (or variables). A specific object of any kind is said to be a *class*. ActionScript allows you to create any type of class that you wish.

Before continuing, let me just tell you that most structures in ActionScript derive from the generic object—even the Movie Clips themselves. This is so much so that even the arrays you created in the last section derived from an object.

What do I mean by *derive*? What I mean is that the objects I've discussed have the same methods and properties as a generic ActionScript object.

Objects are great because you can also assign new methods and properties to them. The ability to do this to your object is part of OOP, or object-oriented programming. This style of programming is usually a mystery for many newbies, but the truth is that it was created so that you can visualize your objects in the program. See Figure 5.7 for a visual.

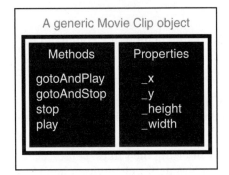

Figure 5.7

Visualizing a generic object

What in the world did I mean by that last sentence? Well, allow me to throw an example at you. Let's say you had a tank main character in your top-scrolling action-adventure. You would want the tank to have a fire function. It is specific to tank objects because they all fire the same (hypothetically) but this same function (method) wouldn't work with another object because it's not part of that object, only part of tank. However, you can have another fire function defined for another object—and make it behave completely differently from the fire function in the tank class. Once the code is written, you would be able to write something like this:

```
tank.fire();

Enemy.fire();

...

Enemy.energy = powerUp;
```

Notice that both functions have the same name. They each belong to different objects. This makes sense because your enemy might fire different missiles from your tank character.

Now look at your enemy's `energy` property. It's really just a built-in object variable. It wasn't declared in the environment but as part of the `Enemy` object. This object could easily be a Movie Clip or even a generic object. How would you create a property just like the energy property? Just like you would any other variable—the only difference is that you aren't creating it under the `_root`, you are creating it as part of an object, so you have to use dot notation unless you are in the object already. In this case, `Enemy` was the object I used to declare the energy variable in.

TIP

It's best to think of OOP as a simpler way to organize your program. After you get used to OOP, you're going to get so close to it that you won't want to program in any other way. (Actually, you've been using OOP all this time in this book.)

What I just explained in the previous paragraph regarding personally hidden properties and methods has a name: *encapsulation*. I didn't throw this name at you before because I don't want you to focus on the vocabulary at this point—I wanted you to grasp the concepts first.

Creating and Initializing Objects

As with arrays, `Objects` can be created in a couple of different ways. By understanding the structure of the generic ActionScript `Object`, you will further understand other derived ActionScript `Objects`.

I'll first show you the long-hand way to create an object, and then I'll show you some expert shortcuts. Sound good?

Creating an object is not much different from creating an array. Check out the code to see why:

```
info = new Object();
```

By writing in this line, you are telling ActionScript that `info` is now of type `Object`. That's great, but the object is pretty much void right now. Let's assign some properties to it.

```
info.Name = "Lewis"
info.Age = "22"
```

Cool—okay, so we just added `Name` and `Age` as part of our `info` `Object`. Would you be surprised that you can do exactly the same with an array? As I mentioned before, an array is derived from a generic `Object`, which is what we created here. This enables us to use the array as a generic object without all the fancy array properties. Interesting.

If you like, you can go ahead and type in this small program and verify that the info was assigned with the `trace` command. You'll know when something went wrong when you go to output something to the screen and the Output Window is blank.

Now for the "cool" way to declare objects:

```
emptyObj = {};
```

This is essentially the same as:

```
emptyObj = new Object();
```

What's the advantage over the longer way? It's a huge advantage, actually—you can initialize and set properties within those curly brackets. For instance:

```
Pos = { x: 50, y: 300 };
```

Doesn't it seem like a completely different language? Who would have thought you would be using the assignment operator in such a way? Did you ever think you would be using a colon as an alternative to assign a value? This line creates an object with two properties, x and y. x is initialized to a value of 50 and y is assigned 300. But where is the assigning happening? Don't be fooled; the colon within—and only within—the curly brackets behaves like the regular assignment operator. Successive properties are separated by a comma as shown in the example above.

It shouldn't come to as surprise that there is more than one way to refer to an object property. As you become more advanced with the language, and as you get more comfortable with it, you will start to see the real advantage to using this way to reference the object property. Take a look:

```
spaceShip.speed = 40;
...
var saveSpeed = spaceShip["speed"];
spaceShip["speed"] = 20;
```

Here I presented the usual dot notation and our new notation using the [] operators. The speed property is initialized to 40. It is then saved to `saveSpeed` and then it is assigned a new value of 20.

Notice that the new notation resembles arrays—don't confuse the two. speed is a property that was created in `spaceShip`. It is then referenced in quotation marks within brackets following the object alias. Once the property is created, it can also be referenced and assigned new values—just like in the last line of my example code.

Using Objects

If you are already familiar with ActionScript, you would have noticed that I have so far failed to mention one type of loop. I've waited this long because I wanted to introduce both arrays and objects so that you'd have a nice grasp of what's going on. This new loop is called a `for-in` loop, and is a more convenient way to traverse objects and arrays, as we'll soon see.

The for-in loop has very simple syntax. It is written in the following format.

```
for (var element in object) {
  object[element];
}
```

As you can see, when the loop initializes itself, it creates a variable—in this case called element. This loop will iterate through all the properties in the object (or elements in an array) and you can use the combination of the object and loop variable to extract the value of the current element—all you have to do is use the loop variable as a reference, or visually, something like this:

TIP

Remember that anything I show you in this section can be applied to arrays in one way or another—including this new for-in loop. Just remember that when you iterate through an object, the loop starts at the top, or end of an array, and ends at the bottom or the first element.

```
object["element"];
```

In order to iterate through each element in an object you can write up a for-in loop like this:

```
for (var attr in spaceShip) {
  trace("spaceShip's " + attr + "contains the value of " + spaceShip[attr]);
}
```

What determines the number of iterations is the number of properties in the object in question.

Let's dive into the statement and see how it works. Besides the keyword for, we see the usual parenthesis. What I did first was declare a variable that the for-in loop will use—a local variable named attr. Following this is the in keyword. The spaceShip object follows the keyword. After that comes the closing parenthesis and the body. What this statement is basically saying is, "For every property in spaceShip, loop once."

Why did I declare attr? Because during each respective iteration, the next property is assigned to attr as a string value. This will allow me to see which property I am working with. For instance, if on the third iteration the property is Ammo, the attr variable will contain "Ammo" as a string value.

I have used a trace command in the body of the for-in loop so you can better understand what I am talking about.

> **NOTE**
>
> The `trace` command probably looks a little complicated. The only reason this is so is because I'm concatenating four strings in one statement. The first one is `spaceShip's`. I am then adding this to the string in `attr`. This string is then added to `contains the value of`. And finally, the value that is returned by `spaceShip[attr]` is also attached to the end of the string and outputted to the window.

The `trace` command is pretty much self-explanatory except for the last piece, `spaceShip[attr]`. This last reference to a property can seem a little confusing because there are no quotation marks around `attr`. You cannot use quotation marks or else ActionScript will be looking for the `attr` property within `spaceship`, and it doesn't exist. `attr` is merely a temporary variable that is being used in the `for-in` loop. Remember that when `attr` is referencing Ammo, it will be in string format. If you rewrite `spaceShip[attr]` at that stage, it will become clear why I wrote it like this: `spaceShip["Ammo"]`. This reference to the property will return the value stored within the Ammo property of `spaceShip`. See how powerful this flexibility is?

A sample output would be this:

```
spaceShip's Ammo contains the value of 50
```

When using objects, you can also create your own class as you would define a function. The name of the structure that creates these classes is called a constructor—just like `new Array()` and `new Object()` are constructors.

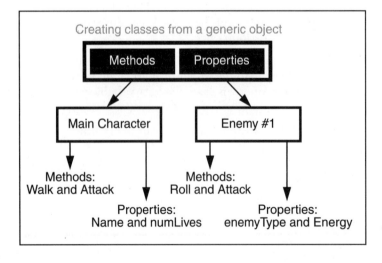

Figure 5.8

Creating a class from a generic object

TIP

An object class is simply a category that you can set up—it's another OOP thing. For instance, you can set up a spaceship class, animal class, human class, and so on. Keep reading and you'll see how you can create object classes.

```
function spaceShip() {

  this.Ammo = 50;

  this.Speed = 25;

}
```

Here, you are essentially creating a class with two properties, Ammo and Speed. You can then use your favorite new keyword to create a new object of this class.

```
XShip = new spaceShip();
```

XShip is automatically initialized with the values you declared earlier in spaceShip. Isn't this cool?

But what if you want to assign a new method, such as the walk method you assigned to the dog earlier?

```
function spaceShip() {

  this.Ammo = 50;

  this.Speed = 25;

  this.Shoot = shootingFunction; // This function was defined somewhere else.

}
```

After defining the class like this and declaring XShip, you should make XShip easily fire by typing in the following line:

```
XShip.Shoot();
```

Additional methods can be assigned in a similar manner. The declaration definition for assigning methods in a constructor function is this:

```
this.method = functionAlias; // functionAlias is defined elsewhere
```

or

```
this.method = function () { // Function code goes here }
```

It's really that simple. Don't forget to unleash your creativity, and don't be intimidated by the second way to assign a method. It's usually only used for shorter functions that you don't want to define elsewhere. This will allow you to skip assigning the method an external name while defining it right in the constructor. If you find the method convenient, use it; if not, just code with what you are comfortable with. ActionScript gives you plenty of choices to code freely.

Summary

Much of the stuff in this chapter cannot be mastered in one day. Notice how I use the stuff in this chapter in the demos to come.

Let's review what you picked up in this chapter. To start off, you learned all about arrays. You learned how to create them as well as to reference them. You also won't be fooled by them because you very well know that the first element in an array is index 0. You also learned how to initialize an array two different ways. You even went to another dimension— you explored multi-dimensional arrays. To finish that section, you learned about some use-ful properties and methods of the Array class.

In the second section, you learned all about objects. This is the very core of ActionScript. You learned how to create objects and even how to create your own classes. And you learned how to create your own class constructor that you can use to initialize your own class with tons of properties and methods.

Question & Answer

Q. I've read about OOP before and I noticed there is something else called inheritance. Will you cover this topic in this book?

A. Inheritance is a very advanced subject and will not be covered in this book. You can, however, find very good sources that explain all about inheritance. Look for other advanced Flash books in Premier's Game Dev series of books.

PART TWO

THE
INTERMEDIATE
INFO

CHAPTER 6

DYNAMIC MOVIE CLIPS

You have entered Part Two of this book and demos will continue to get cooler and "flashier." Are you ready for this chapter? You better be, because I'm about to teach you how create dynamic Movie Clips that seem to act on their own. I will dump demo after demo on you while you learn the concepts you need for a strong foundation. Along the way you'll learn many programming techniques.

In this chapter you'll learn how to do the following:

- Generate random numbers
- Duplicate a Movie Clip
- Duplicate clips from the library
- Improve a particle system

Generating Random Numbers

Believe it or not, random number generation can be very useful for creative results in a game. Random numbers are used to provide random screen locations for objects such as the stars in your star field. Another example of when you want random numbers to affect your game is when you want other game entities, such as enemies, to appear in random locations on the screen. Every time the game is played, they will always appear in a different location if random numbers are used to affect their position attributes. One reason for this is that the game player doesn't want your game to be predictable every time he plays. Even a game like *Tetris* generates a random block, out of 7 total blocks, until you lose the game. Games should be fun and the player should have a different adventure every time he plays (even if he stays at the same level).

So, how do you generate random numbers? I'm not going to get into the complex math that it actually takes to generate them because doing so would take up at least a few chapters. Plus, this isn't a math book—you're reading this to make games, not master mathematical functions.

> **NOTE**
>
> Chapter 11 is full of useful game math, but if you would like further reading, check out other Game Development books published by Premier Press that cover the subject. Enjoy.

Luckily, you don't have to reinvent the wheel. There is a Math object built into ActionScript that you can take full advantage of. I'm only going to touch upon a couple methods of the Math object. One method is:

```
Math.random();
```

This method returns a number from 0 up to the number 1. If called upon twice, the second return will be completely unpredictable, just like the first returned value. Let's test it out.

```
trace(Math.random());
```

I put this statement in a `for` loop that looped 20 times. This was my output:

```
0.96022649621591
0.798773859161884
0.999327154364437
0.441732861567289
0.526776063721627
0.939985535573214
0.126834238413721
0.12000940926373
0.931211666669697
0.688188867177814
0.779313802719116
0.476958607323468
0.5028145625256
0.957195661962032
0.958747376687825
0.932823874987662
0.665031484793872
0.0121707990765572
0.985493869520724
0.8782356120646
```

You could run the script a few times and see that this output would change every time. Zero is a very possible answer—1 isn't. Keep that in mind. The number generated can get very close to 1—and you can also use another method that rounds the result up or down. Either way, you can pretty much generate any possible range you want by multiplying `random`'s result by any number.

To understand how this works, pay close attention to the following explanation. You know that when you multiply a number by 1, you get the number you multiplied by. If we multiply by .5, you get half of the number you multiplied by, and so on.

So what would happen if we were to type in a line like this:

```
trace(Math.random()*10);
```

This would yield a number from 0 to a number very close to 10. In order for you to verify this, you would have to put the resulting number in a loop (just like in the last example). Go ahead and observe the output. I got the following:

```
7.51654958352447
6.19418734684587
8.9927756646648
```

```
9.64880893472582
7.58282233960927
0.215201745741069
5.46044206712395
1.21198146604002
2.19898341689259
1.69041742570698
1.39441115781665
9.54875849187374
4.76128031965345
6.64634562563151
8.05860636290163
0.770040606148541
1.14755514543504
4.76418022532016
8.93458025064319
0.0836741318926215
```

This is very cool—you can now generate a random set of numbers that are useful for all different genres of games. If you're dealing with an action game, you can use random numbers to decide when your enemy wants to fire explosives at you. If you're working on a puzzle game, you can easily use this to decide the next move that the computer opponent will make.

What if you aren't dealing with floating point numbers? What if you were only working with integers? How can you restrain your answers to only integers? It's easily done. After you scale the result from the random method, all you have to do is use the floor method on it. Just so you know, the floor method is specifically named the way it is because it rounds the floating-point value down to the nearest integer. Allow me to show you how this is done:

```
trace(Math.floor(Math.random()*10));
```

Looks complicated, but it's not. All I did was wrap the floor method around the Math.random()*10 result. Type in the following loop in and see what it outputs:

```
for (var index = 0; index < 20; index++)

  trace(Math.floor(Math.random()*10));
```

Take a look at the output I got and observe how neat it is.

```
6
2
7
7
1
6
9
5
```

1
5
6
9
4
2
3
5
0
8
8
8

Cool, eh? Notice something else: I have results ranging from 0 to 9. What if you wanted results from 0 to 10? Even easier! All you have to do is add 1 to the result and you automatically push everything up one. I love game programming—don't you?

Duplicating a Movie Clip

You're probably wondering why you would want to duplicate a Movie Clip. There are many reasons why you might want to do so, but in this chapter, I'm only going to concentrate on particle systems.

Before jumping right into what particle systems are and how to program them, allow me to introduce a smaller demo that will get you acquainted with duplicating Movie Clips. Figure 6.1 shows a small tank demo that I have written showing how you can duplicate an object that is already on the stage—all the code within it also gets duplicated.

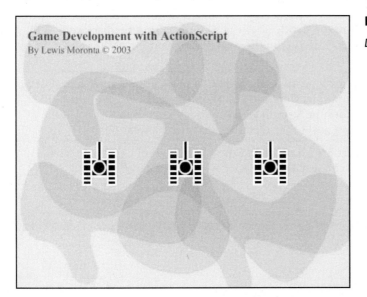

Figure 6.1

Duplicating objects on your screen

Open up GDA_PROG6.1a.fla from the CD. You'll find a nice little tank in the middle of the screen. This tank has been programmed to move up and then wrap around the bottom with the following code.

```
onClipEvent(enterFrame) {
  this._y -= 10;

  if (this._y < -this._height)
    this._y = 400;
}
```

Go ahead and test the SWF and make sure you understand how the code works. This code basically subtracts 10 from the tank's vertical position on each frame—and when the tank hits a position off the top of the screen, the code resets the tank's vertical position to 400.

For the second part of this demo, I modified GDA_PROG6.1a.fla and saved it as GDA_PROG6.1b.fla. This demo duplicates the tank twice on the stage—code and all. It even assigns a different horizontal position to each duplicated tank. How was this done? Let's jump into the following listing, which is code that I wrote on the main Timeline, under the Actions layer, so you can see how it was done.

```
duplicateMovieClip("tank", "tank0", 1);
duplicateMovieClip("tank", "tank1", 2);

tank0._x = 100;
tank1._x = 350;
```

As you can see, the new method duplicateMovieClip was used here to create the two clones. The duplicateMovieClip method takes the name of the instance you want to duplicate in the first parameter—in this case, "tank." The second parameter is the name of the instance clone that you want to create. The third parameter is instance's depth number. Each duplicated instance must have its own unique depth or else the clone cannot be displayed—I'll speak more about this later. I'll introduce the method version of duplicateMovieClip a little later in this section. Which one you use is up to you.

So now that you know how to duplicate Movie Clips, what is a particle system? A *particle system* is a program that can handle multiple, similar types of objects with different properties and attributes. The English translation is: A particle system is a program that can handle elements like snow, rain, sparks, dust and other elements that have similar characteristics.

I have prepared a demo for this section. You can find the SWF file under the GDA_CH06 folder on the CD. The name of the file is GDA_PROG6.2.swf. Check out Figure 6.2.

Figure 6.2

A particle system in action

If you play the demo, you'll see snow falling continuously. If you open GDA_PROG6.2.fla, you'll notice that there is only one snow particle. This snow particle is really a Movie Clip that has an instance name. This Movie Clip instance also has code in it.

If you look on the main Timeline, there is also code embedded in the first frame. This code duplicates the snow particle Movie Clip along with its code, allowing the snow particle Movie Clip to act as it does.

What would happen if you didn't duplicate this Movie Clip? Simple. The clip that is there now would move towards the bottom of the window and it would loop around the top of the window with code that you are already familiar with. When I set it to create additional copies, I made sure the new copies had different speeds and positions. It's a very cool effect, if you ask me. Try playing around with different attributes once you finish this section.

So what is this special method that can duplicate your Movie Clips? It happens to be the aptly-named `duplicateMovieClip`. `duplicateMovieClip` is a built-in method in all Movie Clips. Check out its usage:

```
myMovieClip.duplicateMovieClip("newInstanceName", depth);
```

This definition is true when `myMovieClip` is the instance name of your Movie Clip. So, if your named your instance "particle," you would be able to write:
`particle.duplicateMovieClip("newInstanceName", 1)`.

The first parameter is a string representing the internal name of the new instance. The name could be anything, but be careful to not give the instance the same name as another instance or else Flash won't know what to do with it.

The second parameter is really special, and you have to keep track of it somehow. No two Movie Clips can be on the same internal depth—they all have to be on their own layer or neither will be displayed. As this is the case, you have to be careful to assign a different layer depth to all the Movie Clips you create through ActionScript.

Examine the following listing. It was extracted from GDA_PROG6.2.fla, from the Actions layer. We'll examine the rest of the code (which is in the Movie Clip) in a little while.

```
// GDA_PROG6.2.fla
// Game Development with ActionScript
// This program demonstrates how to
// duplicate a movie clip with built in
// event handlers...

// Initialize the variable that decides
// how many particles will fall
numPart = 50;

// One thing we can do here is
// create some particles.
for ( var index = 0; index < numPart; index++) {
  // Duplicate them!
  particle.duplicateMovieClip("Particle"+index, index);
}
```

The first thing I did in this code is initialize a variable that is set to 50. This variable was set to determine how many particles will be in this system. How will the particles be created? The duplicateMovieClip method was put in a loop that you will soon see.

Once you enter the loop in this example, you will immediately notice that it will loop 50 times. In other words, it will loop while index is less than numPart, which is currently 50. Once in the loop, you'll see the following line:

```
particle.duplicateMovieClip("Particle"+index, index);
```

This is a pretty standard (and slick) way of creating an instance name and assigning a layer automatically when you're in a loop. Let's look at the first parameter of the duplicateMovieClip method. I wrote it as this:

```
"Particle"+index
```

If you look up to the loop, you'll realize that index is the loop's control variable. What this means is that index will be incremented after each iteration, which means a new string will be created in this line—this is what allows this script to assign a different name to the instance each time. To see some of the names that are assigned, look at the following example:

```
Particle0
```

```
Particle1
```

```
...
```

```
Particle4
```

```
Particle5
```

Particle6

...

Particle49

So now that you know how the loop is creating the 50 new particles, how do you assign the layer depths? I'll be nice and give you the answer to that—by using the index variable again. Loops are great! Using the loop's variable allows us to have a variable that's steadily incrementing while killing more than two birds with the same stone. Just like in the last example, Particle0 will be on layer 0, Particle1 will be on layer 1, and so on.

So, after this loop is done, you have 51 identical Movie Clips on your screen. I thought they were all supposed to have different personalities, you're thinking. They do! Let's go through the following listing, shall we?

```
onClipEvent(load) {
  // Initialize
  // Math.random returns a number from
  // 0 to 1. By multiplying a number,
  // you can get it to return a certain
  // range of numbers.
  this._x = Math.random()*320; // Returns
  0-319
  this._y = Math.random()*240; // Returns
  0-239
  speed = Math.random()*2+6;
}

onClipEvent(enterFrame) {
  // Moving code is here =)
```

CAUTION

Try not to confuse the depths and layers that I'm talking about in this section with the layers that you see on your Timeline. These *depths* (as Macromedia refers to them) are internal and have a really complex structure. You don't need more than what is being explained here to be able to completely work with them. Of course, you can move on and do more research if this chapter is not overwhelming enough—who's stopping you?

NOTE

"Why 51?" you might ask. It's because you created 50 duplicates—this does not include the original you duplicated. So, since you have 50 duplicates AND the original instance on your stage, this totals up to 51. Get it?

```
    this._y += speed;

    if (this._y > 240) this._y = 0;
}
```

This listing was extracted from inside the Movie Clip that's in the project file GDA_PROG6.2.fla. This is the code that is duplicated into each of the new instances and that causes them to move themselves. This is also a great example of OOP.

Here we see two familiar event handlers. One is `onClipEvent(load)` and the other is `onClipEvent(enterFrame)`. Just to recap, `onClipEvent(load)` executes its body when the Movie Clip is first created (or duplicated) and loaded. `onClipEvent(enterFrame)` executes on every frame. This is where the motion code is contained.

Let's look at a snippet of what's inside the `onClipEvent(load)` function:

```
this._x = Math.random()*320; // Returns 0-319
this._y = Math.random()*240; // Returns 0-239
speed = Math.random()*2+6;
```

You are familiar with everything here, but let's go through it anyway. The first line in the snippet of code stores a number in the range of 0–319 into `this._x`. In other words, the moment a value is pushed into this property of the Movie Clip it will immediately be placed in the respective screen position. Same thing goes for the _y property—except that a value from 0–239 is being assigned.

Now we encounter this new `speed` variable. You can tell it is global because I didn't use the var keyword. Also, as I created the `speed` variable within a Movie Clip (that is duplicated), it becomes a property of the Movie Clip (and is in each of the Movie Clips that are created).

Let's talk about what's happening in that last line with the calculation. By multiplying 2 by the `Math.random` method, we get a number from 0 to something close to 2—then we add 6 to this result. So what's our new possible range? Our lowest number, 0, is added to 6, so our slowest speed is 6. And as our highest is something close to 2, our highest speed will almost be 8. In conclusion, our range for our speed is 6 to approximately 8. In the actual code, I modified that line so the speed varies exactly from 6 to 8, not approximately 8—check it out. It's a great way to learn.

> **TIP**
>
> You might notice that I did not round before assigning values to the _x and _y properties. You might argue that I should have because there is no such thing as a .5 pixel position. That's true, but I wanted to show you that Flash could interpret these values to give you more of an exact translation. Therefore, you shouldn't worry about the conversion when assigning floats to these properties.

Now that we know what happens when the Movie Clip loads, let's look into what happens every frame thereafter. I stripped down the `onClipEvent(enterFrame)` function and this is what I found inside:

```
this._y += speed;
```

```
if (this._y > 240) this._y = 0;
```

This code is simple but effective. On every frame, the `speed` property is used to increment the _y property of the Movie Clip. If you look in the project file you will notice that I wrote `speed` as `this.speed`. `this.speed` is referencing the same variable, but I wrote it differently so you can get used to looking into other people's code and understanding exactly what it's doing. As far as those calculations go, the `speed` variable sums are accumulated in `this._y` and immediately reflected on the screen.

The next line, `if (this._y > 240) this._y = 0;`, is a conditional statement. It tests to see if _y is greater than 240—this would mean the particle is off the bottom of the screen. If it is, the statement resets `this._y` back to 0—and over we start again. Meanwhile, this very same logic is happening in all the other clips that were duplicated from this one.

And that's how easy the particle system was to create. I must admit though, the concepts were hard for me to grasp the first few times, so don't feel bad if you have to practice a bit to get it down.

Duplicating Clips from the Library

One problem with duplicating an existing Movie Clip is that you have to find something to do with the original clip. Sometimes you don't want an original clip on the stage, and sometimes you might just want to add and remove Movie Clips and not worry about strays in the way. Well, you're in luck—ActionScript allows you to do all of this.

Take a look at the usage of a method called `attachMovie`, which is part of the `MovieClip` class (just like `duplicateMovieClip` is):

```
myMovieClip.attachMovie( "idName", "newClipInstance", depth );
```

It works in very much the same way `duplicateMovieClip` does, except that `attachMovie` creates instances of a symbol in the Library window instead of a copy of another instance on the stage. A big difference is that you can copy the code that's embedded in your duplicated Movie Clips. This isn't possible when attaching Movie Clips from the Library.

Let's skip the explanation of the `idName` parameter for now—I'll just tell you that this is the linkage name for the symbol in the Library.

The `newClipInstance` parameter is very simple—just like in the `duplicateMovieClip` method, this will be the instance name of the new clip. The `depth` parameter defines what internal layer the Movie Clip will be assigned to. Remember that all attached or duplicated Movie Clips should be on unique layers.

> **NOTE**
>
> Remember that `newClipInstance` and `depth` should always be unique.

In order to better explain the `idName` parameter, I have written another demo for you. It is named GDA_PROG6.3.fla. Go ahead and open it and navigate to the second frame. Notice that there aren't any objects on the stage except for the background graphics. See Figure 6.3.

Figure 6.3

The empty playground

Now go ahead and test the movie. Click the button and you'll have a whole bunch of marbles bouncing all over the screen. Nice trick, eh? Take a look at Figure 6.4 for the "after" shots.

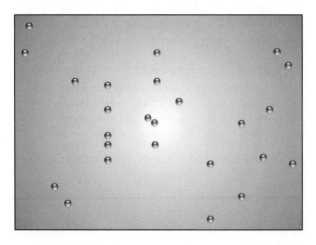

Figure 6.4

There go your lost marbles!

Go back to the project file and access your Library window. (In case you forgot how to do that, press F11.) Once you have the Library window open, stretch it until you see all the fields shown in Figure 6.5.

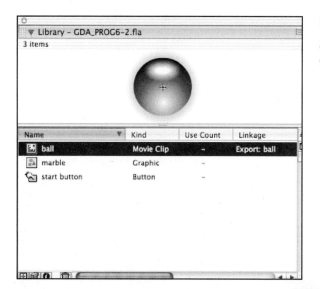

Figure 6.5

Examining the Library window for linkage

Look at the fourth column under Linkage. Notice that the Movie Clip named "ball" has a statement under the linkage column— Export: ball. "ball" happens to be the name `attachMovie` will use to create instances of this clip.

So now that you know how to check what the linkage name is for a symbol, how would you set one up? Let's look into what you already have in front of you. In the Library window, right-click or Control-click (Mac users) on your ball symbol. From the context menu, select Linkage. The Linkage Properties dialog box, shown in Figure 6.6, will open.

NOTE

So what am I making you do here? What you are essentially doing is learning and familiarizing yourself with assigning linkage properties to your Movie Clips so that you can create instances of them in ActionScript. That's all. It sounds complicated, but all you're doing is assigning the symbol an alias that you can use to refer to the symbol in ActionScript.

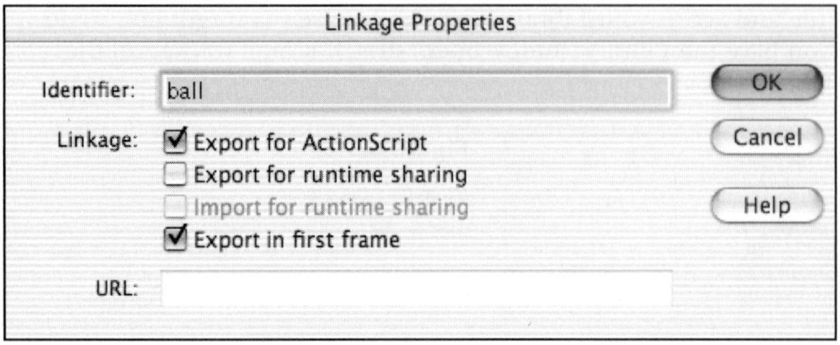

Figure 6.6

Modifying linkage properties

Let me quickly tell you a little about the internals of how Flash writes an SWF file. Flash first examines everything in the library. It makes sure that all the symbols are being used. If they're not, the symbols are not exported with the file. But sometimes when writing a game, you do not want symbols on your Timeline because you want to create dynamic Movie Clips that are created on-the-fly.

So how do you get around this if Flash doesn't export the Movie Clips that aren't being used? This is when you set up the symbols linkage properties from your Library window—in the same Linkage Properties dialog box you see in Figure 6.6.

By setting up the linkage properties, you can let Flash know that you want your symbol included in the first frame. This guarantees that your symbol will be included with the project. You can also assign an alias that you can use from within ActionScript with the `attachMovie` command.

To ensure that ActionScript assigned this exported name, make sure the Export for ActionScript option is selected. To ensure that the symbol is exported with the SWF movie file, select the Export in first frame option. Click OK after you've assigned an ID name and you should be ready to create instances of that symbol dynamically.

NOTE

As you are not duplicating a clip that's already on the stage, `attachMovie` will not copy code into the instances—it will only copy the graphics from the symbol.

TIP

As you probably already guessed, you can remove clips dynamically. You can either use the action or the method way of the `removeMovieClip` command. If you use it as a Movie Clip method (with the dot notation) all you have to do is call this function and your clip disappears. If you use it as an action, all you have to do is call this function with the name of the target clip within its parentheses. If you want more information on this action command, don't hesitate to look it up in the Help file.

The attachMovie Demo

Now that you know how to set up a symbol for the attachMovie Movie Clip method, let's turn to the attachMovie demo. The file name of the SWF is GDA_PROG6.3.swf. It has two frames on the main Timeline. One introduces what the user is about to see in the splash screen, and the other screen is where the action takes place.

The button on the screen you see in Figure 6.7 has the following code:

```
on (release) {
  nextFrame();
}
```

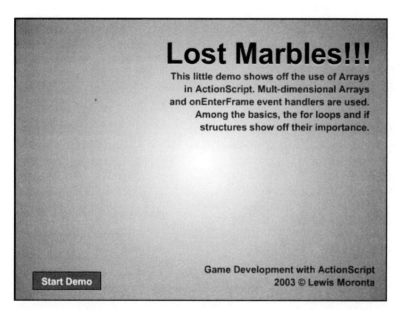

Figure 6.7

Splash screen to the Lost Marbles!!! demo

This code should be familiar enough. The on(release) button handler executes its block when the user finishes pressing a button. The nextFrame() function causes the movie to advance and stop one frame forward. But in order for the user to see this frame, the movie has to pause here until the user clicks this button—how is that done? Easily. Check the first frame on the project file GDA_PROG6.3.fla; I have placed a stop command so that the movie will freeze until the user clicks on the button, executing the nextFrame command.

Now I'm about to introduce the code that really makes this program tick. You already saw the important setup section of the program in the last section of this chapter. Now you're going to see the code that is controlling all the lost marbles at full power. See the following listing, and try to understand it before reading on.

```
// By Lewis Moronta, 2003
// GDA_PROG6.2.fla
// This little demo shows off the
// use of OOP in ActionScript. attachMovie(),
// Mult-dimensional Arrays and onEnterFrame
// event handlers are used. Among the basics,
// the for loops and if structures show off
// their importance.

// IMPORTANT: Feel free to modify...
// This is one of the best ways to learn!

// This is *THE* variable that decides
// how many bouncing balls are in the scene.
numBalls = 25;

// Here we declare a new array called
// bouncingBalls of size numBalls
bouncingBalls = new Array(numBalls);

// Here we loop through numBalls in
// order to initialize each ball.
for (i = 0; i < numBalls; i++) {
  // This line is *VERY* important
  // it declares each item as an object.
  // This allows us to add properties to
  // each item in bouncingBalls
  bouncingBalls[i] = {};

  // These next couple of lines find a number from
  // -20 to 20 and assign it to the new velocity variables
  bouncingBalls[i].xv = Math.round(Math.random()*39+1)-20;
  bouncingBalls[i].yv = Math.round(Math.random()*39+1)-20;

  // "ball" is a Movie Clip we declared and is in our library
  // window. attachMovie() makes copies of it. Once we have
  // a copy, we then initialize x & y by centering them.
```

```
    bouncingBalls[i].mc = attachMovie("ball", "ball"+i, i);
    bouncingBalls[i].mc._x = 550/2;
    bouncingBalls[i].mc._y = 400/2;
}

onEnterFrame = function () {

  for (i = 0; i < numBalls; i++) {

    // These two lines essentially update the screen
    // by updating the bouncingBalls array.
    bouncingBalls[i].mc._x += bouncingBalls[i].xv;
    bouncingBalls[i].mc._y += bouncingBalls[i].yv;

    // The following section is the collision detection section.
    // Try saying that 3x fast! This first "if" checks to see
    // if we are "the balls width" from the right side of the screen
    // if so, then we adjust the ball to that position and we reverse
    // the velocity to get that "bouncing effect."
    if (bouncingBalls[i].mc._x > (549-bouncingBalls[i].mc._width)) {
      bouncingBalls[i].mc._x = (549-bouncingBalls[i].mc._width);
      bouncingBalls[i].xv = -bouncingBalls[i].xv;
    }

    // Now we check the left side of the screen and do the same.
    if (bouncingBalls[i].mc._x < bouncingBalls[i].mc._width) {
      bouncingBalls[i].mc._x = bouncingBalls[i].mc._width;
      bouncingBalls[i].xv = -bouncingBalls[i].xv;
    }

    // And now for the bottom bouncing test...
    if (bouncingBalls[i].mc._y > (399-bouncingBalls[i].mc._height)) {
      bouncingBalls[i].mc._y = (399-bouncingBalls[i].mc._height);
      bouncingBalls[i].yv = -bouncingBalls[i].yv;
    }

    // Finally, we check against the top.
    if (bouncingBalls[i].mc._y < bouncingBalls[i].mc._height) {
      bouncingBalls[i].mc._y = bouncingBalls[i].mc._height;
      bouncingBalls[i].yv = -bouncingBalls[i].yv;
    }
  } // End of for
}; // End of onEnterFrame
```

Looks scary, doesn't it? It won't be after this chapter. As a matter of fact, you can use most of this code to create your own little programs that produce cool effects. I have broken it down for you so that you can understand what each piece does. Look at the following snippet:

```
// This is *THE* variable that decides
// how many bouncing balls are in the scene.
numBalls = 25;
```

This was the variable I defined that the initialization part of the program was written around. Just by changing its value you can determine how many lost marbles will be on stage at any one time.

The following line declares an array. I have formatted the structure of the program so that each of these elements will contain an object (of type Movie Clip) that we can manipulate in order to handle all of what's going on.

```
// Here we declare a new array called
// bouncingBalls of size numBalls
bouncingBalls = new Array(numBalls);
```

Here I enter the very first for loop of the program. It will loop until i is greater than the value in numBalls. What's done in this loop is very interesting—an object is created and initialized into the array I created in the last part. Pay close attention.

```
// Here we loop through numBalls in
// order to initialize each ball.
for (i = 0; i < numBalls; i++) {
```

This following piece of code is something you should also be familiar with. It declares each item in the array as type object. This will allow us to add properties to each of the elements and treat each as a regular object.

```
    // This line is *VERY* important
    // it declares each item as an object.
    // This allows us to add properties to
    // each item in bouncingBalls
    bouncingBalls[i] = {};
```

I immediately created two new properties in the object we generated from the last line. These properties are the x and y velocities that will make the balls move across the screen.

You will also notice a new math method, Math.round. It's similar to Math.floor except that floor only rounds down. Math.round, as the name implies, rounds to the nearest whole number.

You should also notice the number manipulation here. I first scaled the result from random from 0–39. I then added 1 to this result so that I can have a new range of 1-40. I then rounded this result so that I can be sure I'm only dealing with integers. Finally, I subtracted 20 from this result to yield my new range of –20 to 20. Whatever the output of this calculation is becomes my new velocity for the current object being initiated.

```
// These next couple of lines find a number from
// -20 to 20 and assign it to the new velocity variables
bouncingBalls[i].xv = Math.round(Math.random()*39+1)-20;
bouncingBalls[i].yv = Math.round(Math.random()*39+1)-20;
```

Remember when I was talking about regarding linkage properties? That is what has to be done for the following line to work. The ball Movie Clip has the linkage properties setup and the identifier name of "ball." This allows attachMovie to create instances from this symbol.

As I showed you before, I used the loop's variable to dynamically create an instance name and assign a depth to the new object. It's pretty standard, and you should be getting used to it already. There's nothing more to that line.

```
// "ball" is a Movie Clip we declared and is in our library
// window. attachMovie() makes copies of it. Once we have
// a copy, we then initialize x & y by centering them.
bouncingBalls[i].mc = attachMovie("ball", "ball"+i, i);
```

As the new property mc was created in the last line (of type Movie Clip) we can automatically start using the built-in Movie Clip properties _x and _y. I used them in this case to center the object because I didn't want them all stacked up in a corner. These lines were more of
a preference thing than anything else—I just thought it was cool how the balls start moving from the center of the screen. Wouldn't it be boring if they just sprouted out from a corner?

```
bouncingBalls[i].mc._x = 550/2;
bouncingBalls[i].mc._y = 400/2;
```

NOTE

Why did I use 550 and 400 in the last bit of code? That's because those are the dimensions of the viewable that I have in my project file. In other words, if your movie has different dimensions, make sure you use those dimensions to calculate things like center points.

```
}
```

As I wrote this code on the main Timeline, I don't have an onClipEvent(enterFrame) handler. Instead, I have an onEnterFrame handler that has the same function. This is the one I used for frame-to-frame action. Observe how it is defined:

```
onEnterFrame = function () {
```

The first thing I did before moving on in this function was to create a loop that can loop through all my elements in the bouncingBalls array. This way, I can make sure all my elements and objects are being acted upon.

Notice that numBalls is used in the following statement. Also notice that numBalls is global. If the var keyword were to be used, onEnterFrame wouldn't be able to use its value.

```
for (i = 0; i < numBalls; i++) {
```

This next piece of code is the code that makes the balls move. Remember that Movie Clip instances were stored in the mc property of each object. xv and yv properties were also created and initialized (as velocities). These velocities are added to the Movie Clip's current position on every frame—this is what causes the motion. Notice that the for loop's variable is being used to decide which element (or ball) in the array to control. See how flexible this OOP stuff can be?

```
// These two lines essentially updates the screen
// by updating the bouncingBalls array.
bouncingBalls[i].mc._x += bouncingBalls[i].xv;
bouncingBalls[i].mc._y += bouncingBalls[i].yv;
```

Below, there are a series of if statements that test for certain conditions. The first if statement below checks to see if the current ball is off the right side of the screen, by checking for anything past 550 pixels plus the object's width. If the ball is off the right side of the screen, it adjusts the ball position by putting it right on the edge (just in case it went too far out) and then reversing its ball velocity. This reversal causes the ball's velocity to be subtracted from its current position if it's being added, and added if it's being subtracted. In other words, the ball will go in the other direction.

```
// The following section is the collision detection section.
// Try saying that 3x fast! This first "if" checkes to see
// if we are "the balls width" from the right side of the screen
// if so, then we adjust the ball to that position and we reverse
// the velocity to get that "bouncing effect".
if (bouncingBalls[i].mc._x > (549-bouncingBalls[i].mc._width)) {
   bouncingBalls[i].mc._x = (549-bouncingBalls[i].mc._width);
   bouncingBalls[i].xv = -bouncingBalls[i].xv;
}
```

The following segment is very similar to the previous one and the following two. This one checks to see if the ball is off the left side of the screen. If it is, the ball's position will be adjusted and its velocity reversed. I can tell you're getting the hang of this already!

```
// Now we check the left side of the screen and do the same.
if (bouncingBalls[i].mc._x < bouncingBalls[i].mc._width) {
   bouncingBalls[i].mc._x = bouncingBalls[i].mc._width;
   bouncingBalls[i].xv = -bouncingBalls[i].xv;
}
```

The snippet of code to follow tests to see whether the ball is off the bottom of the screen. I know, I know, this seems repetitive, but there are four sides to our screen, and this has to be done to complete the effect. Again, if this tests to true, the position is adjusted and the velocity is reversed.

```
// And now for the bottom bouncing test...
if (bouncingBalls[i].mc._y > (399-bouncingBalls[i].mc._height)) {
   bouncingBalls[i].mc._y = (399-bouncingBalls[i].mc._height);
   bouncingBalls[i].yv = -bouncingBalls[i].yv;
}
```

And the last bit of code checks to see if the ball went off the top of the screen. If it did, the code does what the other statements did—it adjusts the position and reverses the velocity. Crammed into your brain sufficiently?

```
// Finally, we check against the top.
if (bouncingBalls[i].mc._y < bouncingBalls[i].mc._height) {
   bouncingBalls[i].mc._y = bouncingBalls[i].mc._height;
   bouncingBalls[i].yv = -bouncingBalls[i].yv;
}
 } // End of for
}; // End of onEnterFrame
```

I believe you are now ready to create a full-power particle system with your newfound knowledge. You can actually create pretty interesting games with the knowledge you now possess. All you have to do is believe.

Improving the Particle System

So far I've only scratched the surface of what ActionScript can do. When designing a particle system, let your imagination run wild. Get a pen and pad and start writing down attributes of the system you want to imitate.

Let's start our snowing demo for example. I must admit it does look cool, but it gets boring quickly because the snow is coming straight down. It seems as though wind doesn't exist in that world.

How on earth would you do this? It's not like you could just blow on your monitor and make the snow sway to one side. Remember that whole concept of OOP? Well—let's use it. Let's add the WindPush property to each snowflake. This property will hold the direction and velocity (referred to as a *vector quantity*, but I'll discuss that later) of the wind forces.

Once you have this set up, all you have to do is apply these forces to each snowflake horizontally. Apply the force by adding it to its _x property. And that's it.

Now let's stop chatting and whip out the snow demo and modify it. I saved it as GDA_PROG6.4.fla. I modified the code just as I said here. Go ahead and play the file GDA_PROG6.4.swf. It looks much more interesting, and all I did was add wind. Go figure.

Here is the new listing:

```
onClipEvent(load) {

    // Initialize
    // Math.random returns a number from
    // 0 to 1. By multiplying a number,
    // you can get it to return a certain
    // range of numbers.
    this._x = Math.random()*320; // Returns 0-319
    this._y = Math.random()*240; // Returns 0-239
    speed = Math.floor(Math.random()*3)+6;

    // **** NEW LINE ****
    WindPush = 2;
}


onClipEvent(enterFrame) {
    // Moving code is here =)
    this._y += this.speed;

    // **** NEW LINE ****
    this._x += this.WindPush;

    if (this._y > 240) this._y = 0;

    // **** NEW LINE ****
    if (this._x > 320) this._x = 0;
}
```

I have added three new lines that made a world of a difference. I commented over them so you can spot them easily.

The following line is the first that I added in the onClipEvent(load) handler inside the Movie Clip that will be duplicated:

```
    // **** NEW LINE ****
    WindPush = 2;
```

This will cause all additional clips to contain similar code. As a matter of fact, it's the exact same code that produces different results thanks to that Math.random method.

Just like the speed attribute that we added earlier, I added the WindPush property and initialized it to 2. Now that we have a new property, it's time to do something with it.

The next line I added was in the onClipEvent(enterFrame) handler which is also in the Movie Clip that will be duplicated. Here it is:

```
    // **** NEW LINE ****
    this._x += this.WindPush;
```

As `WindPush` is 2 for all the duplicated Movie Clips, they will all move two pixels to the right on each frame. This is where the wind effect is achieved. But what do you do when a snowflake Movie Clip reaches the end of the screen? Simple—just wrap it around the left side. This is the code that I wrote for that:

```
// **** NEW LINE ****
if (this._x > 320) this._x = 0;
```

All it is saying is that if _x is past 320 pixels to the right, wrap the Movie Clip back to 0.

Go ahead and play with the example. Make sure you understand everything that is going on. If you don't, go back to the beginning of this chapter where I explained how the rest of the code works. When you understand that fully, try adding your own properties.

Before I finish up this chapter, I want to show you that a creative mind is never finished with its work. In our world, nothing is perfect. Nothing in nature is uniform. Let's be realistic—the wind should not push our snowflakes at the same rate. As we are defying that concept in our demo, I decided to write some code that would give the snowflakes different velocities by using our random number-generating friend. Check out GDA_PROG6.5.swf for the playable demo and GDA_PROG6.5.fla for the project file.

Observe the following listing. Here you will see the last tweak of the chapter. It can be tweaked even more—it's up to your observation of the real world and your imagination.

```
onClipEvent(load) {
  // Initialize
  // Math.random returns a number from
  // 0 to 1. By multiplying a number,
  // you can get it to return a certain
  // range of numbers.
  this._x = Math.random()*320; // Returns 0-319
  this._y = Math.random()*240; // Returns 0-239
  speed = Math.floor(Math.random()*3)+6;

  // **** NEW LINE ****
  WindPush = Math.floor(Math.random()*6)+1;
}


onClipEvent(enterFrame) {
  // Moving code is here =)
  this._y += this.speed;

  // **** NEW LINE ****
  this._x += this.WindPush;

  if (this._y > 240) this._y = 0;
```

```
// **** NEW LINE ****
if (this._x > 320) this._x = 0;
}
```

As you can see, one little line does make a difference. The line that I'm talking about is the line where the WindPush property is being initialized. Take a look:

```
WindPush = Math.floor(Math.random()*6)+1;
```

This calculation is assigning a value in between the range of 1–6. I'll break it down piece by piece for you. The random method returns a number from 0 to almost 1 and when multiplied by 6 it will yield a number from 0 to almost 6. When you apply the floor method, it will restrict the values to whole numbers from 0 to 5. I added 1 to make the range 1–6. This is the possible range of WindPush values for each snowflake.

> **NOTE**
>
> Doesn't it seem as if there are a lot more snowflakes in this demo than in the first one? Well, there *are* more flakes. I amped up the number to 100 from the original 50. This value can be changed in the code that's on the main Timeline within the first frame. The name of the variable that controls this is numPart.

Now that you get the idea, you're ready to move on to some newer topics. Before you do, go ahead and review what you learned and try the chapter exercise.

Summary

In this chapter, you started off by learning everything that had to do with random number generation, including you learned how to scale them to a specific range of possibilities. You also learned about methods that rounded the numbers for you. You also met the floor method that can round numeric values down to the nearest integer for you when needed.

After you mastered the random number thing, you learned how to duplicate Movie Clips from an instance that is already on the stage. You even learned how to duplicate the code that's inside the Movie Clips using this method. You took advantage of the fact that code also gets copied when you duplicate an instance and you examined a demo that used the embedded code to give each of the duplicated clips their own personalities.

When duplicating clips, you learned all about their internal depth and layer structure. You also learned how to assign unique instance names to them on-the-fly.

As the chapter progressed, you learned how to set up linkage properties and create even more complex dynamic Movie Clip instances from the library window.

As icing on the cake, you got to see the infamous arrays in action. They really didn't show off all their powers that you learned how to use in the last chapter but they were valuable.

As the grand finale, I showed you that it's not in how complex or long the code is, but in how creative you are and how far you are willing to go. You saw how you can take a regular snowy day and convert it to a blizzard. Not too bad, eh?

Question & Answer

Q. All this stuff is really cool but how much longer do you think it will be before I complete my first game?

A. The truth is that after you feel comfortable with what you know, you can create anything you want. Even experts don't know everything, but their confidence allows them to find the information that they don't know—and they learn it. Your programming career will be an ever-learning experience.

Exercise

1. Create a particle system that has motion forces just like in our particle demos. This time, instead of simulating nature on earth, create a star field. Have some stars move really slowly, others at a medium speed, and the topmost layer really fast. Once you complete this, sit back, relax, and enjoy your new creation.

CHAPTER 7

DRAWING WITH A SCRIPT

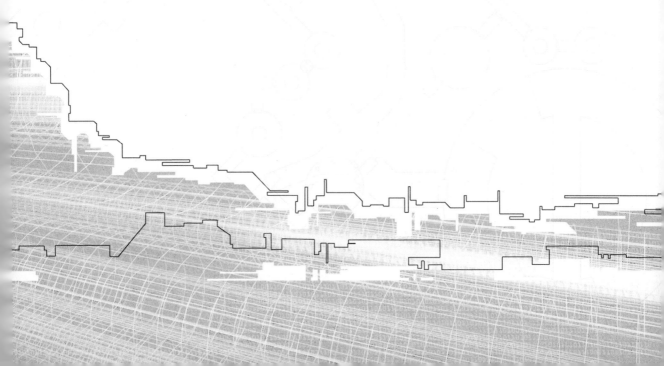

Now that you know that Flash is an extraordinarily powerful program, you won't be surprised to know that you can draw with just a few scripting commands. These commands are not difficult to learn and are extremely flexible. With these creativity-enhancing tools and the information in this chapter, you will learn how to:

- Draw lines, shapes, and curves
- Draw shapes with fills
- Automate patterns
- Draw shapes in Movie Clips

How to Draw a Line

In this section, you're going to learn how to create lines procedurally with ActionScript. Why is it important to learn how to do this when you can just draw lines beforehand with the Line tool? Well, you need to learn how to draw lines dynamically because you want more control over your animations. Everything from advanced screen transitions to the simple hands on an analog clock to a drawing program requires you to program dynamic lines. Think about it, even some advanced patterns and shapes that can take humans tedious days to put together can take a computer less than a second to produce. Once your scripts have control over the objects in your program, you can really make them come alive!

Before you ask Flash to draw a line, you must define the line's width, color, and sometimes even its opacity. This is considered the *style* of the line. The following command is used to set up and/or change a line style:

```
lineStyle(lineWidth, color, alpha);
```

This command prepares subsequent ActionScript drawing commands with these settings. All of the following lines will be drawn with these settings until another lineStyle command is called.

Once you learn this command, you're almost ready to start drawing some lines. Before you can actually draw the line, you should know that Flash draws lines from the position of its "virtual pen." Luckily, this "pen" can be repositioned. And when your program is first run, the position of this pen is not defined—you must define it before you draw anything. The command that you need to use to define the point you want to draw from is the moveTo command which is prototyped like so:

```
moveTo( x, y );
```

This line simply tells ActionScript to move and continue from this new position.

The next command is the actual line-drawing command itself, which looks like this:

```
lineTo( x, y);
```

The following listing demonstrates all the discussed commands. Take a look.

```
// Game Development with ActionScript
// 2003 (c) Lewis Moronta     .
// Drawing with a Script, Chapter 7
// This program demonstrates how to
// draw a line in ActionScript with
// built in drawing commands.

// Setup the line style for the
// following commands.
lineStyle( 5, 0x000000, 100);

// Initialize the initial starting point.
moveTo( 10, 10);

// Draw the line to the final point.
lineTo( 310, 190);
```

Notice that there are only three commands in this listing. Let's see what's happening in the first one:

```
// Setup the line style for the
// following commands.
lineStyle( 5, 0x000000, 100);
```

I assigned the line a thickness of 5, as you can see from the first parameter. The second parameter needs a little explanation. The notation 0x indicates that the number is a hexadecimal number. Hexadecimal numbers are base 16 as opposed to our regular number system, which is base 10. The hexadecimal system goes from 0 to the letter F. In other words, a sample count would be:

0, 1, 2, 3, 4, 5, 6, 7, 8, 9, A, B, C, D, E, F

where A through F represent numbers from 10 to 15.

The color is encoded in hexadecimal format because you can easily separate the red, green, and blue components cleanly within the number places. Allow me to demonstrate. The following line is a sample number for demonstration purposes only (there are no Rs or Gs in the number system):

0xRRGGBB

Any value written within the RR place in the sample number will represent the amount of red in the final color. Anything, including zero, within the GG place would mix in green. And of course, anything within the BB place would represent the blue in the system. If all these areas are blank, or zero, this would cause Flash to output the color black. Black is what is achieved by 0×000000.

TIP

Don't focus on the color system too much. You will eventually catch on as you see more examples of it. Go ahead and open GDA_PROG7.1.fla and play with the color in the `lineStyle` method. See if you can generate a completely red, green, or blue line. Once you achieve that effect, see if you can mix some colors—try to get yellow.

The last parameter is optional. It tells Flash to draw the line with a certain level of transparency. 100 percent would make it completely opaque and 0 percent would make it completely transparent (invisible).

The following line tells Flash the point at which it should start drawing from.

```
// Initialize the initial starting point.
moveTo( 10, 10);
```

The `moveTo` method was set to the coordinates (10, 10). This is near the top left corner. You can easily tell because the topmost left viewable pixel on the corner is (0, 0). Whenever you want to tell Flash a new position, use this command.

Next, we call `lineTo ()` to complete the line:

```
// Draw the line to the final point.
lineTo( 310, 190);
```

When I created the scene, I prepared the layers and the movie's dimensions. I set the dimensions to 320×200. This means that the line will be drawn very close to the bottom rightmost edge.

In the end, what do you get? You get a movie that displays a line from (10, 10) to (310, 190) just like in Figure 7.1.

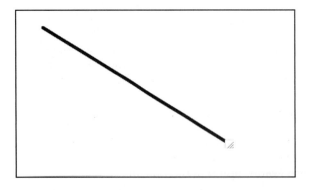

Figure 7.1

A line drawn from
(10, 10)–(310, 190)

How to Draw Shapes

Lines are the basis to almost every computer-aided design. So that you can get an idea of how to create some shapes, I have written another short demo that draws a triangle for you. Check out the following listing.

```
// Game Development with ActionScript
// 2003 (c) Lewis Moronta
// Drawing with a Script, Chapter 7
// This program demonstrates how to
// draw and connect lines to create
// shapes with built in ActionScript
// Commands.

// Setup the line style for the
// following commands.
lineStyle( 3, 0xFF0000);

// Initialize the initial starting point.
moveTo( 160, 20);

// Connect the lines by subsequent commands
lineTo( 80, 170);
lineTo( 240, 170);
lineTo( 160, 20);
```

If you run this program (GDA_PROG7.2.fla) from the CD and you test the movie, you'll see a red triangle on the stage. See Figure 7.2.

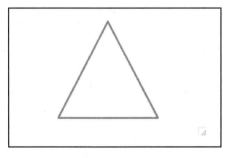

Figure 7.2

A red triangle drawn with a script

Let's step through it to see what's happening. Observe the first method. It's used differently here:

```
// Setup the line style for the
// following commands.
lineStyle( 3, 0xFF0000);
```

The first thing you should notice is that I dropped the final parameter. As I said before, it is optional. If you want your line always to be 100 percent opaque, you could just omit the third parameter.

As you move on to examine the next line, you'll notice that I chose a center point from which to start drawing this triangle:

```
// Initialize the initial starting point.
moveTo( 160, 20);
```

As you move on to the next three lines, you'll see that the next line command will draw from this last line:

```
// Connect the lines by subsequent commands
lineTo( 80, 170);
lineTo( 240, 170);
lineTo( 160, 20);
```

The first lineTo command draws a line from (160, 20) to (80, 170). This causes Flash to draw a line slanting down to the right.

The next lineTo method takes off from the last point at which the last lineTo or moveTo command was called. So, in other words, the next line will be drawn from (80, 170) to (240, 170).

After the line is drawn, all you need is to close the shape. How? Easy—all you have to do is draw another line to the same starting point where the moveTo command was set. This point was (160, 20).

Figure 7.3 shows a breakdown of what's happening behind the scenes.

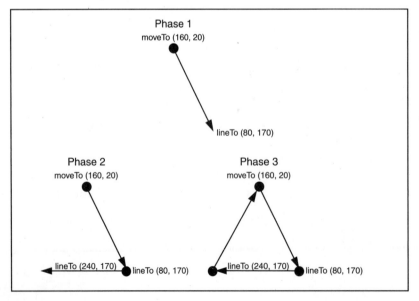

Figure 7.3

Step-by-step images showing how lines connect to each other

How to Automate Patterns

So why am I teaching you how to draw dynamic lines if this book is supposed to teach you how to make games? The reason this chapter even made the cut for this book was because these commands can greatly enhance your gaming and animation experience—for you, the programmer, and your game players. Demos like the ones in this chapter will allow you to get comfortably acquainted with these commands—enough for you to branch off on your own and create your own surrealistic effects.

You'll have to really practice these line-drawing commands in order to get used to using them. Some effects, patterns and designs can be generated by your scripts with loops to create some interesting patterns, as you'll see in this section. We'll start out with simple patterns and then build up from there. To start, I'm going to create a list of horizontal lines on the screen.

GDA_PROG7.3.fla is the file name that's under the GDA_CH07 folder on the CD. This project contains code that produces the output shown in Figure 7.4.

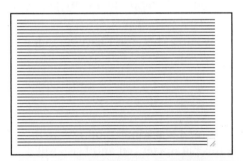

Figure 7.4

A line pattern created with ActionScript

NOTE

Most of the code in these demos is familiar, so that you can just focus on the new parts you're learning about in each section. If you do end up seeing spanking new code, don't worry; I will explain it all.

Take a look at the following listing.

```
// Game Development with ActionScript
// 2003 (c) Lewis Moronta
// Drawing with a Script, Chapter 7
// This program demonstrates how to
// draw and connect lines to create
// shapes with built in ActionScript
// Commands.
```

```
// Setup the line style for the
// following commands.
lineStyle( 1, 0x000000, 100);

// Initialize the initial starting point.
moveTo( 0, 0);

var step = 5; // This is the space between the lines

// Connect the lines by subsequent commands
for (var y = 0; y < 200; y+=step) {
  moveTo( 0, y);
  lineTo( 319, y);
}
```

Notice that this listing is not much longer than the other ones but it does so much more. Gotta thank that for loop. This program basically initializes the line style then sets up the initial point where ActionScript works. Once this is accomplished, the program enters into a loop that draws a line at a different y value each time is passes.

Let's look into the code. The following line, as you already know (because I have pounded it into your brain) sets up the line style:

```
// Setup the line style for the
// following commands.
lineStyle( 1, 0x000000, 100);
```

I decided I wanted 1-point thickness on the lines. I also wanted black lines, and I wanted them 100% opaque (remember, though, you can leave this parameter out and Flash will default to 100% opacity anyway).

The following line also sets up the program before it starts doing any real work:

```
// Initialize the initial starting point.
moveTo( 0, 0);
```

This line moves Flash to its origin point, (0, 0), causing any subsequent line commands to draw from this point.

Before I planned this small demo, I decided that the for loop should be able to control where the next line would be drawn. That's why I use y, the loop counter, as the Y-coordinate of the line as well. This way, I can adjust the value and I'll have a tighter or looser pattern depending on the "step" taken by the loop (in other words, how many pixels separate each line). I put this value in a variable called step, and set it to 5:

```
var step = 5; // This is the space between the lines
```

Before I explain the short loop below, I want you to notice a few things about the setup.

```
// Connect the lines by subsequent commands
for (var y = 0; y < 200; y+=step) {
```

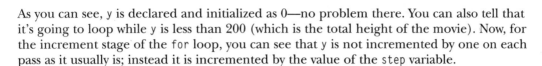

As you can see, y is declared and initialized as 0—no problem there. You can also tell that it's going to loop while y is less than 200 (which is the total height of the movie). Now, for the increment stage of the for loop, you can see that y is not incremented by one on each pass as it usually is; instead it is incremented by the value of the step variable.

You already know that each line will be drawn according to y during each pass. The following two lines help move the movie down while drawing lines every certain number of pixels. Remember that it is the step variable that decides this amount. I have already assigned it to 5.

```
  moveTo( 0, y);
  lineTo( 319, y);
}
```

It might not be immediately clear what is happening here, but I want you to observe how both commands use the for's y variable to decide their next y position. Their x positions will always be 0 to 319, which means that a line will be drawn from left to right on each pass. As the line's y position is the same (on each pass), you can conclude the line will be horizontal.

Let's get a bit more complicated, but use similar code. Before you move on, take a minute and see if you can write up the code that creates a cross pattern just like that in Figure 7.5.

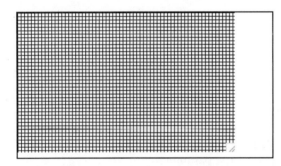

Figure 7.5

Cross pattern created with a script

Now take a look at the following listing. I've made a cross pattern too. You'll be surprised at how this listing is almost identical to the previous listing.

> **NOTE**
>
> A lot of the coding techniques that I use are universal, so if you feel comfortable using another style, feel free. But when learning new topics, try to keep your code as simple as possible so that you can master the concepts before mastering the code writing.

```
// Game Development with ActionScript
// 2003 (c) Lewis Moronta
// Drawing with a Script, Chapter 7
// This program demonstrates how to
// draw and connect lines to create
// shapes with built in ActionScript
// Commands.

// Setup the line style for the
// following commands.
lineStyle( 0, 0x00FF00);

// Initialize the initial starting point.
moveTo( 0, 0);

var step = 5; // This is the space between the lines

// Create the horizontal lines...
for (var y = 0; y < 200; y+=step) {
  moveTo( 0, y);
  lineTo( 319, y);
}

// Create the vertical lines...
for (var x = 0; x < 320; X+=step) {
  moveTo( x, 0);
  lineTo( x, 199);
}
```

This listing creates a cross-wired green-lined pattern. Allow me to break it down for you. lineStyle is the first command I want to go over in the listing. Notice a parameter was omitted—the last one, and the value that was given to the first parameter.

```
// Setup the line style for the
// following commands.
lineStyle( 0, 0x00FF00);
```

Notice that lineStyle has 0 as its line width. Does this mean that the lines won't be visible? No—this means that you want Flash to draw a hairline type of line. A hairline is a line that is exactly one pixel width.

The following line resets the current position to (0, 0):

```
// Initialize the initial starting point.
moveTo( 0, 0);
```

I kept the step variable in this demo. It will be used in both of the following loops.

```
var step = 5; // This is the space between the lines
```

The following loop is really similar to the previous one:

```
// Create the horizontal lines...
for (var y = 0; y < 200; y+=step) {
  moveTo( 0, y);
  lineTo( 319, y);
}
```

This short loop loops through the height of the movie, drawing lines five pixels apart. It's exactly the same loop as in the last example.

I want you notice the final loop. It's very similar to this last loop, but it draws lines going vertically moving horizontally:

```
// Create the vertical lines...
for (var x = 0; x < 320; X+=step) {
  moveTo( x, 0);
  lineTo( x, 199);
}
```

This loop creates the x variable that is initialized 0. As the width of my movie is 320, I set up the loop to loop while x is less than 320. Notice that x is also being incremented by step on each pass. This means that you'll get square shapes when the pattern is finished and drawn.

Now notice the line drawing commands. They're using the x variable to dictate their x position. As their y values are constant, you know that lines will be drawn from top to bottom—left to right.

> **TIP**
>
> Mess with the code. Try changing the color of each line as each new line is created. You'll learn from this exercise.

Right before I finish up this section, let me show you another quick demo. This one is demo GDA_PROG7.5.fla. Notice how I slowly built upon the first demo. This is a great way to work—fun, too.

Check out Figure 7.6 before you examine the listing, so that you can get an idea of what the demo does.

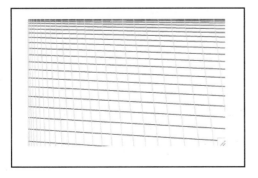

Figure 7.6

A 3D-ish pattern

```
// Game Development with ActionScript
// 2003 (c) Lewis Moronta
// Drawing with a Script, Chapter 7
// This program demonstrates how to
// draw and connect lines to create
// shapes with built in ActionScript
// Commands.

// Setup the line style for the
// following commands.
lineStyle( 0, 0x0000FF);

// Initialize the initial starting point.
moveTo( 0, 0);

var step = 0; // This is the space between the lines

// Create the horizontal lines...
for (var y = 0; y < 200; y+=step, step++) {
  moveTo( 0, y);
  lineTo( 319, y+step);
}

step = 0;
lineStyle( 0, 0x00FF00);

// Create the vertical lines...
for (var x = 0; x < 320; X+=step, step++) {
  moveTo( x, 0);
  lineTo( x+step, 199);
}
```

Now that you're getting the hang of it, let's go through this code a bit more quickly. In the first line you'll see that I'm setting the default line style to a hairline. You can also see that it will be drawn in blue:

```
// Setup the line style for the
// following commands.
lineStyle( 0, 0x0000FF);
```

TIP

All this time I've been assigning colors to these lines and the only value I've been using is 0xFF (in hexadecimal). 0xFF is equivalent to 255, and it's the highest value of that particular color you can mix in with the other two. In other words, you could have a value of 255 for red, 255 for green, and 255 for blue and you would get 0xFFFFFF—this would yield white.

I set up the first point at (0, 0) and the step value to 0:

```
// Initialize the initial starting point.
moveTo( 0, 0);
```

```
var step = 0; // This is the space between the lines
```

Now that we are actually entering a loop, I'll explain what I'm doing during the increment-ing portion of the for loop. Take a look:

```
// Create the horizontal lines...
for (var y = 0; y < 200; y+=step, step++) {
```

Besides incrementing y with the step value, I added another incrementing statement. The step variable is incrementing after each pass, which will create an interesting effect. It's hard to visualize straight from the code but check out the SWF or Figure 7.5 to bet-ter understand what's happening.

TIP

In a for loop, it is possible to initial-ize more than one variable and increment more than one variable. All you have to do is use a comma, just like I did in the last code listing.

I changed the loop's body slightly as well:

```
  moveTo( 0, y);
  lineTo( 319, y+step);
```

Notice that I added the step variable to the y variable to get steadily incrementing spaces to the right side of the stage.

Another difference introduced by this latest script is the mid-program reset code that I put in. It sounds more complicated than it is.

```
step = 0;
lineStyle( 0, 0x00FF00);
```

All I did was reset the step variable and change the line style to green. I did something simi-lar, to the last loop as well. I incremented the step variable along with the x variable. I also added the step value to the x value when drawing the line in order to get nicely incre-mented spaces towards the bottom of the stage.

Drawing Shapes with Fills

Drawing shapes with fills is not that much harder than drawing empty shapes in ActionScript. It's just a matter of learning how to use two more commands. These are the beginFill and endFill methods of a Movie Clip.

I have designed another project for this section, GDA_PROG7.6.fla, which draws a filled triangle. Check it out in Figure 7.7, which shows you how the program internally fills the shape.

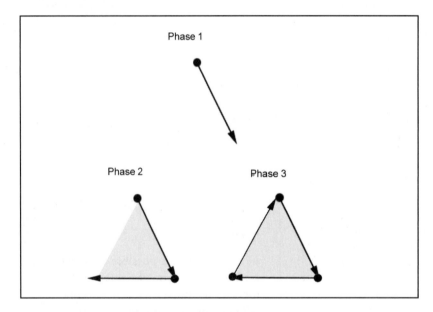

Figure 7.7

Drawing a filled triangle

Now that you know what you're going to learn in this section, let's jump right into the code. Take a look at the following listing.

```
// Game Development with ActionScript
// By Lewis Moronta (c) 2003
// Chapter 7, Drawing with a Script
// This demo demonstrates how to create
// filled shapes with the beginFill
// and endFill methods.

// This line specifies the
// color that the fill should
// be and it also tells Flash
// to draw all closed shapes
// with a fill.
beginFill (0xFFFF00, 80);
```

```
// This sets the line width to 2
// Color to Blue and 100 percent opaque
lineStyle (2, 0x0000FF, 100);

// This draws a triangle
moveTo (160, 10);
lineTo (320, 190);
lineTo (0, 190);
lineTo (160, 10);

// This command ends the filling
// and prevents subsequent commands
// from being filled.
endFill();
```

The beginFill line you see in this listing doesn't do much but tell Flash to set up the fills:

```
// This line specifies the
// color that the fill should
// be and it also tells Flash
// to draw all closed shapes
// with a fill.
beginFill (0xFFFF00, 80);
```

The first parameter indicates the fill's color and the second parameter is the fill's opacity in percent. As I am applying fill style to the _root Movie Clip (which is the highest in the hierarchy), this style will apply for any Movie Clips created within it.

And now, in this following line, the line style is applied:

```
// This sets the line width to 2
// Color to Blue and 100 percent opaque
lineStyle (2, 0x0000FF, 100);
```

As you already noticed, the line thickness is 2 points, the color is blue, and it's completely opaque.

And finally, the moveTo and lineTo commands below draw out the shape (of the triangle). When the script is run, the fill will be there.

```
// This draws a triangle
moveTo (160, 10);
lineTo (320, 190);
lineTo (0, 190);
lineTo (160, 10);
```

Before looking at the last line, notice how drawing a line to the exact point where it was drawn from closes the shape—this part could be omitted because the fill methods automatically close the shape or shapes that you're trying to fill by creating a line between the last point you drew and the first point you drew.

The last command generally stops all fills:

```
// This command ends the filling
// and prevents subsequent commands
// from being filled.
endFill();
```

Any lineTo commands after this point won't generate any fills because of the endFill command. Sweet and simple—just the way I like it.

Drawing Curves

Curves can get tricky because the technique it takes to draw them is one of the most difficult parts of using internal drawing commands. In ActionScript, you can specify a curve with endpoints and a control point. You would assign the two endpoints just as you would with a regular line. The control point is then assigned depending where you want the line to curve.

See Figure 7.8 before reading on; it's a figure showing the relationship between a curve and its control point. The control point is allowed to be anywhere—but remember, wherever you chose to place it, that's the direction where the line will curve to.

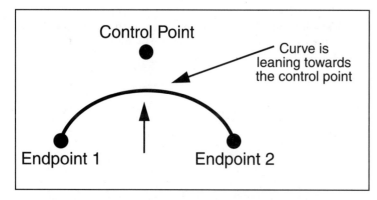

Figure 7.8

Showing off the relationship between the endpoints and the control point of a curve

Figure 7.9 shows a screen shot of the project file GDA_PROG7.7.fla. It demonstrates a curve that is drawn from (0, 100) to (320, 100). So why does the line curve up? There was a control point assigned at (160, 0)—that's why it bends towards the middle-top.

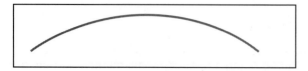

Figure 7.9

Showing off a curve

So what would happen if the line's control point was (0, 0) or (320, 200)? Go ahead and see for yourself in Figure 7.10 and Figure 7.11.

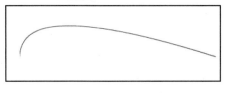

Figure 7.10

Control point set at

(0, 0)

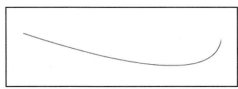

Figure 7.11

Control point set at

(320, 200)

Now you know we can draw curves with the minimum of three points—the two endpoints and the control point. What command can we use for this fabulous curve? Why, the curveTo command, of course. Here's its prototype:

```
myMovieClip.curveTo (controlX, controlY, anchorX, anchorY)
```

Just like the other line commands, curveTo draws from the previous point used (or the point that was given to moveTo).

The controlx parameter specifies the x position relative to the registration point of the parent Movie Clip. In English, that would mean that controlx is the x value of where the control point will be. And of course, controly is the y value that completes the pair. These coordinates are the point that dictates how the curve actually curves.

anchorx and anchory are the endpoints of the curve. This coordinate is a point where the curve will end and where you can continue creating other curves.

> **NOTE**
>
> If you are baffled by where you should place your points, take heed: there is nothing wrong with a little trial and error. Experimentation is part of perfection.

I think you are ready for another listing. The following listing creates the representation of a trigonometric function, sine. Check out the project file GDA_PROG7.8.fla.

```
// Game Development with ActionScript
// By Lewis Moronta (c) 2003
// Demo using ActionScript Curves.

// Set the line style
lineStyle( 0, 0x0000FF);
```

```
// Set the first point (internally)
moveTo( 0, 100 );

// Setup the control point
// and endpoint of the line.
curveTo( 80, 0, 160, 100 );
curveTo(240, 200, 320, 100);
```

The listing's output appears in Figure 7.12.

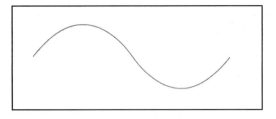

Figure 7.12

Simulated sine wave

By looking at the code, you can quickly see how simple this program really is. The first two lines are the common things we've been doing in this chapter so far:

```
// Set the line style
lineStyle( 0, 0x0000FF);

// Set the first point (internally)
moveTo( 0, 100 );
```

As you can see, I set the color to blue and I have hairline thickness on the curves. The moveTo command set the next point to (0, 100).

There are two curve methods here; check out the first one:

```
// Setup the control point
// and endpoint of the line.
curveTo( 80, 0, 160, 100 );
```

Before we move on, you should know that I moved Flash's "virtual pen" to (0, 100) using the moveTo command.

As the first pair of parameters are the control point's location, you can already tell that this curve is going to bend up. I chose this point so that the line would curve from the center up.

As for the endpoints, I chose points that are centered on the stage. This caused a nice curve up and then down to the middle, where I drew another curve—let's talk about that one now. Take a look:

```
curveTo(240, 200, 320, 100);
```

As the last point was the center of the stage, (160, 100), the line is drawn from this point while curving to (240, 200), its endpoint being (320, 100). As the control point is beneath both of its endpoints, you already know that the curve bends down then comes back up.

And that's all it takes to make complicated curve shapes.

Drawing Shapes in Movie Clips

Creating a shape in a Movie Clip is no harder than what you've already been doing. It's simply a matter of placing the commands inside the clip, or referencing the clip through dot notation. ActionScript not only allows you to draw a shape in Movie Clips, it allows you to create empty Movie Clips that you can fill with wonderful artwork.

```
myMovieClip.createEmptyMovieClip("instanceName", depth);
```

When working with the main Timeline, it's okay to use _parent, _root, and this as the Movie Clip reference. I have used createEmptyMovieClip like this in the upcoming demo:

```
this.createEmptyMovieClip("triangle", 1);
```

This causes an empty Movie Clip with the instance name of triangle and with the depth of 1 to be created on the main Timeline.

Any Movie Clip methods can now be used on triangle with no problem.

Before you look at the listing for the demo in this section, check out the screen shot in Figure 7.13.

> **NOTE**
>
> Empty Movie Clips don't have a set dimension. They adjust to whatever you draw into them. The registration point (0, 0) will always be on the upper left-hand corner.

Figure 7.13

A shape drawn in an empty Movie Clip

```
// Game Development with ActionScript
// By Lewis Moronta (c) 2003
// Creating a shape inside an empty
// Movie Clip with ActionScript.

// Create an empty Movie Clip
// that we are ready to doodle in.
this.createEmptyMovieClip ("triangle", 1);
```

```
// Draw the graphics right into
// the new instance that was created.
with (_root.triangle) {
  beginFill (0x0000FF, 60);
  lineStyle (5, 0xFF0000, 100);
  moveTo (25, 0);
  lineTo (50, 50);
  lineTo (0, 50);
  lineTo (25, 0);
  endFill();
}

// Center the triangle horizontally
triangle._x = 275 - (triangle._height/2);

onEnterFrame = function() {

  // Move it down 10 pixels on every frame.
  triangle._y += 10;

  // If it's off the bottom, wrap it around the top.
  if (triangle._y > 400)
    triangle._y = -triangle._height;
};
```

The screen shot of this demo is not as exciting as the demo itself. This program demonstrates how to create an empty Movie Clip, draw stuff in it, and then manipulate it by using its instance name. I made the shape move vertically in this case. It moves south until it hits the bottom of the screen. And when it does, it pops out of the top. You should have that part of the code memorized already.

The first thing I do in this script is create an empty Movie Clip called "triangle" on the main Timeline—you can tell because I referenced it by the keyword this. It's on depth layer 1 as I mentioned before:

```
// Create an empty Movie Clip
// that we are ready to doodle in.
this.createEmptyMovieClip ("triangle", 1);
```

The next thing you see is a weird new command, called with. Here's how I wrote it:

```
// Draw the graphics right into
// the new instance that was created.
with (_root.triangle) {
```

This command comes in handy when you have a list of commands referencing the same Movie Clip—you can then in turn block out the code where the batch of commands will be

executed and assign those methods to a specific clip. Let's say you had 10 lineTo commands lined up. You want to draw these lines in the Movie Clip called Square. You would literally have to type something in like this:

```
Square.lineTo(x1, y1);
Square.lineTo(x2, y2);
Square.lineTo(x3, y3);
Square.lineTo(x4, y4);
Square.lineTo(x5, y5);
Square.lineTo(x6, y6);
Square.lineTo(x7, y7);
Square.lineTo(x8, y8);
Square.lineTo(x9, y9);
Square.lineTo(x10, y10);
```

The with command can actually save you some typing. You can specify in what Movie Clip you will be executing these methods and just write out the reference once. Check out the following:

```
with (_root.Square) {
  lineTo(x1, y1);
  lineTo(x2, y2);
  lineTo(x3, y3);
  lineTo(x4, y4);
  lineTo(x5, y5);
  lineTo(x6, y6);
  lineTo(x7, y7);
  lineTo(x8, y8);
  lineTo(x9, y9);
  lineTo(x10, y10);
}
```

Notice that Flash knows where to execute these methods because they are enclosed in the with (_root.Square) block.

The commands within the with block initialize the line and the fill styles and draw the shape within the Movie Clip.

```
beginFill (0x0000FF, 60);
lineStyle (5, 0xFF0000, 100);
moveTo (25, 0);
lineTo (50, 50);
lineTo (0, 50);
lineTo (25, 0);
endFill();
```

Just as a review: the line style was set to 5, the color to red, and opacity to 100. Lines were drawn from (25, 0) to (50, 50) to (0, 50) and back to (25, 0). This shape is also filled with the color blue.

After the previous lines of code, you have already created the triangle. The following line positions it—I modified the _x property in our new Movie Clip so that the new graphic is horizontally centered.

```
// Center the triangle horizontally
triangle._x = 275 - (triangle._width/2);
```

How did I calculate the center of the screen? Well, the screen width is 550, so half of it is 275. The center of the triangle would be half its width. If you subtract half of its width from half the stage's width, you would then be able to center the Movie Clip effectively.

The following snippet of the code is a onEnterFrame function that I declared for the main Timeline. You already know that this method is called once every frame. This is the function that helps us animate our—once empty and now filled—Movie Clip.

```
onEnterFrame = function() {

  // Move it down 10 pixels on every frame.
  triangle._y += 10;

  // If it's off the bottom, wrap it around the top.
  if (triangle._y > 400)
    triangle._y = -triangle._height;
}
```

The first line within this function tells you that it's incrementing triangle's _y value by 10 on each frame—this, of course, causes the Movie Clip to move down.

The following if statement checks to see if triangle's _y position is off the bottom of the screen—and if it is, it resets the y position to another value that's above the stage—this causes the triangle to wrap around the top of the stage. It's still cool after so many demos.

Summary

You learned a whole lot in this chapter. You learned how to draw lines with built-in ActionScript methods. You also learned a little regarding hexadecimal numbers. You also learned how to put together basic shapes with your scripts. On top of that, you learned how to use the methods that fill your shapes, and how to create patterns with some ActionScript loops. You ended with a real bang—you even learned how to create complex curves from simple commands. All these methods belong to the Movie Clip class.

And this concludes Part Two of our book.

Question & Answer

Q. Are there any commands to create ovals or circles?

A. Unfortunately, no. But guess what? You can actually create your own functions that you can use later—see the third exercise below.

Exercises

1. Create a program that creates 100 randomly positioned lines on your stage. Use loops to do so. And, if you like, use an empty Movie Clip—but it's not required.

2. Modify the previous program and make the program create each new line in a new color and thickness.

3. Create a function that you can reuse that creates circles of any diameter.

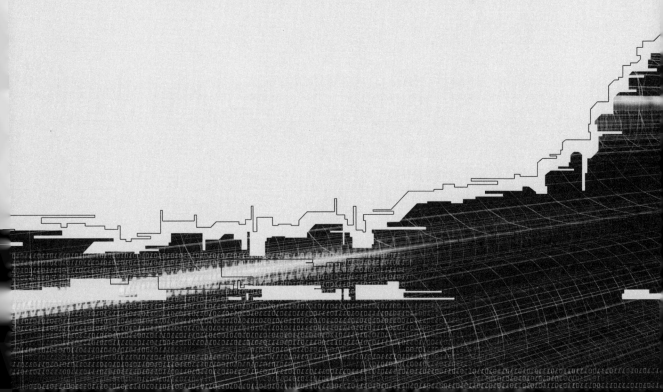

PART THREE

INTERACTIVITY AND SOUND

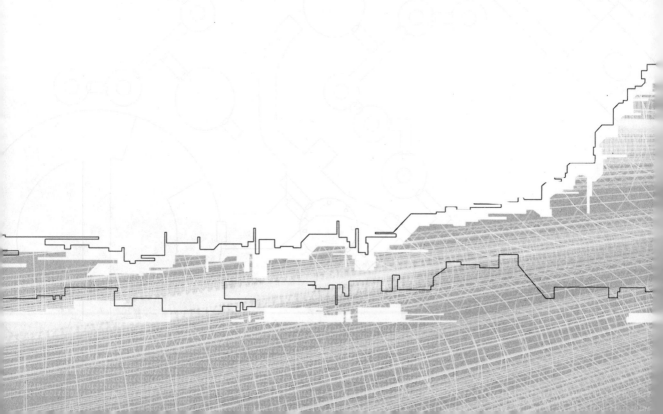

CHAPTER 8

User Interactivity: the Keyboard

Welcome to Part Three of *Game Development with ActionScript*. In this chapter, you will explore many input possibilities within ActionScript that allow you to create customizable keyboard commands. Everything from shortcut button commands to full-blown key listeners—but you'll find out more about those later. For now, take a look at what you'll be learning:

- All about the hidden Keypress
- Using the Key object
- Installing key listeners
- A Key object demo

The Hidden Keypress

In Part One of this book you learned how to create buttons and how to define their on event handler so that the button could execute a block of commands. In this section, you will learn how to create a button that can execute a block of commands with keyboard shortcuts.

I have prepared demo GDA_PROG8.1.fla in the fashion with which you are already familiar. There's a Movie Clip instance in the middle of the screen with the instance name of obj. There are also four buttons on the bottom right of the screen that you can press to move this object up, down, right and left.

Take a look at GDA_PROG8.1.swf, which is shown in Figure 8.1.

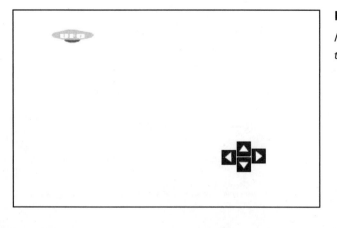

Figure 8.1

Moving an object through custom controls

If you were to pry open one of the button's scripts, you'd see something like this:

```
on (release) {
    obj._x += 5;
}
```

Every time the user presses then releases the button that is associated with that script, the code block will add 5 to the object's x property. This will cause the object to move to the right.

Now that you know what the code does, let's see how I set up the project file. First off, in the Properties panel you can see that I have named the instance of the moveable object.

I have also grouped the four buttons together. If you double-click the group, you'll be able to access the actions for each button—go ahead and do that.

Let's examine the script for the Up button:

```
on (release) {

    obj._y += -5;

}
```

It's very similar to what we have already discussed in previous chapters. This makes the object move up.

Now examine the on handlers for the other buttons.

Here's the Left button code:

```
on (release) {

    obj._x += -5;

}
```

Here's the Right button code:

```
on (release) {

    obj._x += -5;

}
```

Here's the Down button code:

```
on (release) {

    obj._y += +5;

}
```

All this code is very simple, and now that you have seen the demo and are familiar with the project, let's do something more exciting.

I have prepared project file GDA_PROG8.2.fla for this discussion. I didn't include a screenshot because it would look identical to Figure 8.1. The difference in the two demos is that in GDA_PROG8.2.fla, buttons will respond to your keyboard shortcuts—in other words, you can actually use the arrow keys to move the object instead of clicking your life away.

The on handler has a special Keypress parameter. It helps detect a certain key that it will use to trigger the execution of the code block.

Observe the following block:

```
on (Keypress "a") {

  trace("You have pressed the a key.");

}
```

NOTE

Your keyboard has a repeating key feature that allows you to hold down a button so it will be automatically sent to the program as if you were rapidly typing that same key over and over. That feature comes in handy for this demo. You can hold down an arrow key and the object onscreen will continue to move in that direction. Without this feature, you would have to press the key literally every five pixels.

What do you think this handler does? The button waits around for the lowercase "a" to be pressed. Once it is, it outputs, "You have pressed the a key." All you have to do is write out the handler's name, as usual, and in the parameter (between the parentheses) type the keyword Keypress and then, in quotation marks, write out the (case sensitive) letter that you want it to detect.

If you want the handler to detect a special keyboard key, ActionScript has predefined expressions for these keys.

Following is a list of these special expressions:

```
<Left>
<Right>
<Up>
<Down>
<Home>
<End>
<Insert>
<Delete>
<Backspace>
<Enter>
<PageUp>
<PageDown>
<Tab>
<Escape>
<Space>
```

Now that you have a list of all of the possibly detectable keyboard commands, let's look into the code in GDA_PROG8.2.fla. Go ahead and play with the SWF before you move on through this chapter.

Here is the code for the Up button:

```
on (keyPress "<Up>", release) {
  obj._y += -5;
}
```

Before I continue to show you the rest of the code, let's discuss how I formatted the on event handler. Notice that besides setting up the code to detect the Up key, I have also added the release keyword after a comma so that it can also detect the mouse click. This way, if the player decides to use the mouse and/or the keyboard, then he may.

Here is the code for the Left button:

```
on (Keypress "<Left>", release) {
  obj._x += -5;
}
```

Here is the code for the Right button:

```
on (Keypress "<Right>", release) {
  obj._x += +5;
}
```

And the Down button:

```
on (Keypress "<Down>", release) {
  obj._y += +5;
}
```

As you can see, the other buttons handle the input in a similar way. Now you possess the power to add some keyboard functionality to your programs.

Using the Key Object

ActionScript has a special built-in object that doesn't need a constructor to be used. You can just go right ahead and use it. The object I am referring to is called the Key object, and it represents the user's standard keyboard. The Key object can detect key presses and spit back codes. It even has a special built-in set of predefined property constants that can help you in your game venture.

Take a look at our next demo, GDA_PROG8.3.fla, in Figure 8.2. You can see that this program seems to respond when the user presses the Up key.

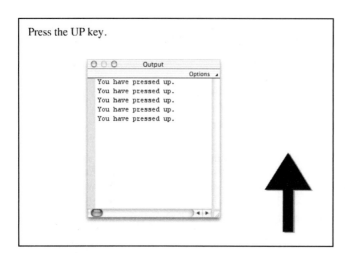

Press the UP key.

Figure 8.2

Using the Key *object to detect keys*

You will like the fact that you won't have to use buttons to detect your key presses—the buttons can get in the way of your graphic presentation. You can use a simple method to check whether the key has been pressed or not:

```
Key.isDown();
```

This function takes the predefined constants defined for the Key object as a parameter. If you wanted to check if the Up key is being pressed, all you would have to do is write:

```
Key.isDown(Key.UP);
```

And this would return either true or false—true if the Up key were being pressed and false if it wasn't.

Since the isDown method returns a Boolean value, you can only put it to use if you use the method in an if statement as shown below.

```
if (Key.isDown(Key.UP)) {

}
```

Now, how would you check to see whether the key is being pressed every frame? That should be simple to answer—remember our old friend, onEnterFrame? If you place this if statement in an onEnterFrame handler, you would be able to literally check for this button press all throughout the program. Cool!

Go ahead and open GDA_PROG8.3.fla. Then check out the following listing.

```
onEnterFrame = function () {
  if (Key.isDown(Key.UP))
    trace("You have pressed up.");
};
```

As you examine this listing, notice that I included everything that we just discussed. I have included an `if` statement that checks to see if the Up key is being pressed. If it is, Flash outputs the message "You have pressed up." to the output window. This condition is checked on every frame because it is within the `onEnterFrame` handler.

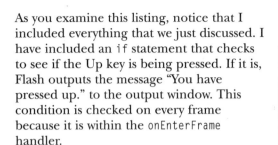

> **TIP**
>
> Don't be confused by all this code talk—there are various codes that are used for information interchange and a standard is the ASCII code. The `isDown` function only accepts ASCII codes—see the appendix for a list of these codes.

How would you handle a regular key press? The `isDown` method accepts the key code as its parameter, so you can't just type in the character within quotes; if you did, that would mean you were passing the ASCII code.

So how do we resolve this problem? Lucky for us, there is another built-in method called `getCode`. Let's see how `getCode` is used:

```
Key.getCode();
```

It seems as though there is no parameter for this method. The method returns a value, and that value is the ASCII code of the last key pressed.

I prepared the following listing for you to play around with. It belongs with demo GDA_PROG8.4.fla.

```
onEnterFrame = function () {
  display = Key.getCode();
};
```

The listing lacks comments, but I'll explain everything. First check out Figure 8.3.

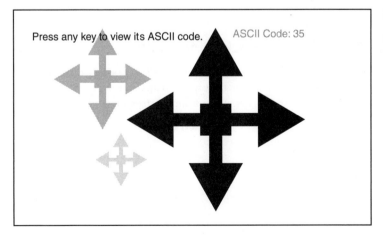

Figure 8.3

Detecting scan codes

I have set up a dynamic text box. In the Properties panel, I assigned a variable to it, display. Then I selected Dynamic from the drop-down box. Once you have these settings, you can adjust what is displayed in the box by modifying the variable's contents.

As this is an onEnterFrame function, it will be executed on every frame. The display variable is being assigned the last ASCII code used. And where is this ASCII code being extracted from? It is being returned by the Key.getCode method.

The following is a list of the built-in constants that represent their respective ASCII codes:

```
Key.BACKSPACE
Key.CAPSLOCK
Key.CONTROL
Key.DELETEKEY
Key.DOWN
Key.END
Key.ENTER
Key.ESCAPE
Key.HOME
Key.INSERT
Key.LEFT
Key.PGUP
Key.PGDN
Key.RIGHT
Key.SHIFT
Key.SPACE
Key.TAB
Key.UP
```

Now that you learned how to use the Key object to detect key presses, you can now move on to the next section where you will learn how to install key listeners.

Installing Key Listeners

A *key listener* is a method that executes its block of code after an event happens no matter what point you are in the program. What this means is that a key listener is a special type of event handler. So what does it exactly do? It responds when a key is pressed and released.

See Figure 8.4 and observe what happens when a key is pressed and released.

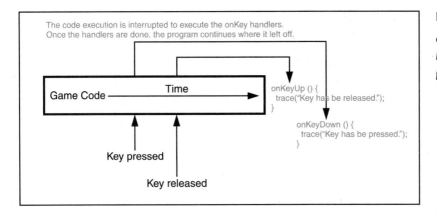

The code execution is interrupted to execute the onKey handlers. Once the handlers are done, the program continues where it left off.

Game Code ——— Time ————→

onKeyUp () {
  trace("Key has be released.");
}

onKeyDown () {
  trace("Key has be pressed.");
}

Key pressed

Key released

Figure 8.4

onKeyDown handler being called after a key press

When would you want to use a key listener instead of the isDown method you learned about in the last section? A key listener is useful when your program is running on a slow computer and your game requires you to process every key stroke—detecting all key strokes can be easily done using key listeners. Now, consider the same program running on the same slow computer. If this game is using the isDown method to test for a key press, problems will arise. The code for this test runs only once every frame, and if it is a slow computer, there is a possibility the key press won't be detected in between frames. You won't have to worry about this situation if you use key listeners.

Open GDA_PROG8.5.fla, and then view the following listing.

```
// Game Development with ActionScript
// By Lewis Moronta (c) 2003
// This program demonstrates how to
// install the Key object's key listener.


// Assign the event handlers to the
// _root object (your main timeline/movie)
Key.addListener(_root);

// Now that you have installed the
// handler, you can define the two handlers.

onKeyUp = function () {
  trace("You have released a key.");
};

onKeyDown = function () {
  trace ("You have pressed a key.");
};
```

Figure 8.5 shows the output I got when testing the code. Notice that the program will stop whatever it's doing to execute these key listeners.

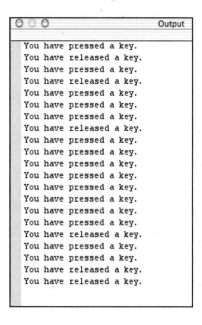

```
You have pressed a key.
You have released a key.
You have pressed a key.
You have released a key.
You have pressed a key.
You have pressed a key.
You have pressed a key.
You have released a key.
You have pressed a key.
You have pressed a key.
You have pressed a key.
You have pressed a key.
You have pressed a key.
You have pressed a key.
You have pressed a key.
You have pressed a key.
You have released a key.
You have pressed a key.
You have pressed a key.
You have released a key.
You have released a key.
```

Figure 8.5

Output from the key event handlers

Before continuing, go ahead and play with this program. Hold down a key, then release it. Hold down multiple keys, and release. Make sure you understand what's happening.

The addListener method accepts an object as its parameter. The object that is passed to it depends on where the onKeyUp and onKeyDown handlers will be installed—all you have to do is define the handlers.

Defining the new handlers isn't very much different from defining the onEnterFrame handler. Check out how I did it:

> **NOTE**
>
> Note that I used the _root object as our target. You could've used any object—even custom objects and classes. In place of _root, I could've used the this keyword because I placed the code on the main time-line.

```
onKeyUp = function () {
  trace("You have released a key.");
};
```

As you can see, all you have to do is assign the function block to the onKeyUp alias.

The block itself consists of a single trace command that tells us that a key was released. This happens because the onKeyUp handler is called when a key is released.

The following handler, onKeyDown, is very similar to the onKeyUp handler:

```
onKeyDown = function () {
  trace ("You have pressed a key.");
};
```

The onKeyDown handler responds and executes its block as soon as any key is pressed.

A Key Object Demo

I created demo GDA_PROG8.6.fla to show off the Key object in action, so you can get a feel for what it's like create a main player in your game. The airtank in the demo has the capability to move forward, backward, left, and right. I even added some scale modifications in there so it would seem as if the aircraft was really flying side-to-side.

See Figure 8.6 for a screen shot of the demo.

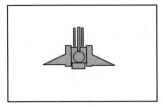

Figure 8.6

The airtank

As you will see from the listing, it is very easy to add features and other goodies to the program—you can even take the code and modify it for yourself.

```
// Game Development with ActionScript
// By Lewis Moronta (c) 2003
// This demo shows off the key object
// that's built in to Flash.

// This onEnterFrame handler
// polls for the keys to see
// which ones are being pressed.
onEnterFrame = function() {

  // Make sure the airtank is
  // always resetting to its
  // original position.
  airtank._xscale = 100;

  // Let's move the tank upward.
  if (Key.isDown(Key.UP))
  {
    airtank._y += -10;
    airtank._xscale = 100;
  }
```

```
// Let's move the tank down.
if (Key.isDown(Key.DOWN))
{
  airtank._y += 5;
  airtank._xscale = 100;
}

// Let's move to the right.
if (Key.isDown(Key.RIGHT))
{
  airtank._x += 8;

  // This creates the illusion
  // of the aircraft moving right
  airtank._xscale = 75;
}

// Let's move to the left.
if (Key.isDown(Key.LEFT))
{
  airtank._x += -8;
  airtank._xscale = 75;
}

// This section prevents the object
// from moving out of the borders of
// the screen.
if (airtank._x < 0)
  airtank._x = 0;

if (airtank._x > 550-airtank._width)
  airtank._x = 550-airtank._width;

if (airtank._y < 0)
  airtank._y = 0;

if (airtank._y > 400-airtank._height)
  airtank._y = 400-airtank._height;
};
```

As you have been reading the book straight through, you should have no problem understanding the code.

The first line, airtank._xscale = 100;, could be confusing if you were not sure what the program was doing—so why is it there? I originally set up the program to move the object in four directions—left, right, up, and down. As the object is an aircraft, it didn't look

natural for it just to move left and right without tilting. I resolved the problem in a very quick and effective way—perhaps not the best way, as it still looks a bit cheesy, but it works for the demo.

When the user presses either the Left or Right arrow on the keyboard, the graphic shrinks to 75 percent and creates the illusion of actually tilting to one side. As the airtank is symmetrical, the tilting works for both sides.

So back to this first line:

```
// Make sure the airtank is
// always resetting to its
// original position.
airtank._xscale = 100;
```

If the object starts out at 100 percent, then why do I need this assignment? Well, it turns out that when the user presses either the Left or Right arrow—and then stops pressing in that direction—the aircraft stays in the direction last pressed. One way to reset the aircraft to its original position is by making sure it always goes back to 100 percent—and it will always look normal when left alone.

NOTE

Keep in mind that you are in a block of code that is executed on every frame; if you have problems visualizing something, try to play out a few frames before moving on.

The `if` structure used in the demo is new, so let's examine it:

```
// Let's move the tank upward.
if (Key.isDown(Key.UP))
{
  airtank._y += -10;
  airtank._xscale = 100;
}
```

The `Key.isDown` method returns true if the Up key is being pressed, and if the Up key is being pressed, then the `if` block executes. So what's happening in the block? Well, when the user presses the Up key, the `airtank` moves up by 10 pixels because 10 is being subtracted from the `_y` property of `airtank`. And to make sure that the `airtank` has the proper orientation, make sure that the scale is at 100 percent.

As the user plays around with the controls, he will eventually press Down and the aircraft will move down. Amazing isn't it? What's the secret behind this magic?

```
// Let's move the tank down.
if (Key.isDown(Key.DOWN))
{
  airtank._y += 5;
  airtank._xscale = 100;
}
```

This is very similar to the last piece and not too difficult to understand. The `if` statement tests to see if `Key.Down` is being pressed. If the test results to true, then the `airtank` is moved down by adding 5 to its `_y` property.

Now let's see what happens when the user presses Right:

```
// Let's move to the right.
if (Key.isDown(Key.RIGHT))
{
   airtank._x += 8;

   // This creates the illusion
   // of the aircraft moving right
   airtank._xscale = 75;
}
```

Just as you guessed, 8 is added to its `_x` property, causing the tank to move 8 pixels to the right. The `_xscale` is brought down to 75 percent in order to create the tilting illusion I mentioned previously.

Moving left is not much different from moving right. All you have to do to activate left movement is press the Left arrow key on your keyboard. The scale is also adjusted to 75 percent for the same visual reasons.

```
// Let's move to the left.
if (Key.isDown(Key.LEFT))
{
   airtank._x += -8;
   airtank._xscale = 75;
}
```

One of the things I did to this program was the classic "prevent the object from going through the borders of the screen" routine. The following demonstrates how to prevent the object from going off the left side:

```
// This section prevents the object
// from moving out of the borders of
// the screen.
if (airtank._x < 0)
   airtank._x = 0;
```

This checks to see if the `airtank._x` property is less than 0, and if it is, it will keep it at 0.

The next thing I did was make sure that the tank is within the right side of the screen:

```
if (airtank._x > 550-airtank._width)
   airtank._x = 550-airtank._width;
```

The width of my movie is 550 pixels, and subtracting my object's width ensures that the `airtank` will remain visible.

Now that I handled the horizontal motion, it is time to take care of the vertical motion:

```
if (airtank._y < 0)
    airtank._y = 0;
```

With this `if` statement, I'm preventing the `airtank` from moving off the top of the screen. If the `airtank` is off the top, I adjust it back to 0.

And finally, I protect the aircraft from going off the bottom of the screen:

```
if (airtank._y > 400-airtank._height)
    airtank._y = 400-airtank._height;
}
```

If its `_y` value is passed 400 (minus its height) then it's too far off the edge, and I must adjust it (or keep it at 400 minus its height).

Have a happy flight!

Summary

You can now move your objects with the press of a key. You learned all about button short-cut keys and how to set them up to control external objects. You even learned how to make the button react to a click, release, and/or shortcut all at the same time—you pretty much mastered the `on` event handler in this chapter. You also learned how to install keyboard handlers that respond and execute code as soon as a key has been pressed or released. And to finish up, you dissected a program that made full use of the key commands within the `Key` object. You can now take this information and create your very own demos and mini-games that users can control from their own keyboards. How cool is that?

Questions & Answers

Q. So are you saying I'm ready? Ready to create games?

A. You're mighty close. With the stuff you picked up in this chapter, you have all the inter-activity you can want in a game. But stay tuned—you still need to learn how to program the mouse and some sound effects.

Q. What if I don't know the ASCII code for a character I want to use?

A. Simple, look it up in the ASCII table that's in Appendix A.

Q. When would you install a listener instead of using the rest of the `Key` object methods?

A. I would use a listener in a case where the speed of the computer is important. If you have a heavy game and it's running on a slow computer, then there is a good chance that there will be some input delay. If you install a listener, you can guarantee that your key press won't be missed.

Q. So are you saying a key listener is better than using anything else?

A. They are more reliable but not necessarily better—it always depends on the situation and the game.

Exercises

1. Create a demo similar to the aircraft demo I created but this time add some rain or snow. Make the aircraft seem as if it is really flying forward.

CHAPTER 9

MORE INTERACTION! THE MOUSE

Getting input from the player via the computer's I/O devices is a mystery to most—and the mouse is no exception. In this chapter, you will discover how to detect the cursor's exact position on your stage—you'll even be able to detect its exact position within a Movie Clip. You will learn how to code familiar, yet mysterious, things like drag and drop. Overlap detecting will also be discussed. Here are the topics that will be covered in this chapter:

- Detecting the mouse cursor position
- Replacing the mouse cursor
- Drawing lines to the cursor
- Dragging and dropping

> **NOTE**
>
> The mouse was originally invented in the 1960s by a pioneering computer scientist named Doug Engelbart. From 1962 to 1968, Doug and his team of fellow scientists built a revolutionary computer system called NLS, which introduced many of the technologies we take for granted today in an era when even simple desktop computers themselves were still alien technology. In addition to the mouse, the 1968 public demonstration of NLS introduced hypertext, objects, and even split-screen video conferencing! Pretty surreal to imagine such technology existing in a fully operational state at around the same time as Woodstock!

Detecting the Mouse Cursor Position

One of the greatest things about Flash is its ability to use much of the operating system's resources and functionality. What I mean by this is that with simple commands, you can get information and perform tasks that programmers in other languages have to work much harder for—including information about the mouse like the cursor's current on-screen position.

See Figure 9.1 for a visual explanation of a mouse cursor position.

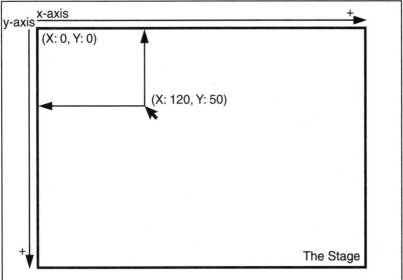

Figure 9.1

Screen cursor positions

Figure 9.2 shows the relationship between the mouse on your desk and the position of the cursor on the screen.

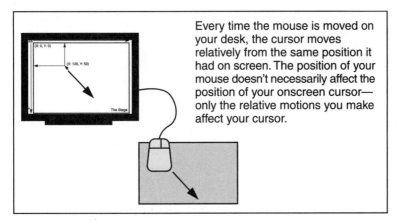

Every time the mouse is moved on your desk, the cursor moves relatively from the same position it had on screen. The position of your mouse doesn't necessarily affect the position of your onscreen cursor— only the relative motions you make affect your cursor.

Figure 9.2

Physical and on-screen positions

Why would anyone want to know exactly where the mouse cursor is? Just think of the possibilities. For example, imagine creating a skeet-shooting game in which the mouse cursor becomes a crosshair that the user can position over flying projectiles. The virtual rifle could then be fired by clicking the mouse, and if the cursor and the projectile line up closely enough, the projectile could explode to illustrate the impact. This is just one of the many examples of why you want to know exactly where the mouse cursor is—otherwise games like these wouldn't be possible.

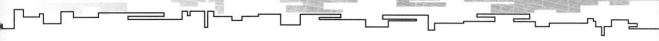

Figure 9.3 shows demo GDA_PROG9.1.fla, which I wrote for this chapter. It tracks the current cursor position and displays its location on the X and Y axes in a couple of text boxes.

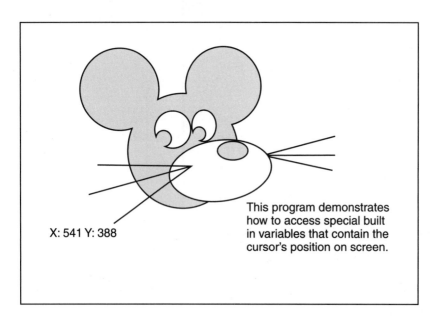

X: 541 Y: 388

This program demonstrates how to access special built in variables that contain the cursor's position on screen.

Figure 9.3

Tracking the cursor's position

A big plus about the way that information is passed on from the operating system is that there is no setup. In other words, you don't have to write any "initialization" code to get mouse support up and running—it's always available for you to use! You can use built-in, property-like variables that the operating system constantly updates, allowing you to straighten your learning curve by skipping all the system specifics and low-level programming.

The mouse position variables are the following:

`_xmouse`

and

`_ymouse`

These properties are part of the Movie Clip class. They are the x and y pair of the current cursor position.

If you take a quick look at Figure 9.4, you'll see how I set up the two dynamic textboxes on the stage that I use to output the information.

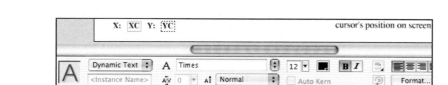

Figure 9.4

Setting up dynamic textboxes for output

Let's jump right into the code, which was placed on the Actions layer of the main Timeline. See Listing 9.1.

```
// Game Development with ActionScript
// By Lewis Moronta (c) 2003
// This program demonstrates how to
// detect the cursor's position on
// the _root movie.

// Setup a frame handler so we
// can check the mouse position
// on every frame.
onEnterFrame = function () {

    // xcoord is the name of
    // a dynamic textbox that
    // is on the stage.
    // _xmouse is being assigned
    // on every frame, which in turn
    // updates the screen's contents.
    xcoord = _xmouse;

    // ycoord also is the name of a
    // dynamic textbox that is used to
    // display the y coordinate of
    // the mouse cursor.
    ycoord = _ymouse;
};
```

The first thing you'll notice is that I set up an onEnterFrame handler. This helps me track every frame. The second thing I did was assign _root._xmouse to xcoord. _xmouse is the built-in property that has the current mouse position and xcoord is the variable that's attached to the textbox on the stage. That being so, it makes sense to say that we are outputting the results by using this line:

```
// xcoord is the name of
// a dynamic textbox that
// is on the stage.
// _xmouse is being assigned
```

```
// on every frame, which in turn
// updates the screen's contents.
xcoord = _xmouse;
```

> **TIP**
>
> **_root._xmouse and _root._ymouse will always return the cursor positions relative to the main movie's top-left corner. If you use another object, it will return values relative to the registration point [(0, 0)] of that Movie Clip.**

The last thing I did here was assign the y value of the cursor's position to its respective dynamic textbox, ycoord.

```
// ycoord also is the name of a
// dynamic textbox that is use to
// display the y coordinate of
// the mouse cursor.
ycoord = _ymouse;
```

This causes _root._ymouse to be output to the dynamic textbox on stage. Simple, isn't it? It only gets better.

> **NOTE**
>
> You might have noticed that sometimes I rewrite the same thing in a couple of different ways. I want you to get used to recognizing the code in all formats. Notice that when writing _ymouse on the main Timeline, it's the same thing as writing _root._ymouse or this._ymouse because you are still referencing the same object.

Replacing the Mouse Cursor

In the Windows operating system, the mouse cursor is normally an arrow. This is all fine and good for a spreadsheet, but game cursors need to be a lot more interesting! Wouldn't it be nice to replace that drab arrow with a crosshair, or perhaps a rusty blade? Flash makes this easy. All you have to do is hide the real cursor and program a Movie Clip to follow your mouse cursor position properties. Doesn't sound too bad. Let's see what it takes to do it.

Let's talk about the setup of the mouse cursor: it must be specific. What do I mean by that? The registration point has to be in a certain place. Open the demo file GDA_PROG9.2.fla to see what I mean, then check out Figure 9.5.

Figure 9.5

Replacing the cursor

TIP

When you create a Movie Clip, you have the option of selecting where its (0, 0) coordinates should be placed; this is referred to as its *registration point*. In previous demos, we've kept the registration point to the upper-left of the Movie Clip because of its ease in programming. But in this demo I placed the cursor's graphics right under the registration point in the Movie Clip so that I can use this point as the hot spot. A cursor's hot spot is the location on the cursor graphic that the user uses to click with.

That mouse silhouette in the middle of Figure 9.5 is my cursor. Double-click it when you get the chance and observe where I placed all of the graphics—below the registration point, so the hot spot, the spot on the cursor that you click with, becomes the mouse's nose.

I have highlighted the Movie Clip in Figure 9.6 so that you can see where the registration point is.

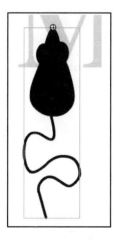

Figure 9.6

Setting up your cursor's registration point

Okay, enough play—check out the following listing and see what it really takes to replace the mouse cursor.

```
// Game Development with ActionScript
// By Lewis Moronta (c) 2003
// This program demonstrates how
// to hide your current mouse
// cursor and replace it with one
// in your Flash movie.

// Initialize
onLoad = function () {
  // Hide the mouse cursor
  Mouse.hide();

  // Make sure the cursor is on top
  // of all other objects
  cursor.swapDepths(1000);
};

// Follow the mouse position
// on every frame.
onEnterFrame = function () {
  cursor._x = _xmouse;
  cursor._y = _ymouse;
};

// Once done, do a little cleaning.
onUnload = function () {
  Mouse.show();
};
```

If you look carefully you can see that I whipped out a handler that I haven't used in a while, the onLoad handler. This handler is the very first thing that executes when the project file is loaded. I also used the onUnload handler—and that's the very last thing that executes. I used the onLoad function to hide the cursor and to bring it all the way to the front. I used the onUnload function to reveal the cursor. Let's see how:

```
onLoad = function () {
  // Hide the mouse cursor
  Mouse.hide();

  // Make sure the cursor is on top
  // of all other objects
  cursor.swapDepths(1000);
}
```

The Mouse.hide method is very simple; all it does is hide the mouse cursor. Now what's this other method? cursor.swapDepths? When I set up the file, I gave the instance name of cursor to my mouse silhouette. As every object is organized in internal layers, our cursor was also

placed in a layer. So what does
`cursor.swapDepths` do? It swaps the layer
position with whatever object is in the layer
you request in the parameter. Requesting a
ridiculously high number will almost guarantee that your cursor will be on top of
everything else—and that's what you want.

Now that you performed all this setup, all
you have to do is make the Movie Clip follow your cursor position. Take a look:

```
// Follow the mouse position
// on every frame.
onEnterFrame = function () {
  cursor._x = _xmouse;
  cursor._y = _ymouse;
};
```

It's a simple matter of passing on the current cursor position to the current Movie
Clip position.

Now what happens if you want the cursor
back? There's a command for that, of
course—`Mouse.show`. This is exactly what I
used in the `onUnload` function.

```
// Once done, do a little cleaning.
onUnload = function () {
  Mouse.show();
};
```

> **TIP**
>
> Use `swapDepths` on any Movie Clip
> you need to appear in front of
> another Movie Clip. For example,
> let's say you had a set of explosions
> programmed into your shooter, then
> you programmed the main player
> after the explosions. When you play
> the game, the explosions seem to
> burst behind the main player
> because of the order in which you
> created them. A nice way to fix this
> is by swapping the position of the
> first explosion with the player's posi-
> tion and the game will look like it
> should. Next time you play the
> game, the explosions will explode
> over the player's layer. By using this
> method, you swap the internal layer
> positions, of course.

As `Mouse.show` is the last thing that executes within the whole Flash program, the cursor will
be revealed.

Drawing Lines to the Cursor

Drawing dynamic lines to the current cursor's position will reinforce everything you know
so far. A case in which you might use this technique would be when you are working on
some tools for your game project. One of those tools could be a character creation program
that requires you to draw dynamic lines that the programs logs, and later saves. Using a program like this would nearly be impossible with the keyboard, so learning how to program
the mouse *and* dynamic lines is essential.

The demo I have prepared for this section is pretty cool because you get to interact with it,
as you'll soon see. You, the user and programmer, get to control the program's behavior.
See Figure 9.7 for a shot of this demo in action.

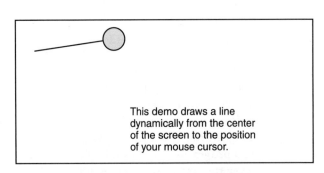

Figure 9.7

Drawing dynamic lines
to the cursor

This demo draws a line dynamically from the center of the screen to the position of your mouse cursor.

Would you believe that the longest block in this demo is four lines and that there is only one block of code here? See the following listing.

```
// Game Development with ActionScript
// By Lewis Moronta (c) 2003
// This program demonstrates how
// you can have a line drawn to your
// curor's position dynamically.

// Let's prepare a function that's
// constantly executed
onEnterFrame = function () {

   // Let's clear all the lines
   // off the screen.
   clear();

   // Let's setup the line style
   lineStyle(0, 0xFF0000);

   // Let's move back to the center
   moveTo (274, 199);

   // Let's finally draw the line to
   // the mouse cursor position.
   lineTo(_xmouse, _ymouse);
};
```

There is only one new command in this listing that I haven't taught you yet, the `clear` method of a Movie Clip. It clears the screen from all lines drawn dynamically. This command is the first that I placed within the `onEnterFrame` handler on the main Timeline. I did this to ensure that every time I enter this function, the main stage will always be clear (from dynamic art) before drawing another line.

Next up, I change the line style, which you know how to do very well:

```
// Let's setup the line style
lineStyle(0, 0xFF0000);
```

I gave the line a hairline thickness and assigned a red color to it.

The next thing I did was add a `moveTo` command to make sure that the line is always drawn from the center.

```
// Let's move back to the center
moveTo (274, 199);
```

As my movie is 550 and 400, I approximated its center by using 274 and 199.

The next thing I did was draw the line to the current cursor position using the `_xmouse` and `_ymouse` properties of the main Timeline:

```
// Let's finally draw the line to
// the mouse cursor position.
lineTo(_xmouse, _ymouse);
```

That's it. Now all you have to do is work up to doing this in your sleep.

Programming Lines Chasing the Cursor

Before going on and improving this program in the next section, let's see how you can modify the last example program so that you can get your juices flowing and design the next popular game design program.

See Figure 9.8, which shows my next demo. This demo is very similar to the previous one; as a matter of fact, I took the last demo and modified it to get completely different results.

So what does the demo do? Nothing but draw lines as you move your mouse cursor. Interesting, very interesting.

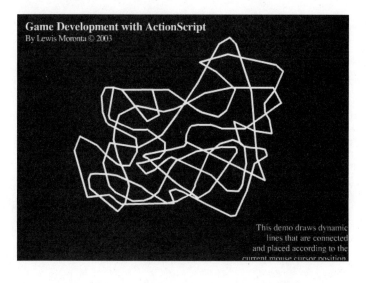

Figure 9.8

Lines chasing your mouse

Take a look at the changes that I made from the last listing.

```
// Game Development with ActionScript
// By Lewis Moronta (c) 2003
// This program demonstrates how
// you can set up the program to
// initialize and then draw consecutive
// lines that are connected.

// Initialize...
onLoad = function () {
  // Let's setup the line style
  lineStyle(3, 0xFFFFFF);

  // Let's move back to the center
  moveTo (274, 199);
};

// Let's prepare a function that's
// constantly executed
onEnterFrame = function () {
  // Let's connect the lines...
  lineTo(_xmouse, _ymouse);
};
```

As you can see, what I did was move most methods to the initialization function, onLoad. This causes the program to set up once and then move on with its short life.

```
// Initialize...
onLoad = function () {
  // Let's setup the line style
  lineStyle(3, 0xFFFFFF);

  // Let's move back to the center
  moveTo (274, 199);
};
```

In this function, I have set the line thickness to 3 and its color to white. I have also initiated the first line to be drawn from the center of the stage.

As you can see from the onEnterFrame handler, all you have is a lineTo command in there. And as this command is executed on every frame, it will end up drawing lines connecting the previous line. All of the lines will be relative to where the mouse was and to where it was moved.

I know all of this is giving you ideas—just because I'm such a nice guy, we'll take it a step further in the next section. Read on.

Allowing the User to Draw

You probably want to explore more mouse-driven interaction, so let's check it out. For this section, I have prepared two demos that show you how to build a program that will give the user control over a "virtual pen" that will allow him to draw on the stage.

Simple Drawing

In the following listing, the user only gets to draw in one line thickness and color, but he will be able to draw lines whenever he wants.

```
// Game Development with ActionScript
// By Lewis Moronta (c) 2003

// This program demonstrates how
// to allow the user to draw on your
// Flash movie with minimal setup.
// This is pretty much a skeleton
// for a full-blown drawing program.

// In our onLoad function, we set up
// our lineStyle and global variables
// that we will end up using later.
_root.onLoad = function() {

  // The usual setup...
  lineStyle (2, 0xFFFFFF);

  // This variable will alert
  // other parts of the program
  // and let them know if the
  // mouse is being pressed or
  // not. This will decide if
  // it should or shouldn't draw
  // the connected line.
  mousePressed = false;
};

// This line is very important.
// It is used to install the mouse
// listener in your _root Movie Clip.
// This includes three methods: onMouseDown
// onMouseMove and onMouseUp.
Mouse.addListener(_root);
```

```
// Here I defined the onMouseDown
// handler, which will execute as
// soon as the user clicks the mouse.
_root.onMouseDown = function() {

  // Since the mouse was pressed
  // I set this boolean variable to
  // true--it will help us draw the line.
  mousePressed = true;

  // This method prepares the line
  // from the current location.
  moveTo(_xmouse, _ymouse);
};

// This mouse handler responds
// when the mouse is moved.
_root.onMouseMove = function() {

  // If this variable is true,
  // then you are allowed to
  // draw the line. In other words
  // if the mouse isn't pressed, don't draw.
  if (mousePressed)
    lineTo(_xmouse, _ymouse);
};

// The onMouseUp handler responds
// when the user releases
// the mouse button.
_root.onMouseUp = function() {

  // To prevent any line-drawing
  // you reset this variable.
  mousePressed = false;
};
```

I have initialized a couple of things in the onLoad handler, including a special flag variable, which is mousePressed, and the line style for the program. The thickness was set to 2, the line color was set to white, and opacity to 100 percent.

```
// In our onLoad function, we setup
// our lineStyle and global variables
// that we will end up using later.
_root.onLoad = function() {
```

```
// The usual setup...
lineStyle (2, 0xFFFFFF);

// This variable will alert
// other parts of the program
// and let them know if the
// mouse is being pressed or
// not. This will decide if
// it should or shouldn't draw
// the connected line.
mousePressed = false;
};
```

The next thing I did was install the mouse listener so that I can use those special built-in methods, onMouseDown, onMouseUp and onMouseMove.

```
// This line is very important.
// It is used to install the mouse
// listener in our _root Movie Clip.
// This includes 3 methods: onMouseDown
// onMouseMove and onMouseUp.
Mouse.addListener(_root);
```

I defined the onMouseDown handler—I used it to set up the "drawing from" position and to flag the rest of the program that the user wants to draw a line because he has clicked the mouse button.

```
_root.onMouseDown = function() {

    // Since the mouse was pressed
    // I set this boolean variable to
    // true--it will help us draw the line.
    mousePressed = true;

    // This method prepares the line
    // from the current location.
    moveTo(_xmouse, _ymouse);
};
```

The onMouseMove will execute every time the mouse moves, but I didn't want onMouseMove to draw a line every time, so I used the flag variable, mousePressed, to check whether the user is clicking the mouse. If he is, then the line drawing is allowed.

```
_root.onMouseMove = function() {

    // If this variable is true,
    // then we are allowed to
    // draw the line... In other words
```

```
    // if the mouse isn't pressed, don't draw.
    if (mousePressed)
      lineTo(_xmouse, _ymouse);
};
```

Once the user is done, the flag variable must be updated so that the `onMouseMove` function will suppress the line drawing. I set up the `onMouseUp` handler to detect when the user releases the mouse and I set the flag variable to false so no lines are drawn when the mouse is moved.

```
_root.onMouseUp = function() {

    // To prevent any line drawing
    // we reset this variable.
    mousePressed = false;
};
```

Now that you know what it takes to let the user decide what lines he wants to draw, let's see if you can allow the user to change some line style settings, such as the line color.

Improved Drawing

The revised version of this demo was saved as GDA_PROG9.6.fla. Figure 9.9 shows the new enhancements.

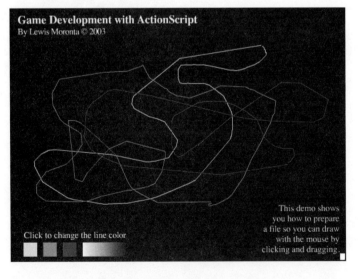

Figure 9.9

New and improved drawing

As you can see from the figure, I have added three new buttons. When the user clicks on one of them, the color of the line is changed to the color of the button. The user has complete control over where he chooses to draw lines and what color he wants the lines to appear. Note that the white-to-black gradient next to the other color buttons doesn't do anything.

Go ahead and have some fun with the demo before we discuss the following listing.

```
// Game Development with ActionScript
// By Lewis Moronta (c) 2003

// This program demonstrates how
// to allow the user to draw right
// on your movie like a canvas.
// He also has the option of
// changing the color of his lines.

// This function is the first
// one to execute. This is
// where everything is initialized.
_root.onLoad = function() {

    // Flag the program not to draw lines.
    mousePressed = false;

    // Initialize the line color to green.
    lineColor = 0x00FF00;
};

// Install the mouse listener methods.
Mouse.addListener(_root);

// Let's set up the line as soon
// as the user clicks the mouse.
_root.onMouseDown = function() {

    // This tells onMouseMove that
    // it's ok to draw the line.
    mousePressed = true;

    // This sets the current position
    // so the program can have a place
    // to which to draw a line.
    moveTo(_xmouse, _ymouse);
};

// This function responds to any
// mouse motion--even the squeaky sounds.
_root.onMouseMove = function() {

    // Here we update the line style
    // because line color might have
```

```
    // been updated.
    lineStyle (0, lineColor);

    // If the mouse is being pressed
    // then go ahead and draw the line.
    if (mousePressed)
      lineTo(_xmouse, _ymouse);
};

// Disable line drawing if the
// user releases the mouse.
_root.onMouseUp = function() {
  mousePressed = false;
};
```

In order to make this program work, I initialized the line style and the line color within the onLoad handler. I set up the color to be green.

```
_root.onLoad = function() {

    // Flag the program not to draw lines.
    mousePressed = false;

    // Initialize the line color to green.
    lineColor = 0x00FF00;
};
```

I installed the mouse listeners for those infamous methods:

```
// Install the mouse listener methods.
Mouse.addListener(_root);
```

Below you'll see the setup for when the user clicks the mouse button—it flags the program that the button has been pressed and it relocates the current drawing position to the current cursor position:

```
_root.onMouseDown = function() {

    // This tells onMouseMove that
    // it's ok to draw the line.
    mousePressed = true;

    // This sets the current position
    // so the program can have a place
    // to draw a line to.
    moveTo(_xmouse, _ymouse);

    // Here we update the line style
    // because line color might have
```

```
// been updated.
lineStyle (0, lineColor);
};
```

The onMouseDown function also contains a lineStyle method with the global lineColor variable, which is updated with the current color information (every time the user clicks).

The line, once again, is only drawn if the button is clicked:

```
_root.onMouseMove = function() {

  // If the mouse is being pressed
  // then go ahead and draw the line.
  if (mousePressed)
    lineTo(_xmouse, _ymouse);
};
```

> **NOTE**
>
> Where do you think this lineColor variable is being modified? In the buttons, of course. Hold on—I'll review that code soon.

The last block of code that we have on this frame on the main Timeline is the following:

```
_root.onMouseUp = function() {
  mousePressed = false;
};
```

All this function does is flag the program to stop drawing lines.

Now let's look into the button code. They are all similar; here's the Green button:

```
on (release) {
  lineColor = 0x00FF00;
}
```

Once the user clicks on this button, the button's code will adjust the lineColor (which is a global variable) by giving it the hexadecimal representation of green. The other two buttons are similar but they adjust to red and blue, respectively. Remember that the line style is updated when the user clicks on the stage—this is when the onMouseDown function calls the lineStyle method.

Dragging and Dropping

Dragging and dropping techniques enhance your user's interactivity factor by 100 percent. Imagine a space shooter in which a player can upgrade their ship with new weapons and engines. How cool would it be if they could literally drag weapon and engine graphics over an image of their ship, and see a new image appear with the upgrades taken into account! This would not be possible without first understanding how drag-and-drop techniques work. I have written a list of demos that will teach you how to set up your own dragging and dropping demos from scratch.

Using startDrag and stopDrag methods

Open GDA_PROG9.7.fla and test the movie. Drag the clip around, and drop it someplace and then pick it up again. Don't you just love the dynamics? Check out the following listing and see how I did it.

```
// Game Development with ActionScript
// By Lewis Moronta (c) 2003

// This program demos how to use
// the mouse listener methods along
// with the startDrag and stopDrag methods.

// Add the listeners...
Mouse.addListener(_root);

// Once the user clicks, start the drag.
_root.onMouseDown = function () {
  dragme.startDrag();
};

// Once the user releases, stop the drag.
_root.onMouseUp = function() {
  dragme.stopDrag();
};
```

Figure 9.10 shows the Drag Me demo.

This demo allows you to drag and drop the "Drag Me" object in the middle of the stage. You can drag it by clicking ANYWHERE on the stage.

Figure 9.10

The Drag Me demo

Luckily for you, you get to learn how to drag and drop the easy way before you continue on to the more advanced methods. Doing it the easy way means using two convenient methods especially designed for dragging and dropping, startDrag and stopDrag.

The first thing I did in this demo was install the mouse listener so that I can use its onMouseDown and onMouseUp methods. After that I defined the onMouseDown method as follows:

```
// Once the user clicks, start the drag.
_root.onMouseDown = function () {
  dragme.startDrag();
};
```

This function only executes when the mouse is clicked, causing the clip to follow the mouse position, because that's exactly what startDrag is meant to do.

So what about when the user wants to put the clip down—drop it? I put a stopDrag command within an onMouseUp handler. This causes the clip to stop following the mouse when the user releases the mouse button.

That's not all there is to dragging and dropping; if you carefully try different things with this program, you will notice that when you click *anywhere* on the screen, the clip will start following the mouse position relative to where you clicked. You do not want this.

Because of this issue, I wrote another demo, GDA_PROG9.8.fla. This demo, unlike the last one, contains the code within the Movie Clip instead of in the main Timeline. Note that when the movie is tested, you can still click completely outside the object and drag it. Also note how the same program is written in two completely different ways.

```
// Game Development with ActionScript
// By Lewis Moronta (c) 2003

// This program demos how to use
// onClipEvent mouseDown and mouseUP
// with the startDrag and stopDrag methods.

// Once the user clicks, start the drag.
onClipEvent(mouseDown) {
  this.startDrag();
}

// Once the user releases, stop the drag.
onClipEvent(mouseUp) {
  this.stopDrag();
}
```

It's customary to always include the code that pertains to the Movie Clip inside the Movie Clip. This is the first time you have encountered these onClipEvent methods, but they behave just like the onMouseUp, onMouseDown and onMouseMove functions, so they shouldn't be too scary.

The following `onClipEvent(mouseDown)` method executes when the mouse is pressed and automatically starts the drag:

```
onClipEvent(mouseDown) {
  this.startDrag();
}
```

The `onClipEvent(mouseUp)` detects when the user doesn't want to drag anymore and then releases the clip from following the cursor:

```
onClipEvent(mouseUp) {
  this.stopDrag();
}
```

The hitTest Method

So let's find out how to have the clip detect where the mouse position is. We need to make sure that the mouse only drags when it's over the clip. The dragging and dropping doesn't behave properly when the user is allowed to move the clip and the mouse isn't even over the darn thing.

Check out GDA_PROG9.9.fla. It's not perfect, but we're getting there. The user can actually click on the shape and the code will do what it's been designed to do. If the user clicks outside the shape, the code does nothing—or at least that's what I'm telling you now. We'll come back to that.

Let's jump into it—this listing is the code that's inside the draggable Movie Clip.

```
// Game Development with ActionScript
// By Lewis Moronta (c) 2003

// This program demos how to use
// onClipEvent mouseDown and mouseUP
// with the startDrag and stopDrag methods.

// Once the user clicks, start the drag.
onClipEvent(mouseDown) {
```

> **TIP**
>
> There is an easier way to detect whether the user has clicked your Movie Clip. You can use the `onPress` method, which executes when the click is inside the Movie Clip's boundaries. With this method, you can avoid using `hitTest` to test whether the user really clicked on your clip or not. If you want more info on `onPress` check out the Flash Help files—you will learn how to use `onPress` later in this book.

```
    if (this.hitTest(_root._xmouse, _root._ymouse, false))
      this.startDrag();
}

// Once the user releases, stop the drag.
onClipEvent(mouseUp) {
  this.stopDrag();
}
```

What's this? A new method? They seem to come out of nowhere, don't they? But that's one of the best things about ActionScript—there's almost nothing you can't do with the language.

```
onClipEvent(mouseDown) {

  if (this.hitTest(_root._xmouse, _root._ymouse))
    this.startDrag();
}
```

Briefly stated, this event handler checks to see if the mouse position is within the Movie Clip's area—and if it is, it starts to drag it when the user presses the mouse.

Let's check out the heart of this functionality—the hitTest method:

```
myMovieClip.hitTest(x, y, considerShape);
```

As you can see, this is a method of the Movie Clip class. It returns true if the point that was passed to it lies within the Movie Clip. If it doesn't, it returns false. The last parameter, considerShape, is a Boolean value that tells the function whether or not to consider the irregular shape of the Movie Clip. If the point that was passed to it doesn't lie within the Movie Clip, it evaluates the Movie Clip as a bounding box. Grab the Movie Clip by the corners, in the demo, and you'll be able to drag it even though it seems as if you aren't grabbing anything. See Figure 9.11 for a look at Movie Clip's bounding box.

Figure 9.11

A Movie Clip's bounding box

I have modified this demo into GDA_PROG9.10.fla to achieve the solid dragging and dropping that we originally wanted.

```
// Game Development with ActionScript
// By Lewis Moronta (c) 2003

// This program demos how to use
// onClipEvent mouseDown and mouseUP
// with the startDrag and stopDrag methods.

// Once the user clicks, start the drag.
onClipEvent(mouseDown) {

  if (this.hitTest(_root._xmouse, _root._ymouse, true))
    this.startDrag();
}

// Once the user releases, stop the drag.
onClipEvent(mouseUp) {
  this.stopDrag();
}
```

As you can see, the only change is the last parameter in the hitTest method, which was set to true. Run the program and test the movie and see how everything works solidly.

A Solid Drag-and-Drop Demo

And now for the last drag-and-drop demo of the chapter—see Figure 9.12 before I explain what it does. Also play GDA_PROG9.11.swf to see it in action.

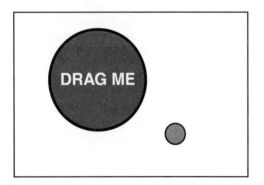

Figure 9.12

Interaction between objects

This listing was extracted from the Drag Me Movie Clip in GDA_PROG9.11.fla.

```
// Game Development with ActionScript
// By Lewis Moronta (c) 2003

// This program demos how to use
// onClipEvent mouseDown and mouseUP
// with the startDrag and stopDrag methods.
```

```
// Once the user clicks, start the drag.
onClipEvent(mouseDown) {

  if (this.hitTest(_root._xmouse, _root._ymouse, true))
    this.startDrag();
}

// Once the user releases, stop the drag.
onClipEvent(mouseUp) {
  this.stopDrag();
}
```

As you can see, this listing is identical to the previous one except that I modified the actual Movie Clip timeline for some effects. I set the project up so that when the other bouncing Movie Clip touches this one, this Movie Clip will play a red frame to show a hit.

Take a look at what's inside the bouncing Movie Clip in the following listing.

```
// Game Development with ActionScript
// By Lewis Moronta (c) 2003
// This is a bouncing projectile
// that makes the dragme clip blink
// everytime they overlap. How is it
// done? The dragme clip is played
// like a regular movie--to make sure
// it resets when there is no contact
// a stop() command is place at the
// first frame of the dragme clip.

onClipEvent(load) {
  xv = 10;
  yv = 10;
}

onClipEvent(enterFrame) {
  if (this.hitTest(_root.dragme))
    _root.dragme.play();

  this._x += xv;
  this._y += yv;

  if (this._x > 550) xv = -xv;
  if (this._x < 0) xv = -xv;

  if (this._y > 400) yv = -yv;
  if (this._y < 0) yv = -yv;
}
```

The first thing I did in this Movie Clip was initialize some velocity variables. The ball will go at an even 10 pixels per frame in any direction while bouncing off walls. I kept the variables global so that I can access them elsewhere in the clip.

```
onClipEvent(load) {
    xv = 10;
    yv = 10;
}
```

In the enterFrame handler, you will notice that the hitTest function is being used completely differently from the way I originally showed you. Check out its other usage:

```
myMovieClip.hitTest(targetMovieClip);
```

myMovieClip is the clip you want to test and targetMovieClip is the clip you want to test against. The function returns true if they overlap and false if otherwise.

In this case, I am testing to see if the bouncing projectile hits the dragme clip at any point. If it does, the bouncing projectile executes the play method in the dragme clip for a flashing effect.

The next thing you see here is the motion code—the velocities are being added to the current clip position in order to move the projectile.

```
    this._x += xv;
    this._y += yv;
```

The next couple of if structures test to make sure that the ball bounces from the left and right sides of the screen:

```
    if (this._x > 550) xv = -xv;
    if (this._x < 0) xv = -xv;
```

I also wanted the ball to bounce off the top and bottom of the screen, so I wrote these lines:

```
    if (this._y > 400) yv = -yv;
    if (this._y < 0) yv = -yv;
```

What they basically do is check if the projectile is past a side and if it is, it reverses the velocity. This, of course, forces it to move in the opposite direction.

Summary

I'm loving it—how about you? You started out simple by detecting the mouse cursor position and you built on that from there. You even learned how to make the mouse cursor disappear and to replace it with your own—that's a very cool thing to know. You became more accustomed to more of the dynamics of line drawing and you even learned a command that clears the screen. You got so advanced in this chapter that you even set up a file that allows the user to draw on the screen and change his line color. On top of that, you learned all about dragging and dropping. You pretty much mastered the mouse. Congrats!

Question & Answer

Q. Is there a method that can alert the Movie Clip when the user clicks within its boundaries?

A. Yes. You can use the onPress method. You can also use its buddy methods, such as `onRelease` and `onReleaseOutside`. Check out the Flash Help file for more info.

Exercise

1. Take the drawing program created in this chapter and add functionality to it. Allow the user to change his line thickness and also allow him to clear the screen when he wants.

CHAPTER 10

Sound Effects and Music

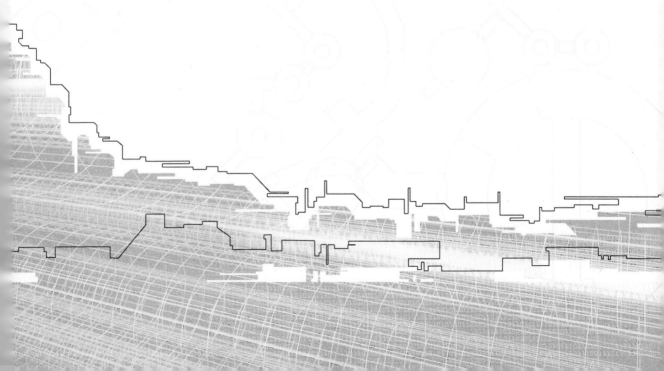

B ack in the day, sound was the missing link in many games, but now it's an essential part of any game. Sound enhances the gaming experience and helps immerse the player in the world you've created. Not only can a game be visually stimulating, but it can also be audibly pleasing as well.

Imagine playing a game where you can see the explosion but not hear it. How dull would that be? Can you imagine a Star Wars game without its crazy classical-adventure music? I don't think so. A game without sound can dull the moment and kill the experience. And in this chapter you will learn how to set up and play sounds through your ActionScript code. Among the topics I'll discuss are the following:

- Using library sounds
- Setting up a sound Movie Clip
- Attaching sounds dynamically
- Creating a volume slider
- Panning, transforming, and monitoring sounds

Using Library Sounds

Macromedia Flash includes built-in libraries that contain plenty of stock buttons and sounds. They can easily be used in any project simply by dragging the object onto your stage.

To access these common libraries, go to your Window menu, Common libraries, Sounds.fla. The Library window, shown in Figure 10.1, should open.

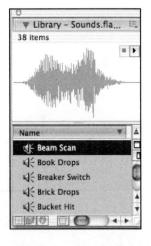

Figure 10.1

Accessing common libraries

To make a sound play at a certain frame, make sure there is an empty keyframe on the layer you're working in and drag the sound from the library onto your stage while selecting that frame on the timeline. You will get a graphical representation of the sound drawn in the timeline, just like in Figure 10.2.

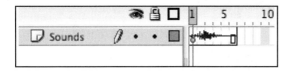

Figure 10.2

A sound event within the Timeline

Once the sound is in your movie, it will automatically be loaded into your movie's Library window. When the movie is played, the sound will be played unless ActionScript controls it otherwise. And that's all that there is to that.

What if you have a sound that you would like to use on your hard drive? Or even a song that you wrote and saved as a WAV or MP3 file? The easiest way to do this is by going to File, Open as Library. Once you open the sound file you will have another Library window with nothing but the sound you opened. To import the sound to your project, just drag it to the frame you want or to your movie's library.

Once you have a sound on your Timeline, you can adjust its properties and its behavior. Figure 10.3 shows what a sample Properties panel would look like when a keyframe that is selected contains a sound.

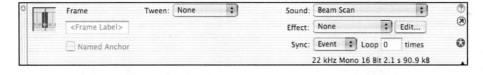

Figure 10.3

Adjusting a sound's properties

The Sound drop-down menu allows you to select a sound that is within the movie's library. The currently selected sound is the one that will play when the frame is played.

The sound can also be edited. The Edit drop-down box adds predefined effects, such as fade-in and fade-out, to the sound. You can either choose custom from the list or click on the Edit button next to the drop-down box to edit the sound envelopes yourself. See Figure 10.4.

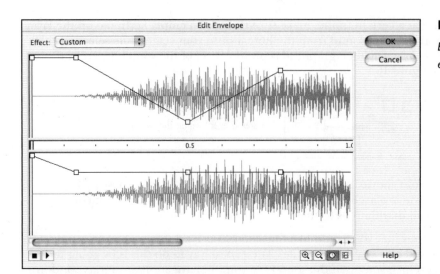

Figure 10.4

Editing a sound's envelopes

An important term you should know is *sound envelope*. A sound envelope is like a chain of points, often expressed visually as a spline curve or a series of connected lines (like a graph) that represent changes made to some property of a sound. For example, if you draw a volume envelope over a sound, the higher parts of the envelope mean the sound will be played louder at that point, while the lower points mean the sound will be played quieter.

The next drop-down box that you see in your Properties window is labeled Sync. Your selection in this box determines how the sound is played. If it's a short sound that should play when an event happens, then choose Event. If the event occurs more than once and the first sound hasn't finished playing, all the subsequent sounds will play along simultaneously. If you set the Sync to Start it won't let any other Start sounds play along with this sound. If you choose Stop, the specific sound will be silent. If you choose Streaming, the sound will be synchronized to your frames. This is handy for Web sites—if the user's computer is too slow to process all the frames on time while the sound is playing, the Flash player will skip frames to compensate for the time lost.

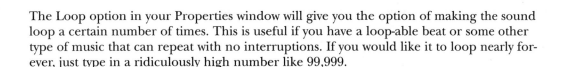

The Loop option in your Properties window will give you the option of making the sound loop a certain number of times. This is useful if you have a loop-able beat or some other type of music that can repeat with no interruptions. If you would like it to loop nearly forever, just type in a ridiculously high number like 99,999.

Setting Up a Sound Movie Clip

There are many ways to do perform the same task in Flash. You always have the option of choosing the most effective and efficient setup for yourself. In this section, you will learn how to prepare a project that can play a sound with minimal ActionScript. The advantage? There's very little coding to this method. When you're writing a complicated game and you need to squeeze in some sound effects at the last minute, this method never fails.

So I set up a file that allows you to click buttons and trigger built-in sounds with minimal ActionScript. Once you master the way I've set it up in the file, I will introduce the Sound object. But for now, open up GDA_PROG10.1.fla and examine it. See Figure 10.5 for the visual.

Test the movie and click on the buttons—you should hear sounds play. If you click the buttons fast enough, you should hear the sounds play simultaneously. This is because all of the sounds are set up as Event sounds in the Sync properties drop-down menu.

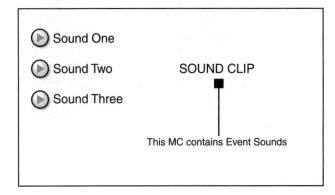

Figure 10.5

Demo 10.5 in action

The heart of this program lies within the Movie Clip labeled Sound Clip. Double-click on it and look into it. Figure 10.6 shows its timeline.

Figure 10.6

Sound clip's timeline

As you can see in Figure 10.6, frames are labeled (noted by the red flags on the timeline) and there are scripts embedded (noted by the "a" over the keyframes). You can also see that there are three sounds embedded in three different keyframes. Let's see what each label is and what scripts are embedded.

Select the first frame and observe the Properties panel—the frame is labeled FrameOne. Now that you know that, look into the Actions panel—there's only one command in there, a `stop` command. The `stop` command causes the Movie Clip to pause at FrameOne when loaded. As there is a graphic on that frame as well, the Movie Clip will display that graphic (which happens to be the text of Sound Clip).

Frame 5 is labeled `soundone` and has a sound embedded on that frame—no actions.

Frame 9 has the following script:

```
goToAndPlay("FrameOne");
```

This allows the sound to play starting at Frame 5 and returning to Frame 1 when it hits Frame 9. As there is a `stop` command on Frame 1, everything returns to normal. A lot of jumping around, huh?

Frame 10 is labeled `soundtwo` with another sound embedded within—the frames will play until Frame 14 where Flash encounters some more ActionScript. Here's what Flash executes:

> **NOTE**
>
> The gap between Frame 5 and 9 isn't necessary; I just wanted a neat file that can display the label—a crammed file is never a good thing. Always allow yourself enough space to work with.

```
goToAndPlay("FrameOne");
```

This causes Flash to retreat once the program plays the sound.

By now, you can pretty much guess how the third sound was placed and organized into the project. Frame 15 is labeled `soundthree` and also has a sound embedded within. Frame 20 also has the following code:

```
goToAndPlay("FrameOne");
```

For the very same reasons as before,—this last `gotoAndPlay` command causes the clip to rest at the first frame and wait for another `play` command.

So now that you have a great idea of how the Movie Clip is set up to play our sounds, let's see the code that it takes to actually play these sounds individually.

Go back up to the main Timeline. Check out the first button on Actions panel. This is what you will see:

```
on (release) {
  sounds.goToAndPlay("soundone");
}
```

As you can see, when the user releases the button, the gotoAndPlay command is called from the Movie Clip instance named sounds. The Movie Clip instance named sounds is the same Movie Clip that we just went over, and if you remember correctly, one of the frames within it was named soundone. This will cause the clip to play the sound clip embedded within soundone and return to Frame 1 within that Movie Clip when it's done.

The second button down on the stage has similar code—except this time it's playing from where the second sound clip is embedded.

```
on (release) {

  sounds.goToAndPlay("soundtwo");

}
```

The third button plays the third clip with help of the following code:

```
on (release) {

  sounds.goToAndPlay("soundthree");

}
```

Feel like it's starting to sink in? Let's get even deeper into this sound stuff.

Attaching Sounds Dynamically

In ActionScript, you can load and link sounds from your library and play them whenever you wish. All you have to do is create a Sound object that you can manipulate with its built-in methods. For example, imagine you created a puzzle game that plays fun music while the user is playing. To make the game more exciting, when the player is about to lose, you can have the program switch to ominous music by loading in the appropriate track from the library.

You would have to create a Sound object and to do this, you must declare it; all you have to do is write the following line:

```
var mySound = new Sound();
```

and you have yourself a Sound object of the Sound class.

Before you can play a sound from this object, you must attach the sound to the object. For this to work, you must have a sound imported into your library and have its linkage properties set up.

Import a sound into your library and access its Linkage Properties dialog box by accessing the context menu. The Linkage Properties dialog box should look like that in Figure 10.7. Give your sound a name and make sure you export it in the first frame. This name should be reflected in your Library window.

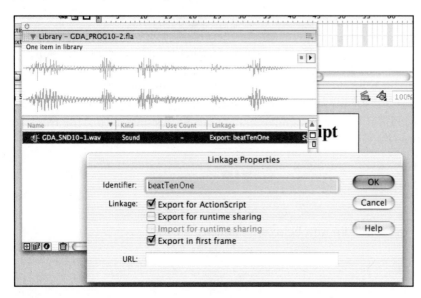

Figure 10.7

Adjusting the linkage properties for a sound

Once your file is prepared, you can either type in the following listing or play with demo file GDA_FIG10.2.fla. It takes an imported sound and loops it 9,999 times.

```
// Game Development with ActionScript
// By Lewis Moronta (c) 2003
// In this demo you are shown
// how to create a sound object
// so you can control sounds
// from within ActionScript.

// Create the new Sound object
mySound = new Sound();

// Attach a sound to play from the library
mySound.attachSound("beatTenOne");

// Play the sound starting at 0 pos
// looping for 9,999 times.
mySound.start(0, 9999);
```

As I said before, when you create a new Sound object, you need to attach a sound to the object so it can play something. I have done this with the following line:

```
mySound = new Sound();
```

Then I used the linkage name as the `attachSound` parameter to attach that sound to the `mySound` object like this:

```
mySound.attachSound("beatTenOne");
```

The `start` method of the `Sound` class of object can actually be used with no parameters, as shown below—this will cause the sound to be played once straight through. However, the way I used the `start` method in this demo is a different—the first parameter indicates how far along (in milliseconds) the `Sound` object should start playing the sound. This is good for sounds that have silent gaps in front of the actual contents. The second parameter actually indicates how many times you want the sound to loop.

```
mySound.start();
```

Play the SWF; you'll find that it does what I just explained. It loops the sound 9,999 times because of this line:

```
mySound.start(0, 9999);
```

By the way, the sound you hear is my voice before I modified it—you can get really creative once you have a mic in front of your face.

> **TIP**
>
> Try modifying demo **GDA_PROG10.2.fla**—execute the `start` method with no parameters and hear what happens.

Creating a Volume Slider

Creating a slider can benefit your game in many ways. A slider can allow the player to adjust the overall sound level of the game. A slider in the Options menu can be used to control difficulty level control—the higher up the slider button, the harder the game, the lower the slider button is, the easier the game.

What is a slider control anyway? If you take a look at Figure 10.8 right now, you'll notice that I broke down the slider anatomy.

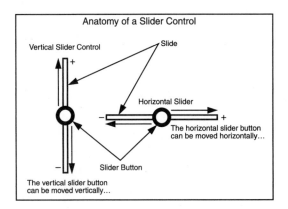

Figure 10.8

The anatomy of a slider control

A slider can be vertical or horizontal. Obviously, the slider button will move vertically on the vertical slider and horizontal on the horizontally positioned slider.

Before jumping into creating slider code, let me show you how to adjust the sound's volume first. All you have to do is use the setVolume method on the Sound object with a parameter ranging from 0 to 100, with 0 being no sound and 100 meaning full blast. Check out GDA_PROG10.3.fla and the following listing.

```
// Game Development with ActionScript
// By Lewis Moronta (c) 2003
// In this demo you are shown
// how to create a sound object
// so you can control sounds
// from within ActionScript.

// Create the new Sound object
mySound = new Sound();

// Attach a sound to play from the library
mySound.attachSound("beatTenOne");

// Play the sound starting at 0 pos
// looping for 9,999 times.
mySound.start(0, 9999);

// Lower the volume
mySound.setVolume(30);
```

How simple can it get? The creative side of it all starts with you. This program is not interactive and dynamic enough—let's make it more so.

Demo GDA_PROG10.4.fla starts off on the main Timeline in a similar way to the last program example, except that I added a custom control, a volume slider. See the following listing and see how similar the code is.

```
// Game Development with ActionScript
// By Lewis Moronta (c) 2003
// In this demo you are shown
// how to create a sound object
// so you can control sounds
// from within ActionScript.

// Create the new Sound object
mySound = new Sound();

// Attach a sound to play from the library
mySound.attachSound("beatTenOne");
```

```
// Play the sound starting at 0 pos
// looping for 9,999 times.
mySound.start(0, 9999);
```

Looks like the usual—create a sound object, attach the sound, then use the `start` command to play it. So where is the volume code? Test and run the movie and see for yourself. The volume code is actually in a Movie Clip that responds to the mouse's position and adjusts the volume according to its on-screen position—in other words, a slider.

Listing 10.4 contains the rest of the code, which is inside that sliding clip. To see the slider, check out Figure 10.9.

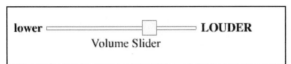

Figure 10.9

The volume slider

```
// The onClipEvent(load) handler
// initializes all other handlers
// in this Movie Clip.
onClipEvent(load) {

  // These properties
  // are used and can be
  // adjusted to where you
  // want your slider min
  // and max to be on the
  // x axis.
  this.minX = 100;
  this.maxX = 300;

  // Define another sound
  // object to control the
  // sound globally--this is
  // why it's declared on _root.
  _root.music = new Sound();
  _root.music.setVolume(50);

  // This handler is declared
  // and executed for when the
  // mouse clicks on the mc--
  // it then flags its variable
  this.onPress = function() {
    this.active = true;
  };
```

```
// This flags the rest of the
// handlers that the mouse was
// released.
this.onRelease = function() {
  this.active = false;
};

// This function was also declared
// for when the user releases the
// mouse outside of the clip.
this.onReleaseOutside = function() {
  this.active = false;
};

// This is the heart of it all--
// It is executed when the mouse is
// moved and if pressed.
this.onMouseMove = function() {

  // This only executes if the mouse
  // is being pressed (and flagged)
  if (this.active) {

        // Follow the _xmouse to
        // simulate dragging.
        this._x = _root._xmouse;

        // Constrain this position to
        // the max property that we set.
        if (this._x > this.maxX) {
         this._x = this.maxX;
        }

        // Also constrain our position
        // to the min property we set.
        if (this._x < this.minX) {
         this._x = this.minX;
        }

        // Set the volume of our music object depending on what percent along
        // the slider our mc is. See the text for an explanation of the formula.
_root.music.setVolume(Math.floor((this._x-this.minX)/(this.maxX-this.minX)*100));
    }
  };
}
```

It looks overwhelming, but you are more than ready for code like this—this is the cool stuff that you can impress your novice programmer friends with!

Even though much of the code is understandable, it does include a few functions and handlers that I haven't shown you yet. These handlers are commonly used for tasks like creating sliders and other similar controls so don't be a stranger to them. Let's dive in.

Notice that all the handlers are being defined within the main handler, onClipEvent(load). This causes the clip to take a life of its own once everything is set into place.

One of the first things I did within the loading handler was initialize new variable properties that hold the minimum and maximum pixel values of where the slider can slide.

```
// These properties
// are used and can be
// adjusted to where you
// want your slider min
// and max to be on the
// x axis.
this.minX = 100;
this.maxX = 300;
```

The next thing I did was create a sound object on the _root of the movie so it can be accessed anywhere. As the regular Sound constructor was used, any adjustments to the sound here will affect other sound objects as well. In other words, this Sound object will be used as a global sound control.

```
// Define another sound
// object to control the
// sound globally--this is
// why it's declared on _root.
_root.music = new Sound();
_root.music.setVolume(50);
```

I know you're not used to defining a function within another function, but this is possible in ActionScript, and I did so. I declared the onPress handler here; it sets a flag that tells the rest of the program that it has been clicked.

```
// This handler is declared
// and executed for when the
// mouse clicks on the mc--
// it then flags its variable
this.onPress = function() {
  this.active = true;
};
```

The onPress handler will only be called when the mouse clicks within the Movie Clip area. This saves you from having to use the hitTest function.

```
// This flags the rest of the
// handlers that the mouse was
```

```
// released.
this.onRelease = function() {
  this.active = false;
};
```

The onRelease even handler detects when the Movie Clip is released (within the Movie Clip). This handler tells the rest of the program that the mouse has been released, so it should stop dragging the clip.

The next thing I did was use the onReleaseOutside method to prevent any weird functionality with the clip. I will be restricting the slider from following certain mouse positions; to do so, mouse release in those off-limits areas must be detected.

```
// This function was also declared
// for when the user releases the
// mouse outside of the clip.
this.onReleaseOutside = function() {
  this.active = false;
};
```

The next thing I declared was the onMouseMove method. Notice that I didn't install the listener—Flash 6 allows you to declare onMouse event handlers in Movie Clips without a mouse listener. This is bad practice, though. The future version of Flash won't let you get away with missing code so don't do it. I did it to prove that Flash MX will let you get away with a lot—so be careful.

```
// This is the heart of it all—
// It is executed when the mouse is
// moved and if pressed.
this.onMouseMove = function() {
```

I used the flag variable to determine if the mouse is down—if it's not, Flash won't execute any commands. If it is, the program enters the following if statement:

```
// This only executes if the mouse
// is being pressed (and flagged)
if (this.active) {
```

The first obvious thing I do if the mouse is down is make the clip follow the mouse position. This would make it seem as if the user is really dragging the clip:

```
// Follow the _xmouse to
// simulate dragging.
this._x = _root._xmouse;
```

I wanted solid code, so I decided to restrict the directions in which the user can slide this Movie Clip. This is why the slider is following the mouse only on the x-axis.

```
// Constrain this position to
// the max property that we set.
```

```
    if (this._x > this.maxX) {
     this._x = this.maxX;
   }
```

The previous if statement makes sure that the clip's current position doesn't go past the predefined maxX position. This forces it within boundaries.

The following if statement does something similar, except that it restricts the Movie Clip to the predefined minX position.

```
     // Also constrain our position
     // to the min property we set.
     if (this._x < this.minX) {
      this._x = this.minX;
    }
```

The last line of the onMouseMove function is the most important of all—it uses all the information in this system to decide the volume of all the sounds being played. It's the master volume control, if you will.

```
_root.music.setVolume(Math.floor((this._x-this.minX)/(this.maxX-this.minX)*100)));
```

Seems very complicated, but let's break it down and you'll see how simple it really is. You know setVolume requires a parameter that goes from 0 to 100, so you already know that you have to work with percent amounts but take a look at the following visual to help you with them—Figure 10.10.

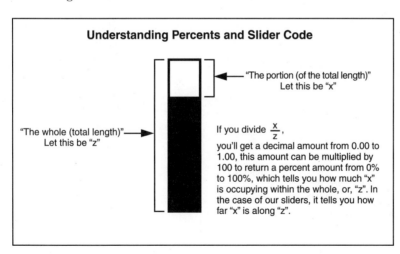

Understanding Percents and Slider Code

"The portion (of the total length)"
Let this be "x"

"The whole (total length)"—▶
Let this be "z"

If you divide $\frac{x}{z}$, you'll get a decimal amount from 0.00 to 1.00, this amount can be multiplied by 100 to return a percent amount from 0% to 100%, which tells you how much "x" is occupying within the whole, or, "z". In the case of our sliders, it tells you how far "x" is along "z".

Figure 10.10

Working out a fraction

If you take the position of the slider button along the slide and you divide that by the length of the slide, it returns a decimal, from 0.00 to 1.00, that can be multiplied by 100— this returns the amount in percent, along the slider, which is what we need.

For instance, if the slider button is 50 pixels along a slider bar that is 300 pixels long, then divide 50 by 300 to find out what the scalable amount is. It's roughly 0.17—this number can be scaled or multiplied by 100 to return 17 percent. If this value is passed on to setVolume, it will make the volume 17, which will be a very low volume.

Experiment with a few values until you understand what's going on. In essence, I subtract minX from the current x-position to get the distance along the slider (this._x-this.minX). This could be anything from 0 to 300, if the slider is 300 pixels long. minX is subtracted from maxX to figure out the real length of the slider (this.maxX-this.minX)—let's say it's 300. The distance along the slider—let's say it's currently 150—is divided by the length of the slider ((this._x-this.minX)/(this.maxX-this.minX)), which is now 300. This would yield 0.50, which can be multiplied by 100 to equal 50 percent. This would be the value passed on to setVolume to make your volume 50 percent. Get it?

The good part about this slider is that you can copy and drag it to any of your movies and it will work with minimal modification—what you choose as the graphic for the slider is up to you.

Panning Sounds

What does it mean to *pan* a sound? It simply means to control the left and right speakers independently by individually adjusting their volume levels. This allows you to make really cool effects—for example, if you ever create a game with explosives, such as a war game, you can have the explosions near the right side of the screen sound at a higher volume from the right speaker than the left. Same thing with the explosions towards the left side of the screen—you can make the sound at a higher volume from the left speaker than the right. This, of course, will help your player disappear into your game. This is the essence of stereo sounds—see Figure 10.11.

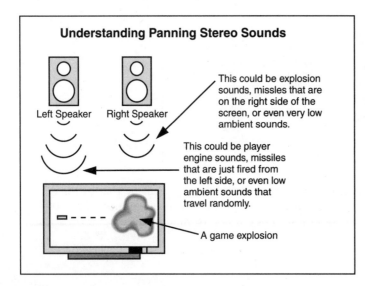

Figure 10.11

The effects of using stereo sounds

I modified the previous program so that instead of the slider adjusting the volume, you have a slider that adjusts the panning from the left and right speakers. It's pretty cool, if you ask me. Open the demo GDA_PROG10.5.fla and review the code. I have posted it here as well. I didn't post the code that's on the main Timeline, because all it does is create a Sound object, attach the sound from the library, and then loop the object for a long time.

```
// The onClipEvent(load) handler
// initializes all other handlers
// in this Movie Clip.
onClipEvent(load) {

  // These properties
  // are used and can be
  // adjusted to where you
  // want your slider min
  // and max to be on the
  // x axis.
  this.minX = 100;
  this.maxX = 300;

  // Define another sound
  // object to control the
  // sound globally--this is
  // why it's declared on _root.
  _root.music = new Sound();

  // This handler is declared
  // and executed for when the
  // mouse clicks on the mc--
  // it then flags its variable
  this.onPress = function() {
    this.active = true;
  };

  // This flags the rest of the
  // handlers that the mouse was
  // released.
  this.onRelease = function() {
    this.active = false;
  };

  // This function was also declared
  // for when the user releases the
  // mouse outside of the clip.
  this.onReleaseOutside = function() {
    this.active = false;
  };
```

```
// This is the heart of it all--
// It is executed when the mouse is
// moved and if pressed.
this.onMouseMove = function() {

        // This only executes if the mouse
        // is being pressed (and flagged)
    if (this.active) {

            // Follow the _xmouse to
            // simulate dragging.
            this._x = _root._xmouse;

            // Constrain this position to
            // the max property that we set.
            if (this._x > this.maxX) {
             this._x = this.maxX;
        }

            // Also constrain our position
            // to the min property we set.
            if (this._x < this.minX) {
             this._x = this.minX;
        }

            // Set the pan of our music object depending on how far along
            // the slider our mc is. See the text for an explanation of the formula.
_root.music.setPan(Math.floor(((this._x-this.minX)/(this.maxX-this.minX)*200)-100));
        }
    };
}
```

As you can already tell, most of the code is the same. Just to recap, I'll briefly explain the sections.

All of the event handlers used are declared in the load event handler of the Movie Clip slider.

Properties were created to keep track of the minimum and maximum positions that the slider should be within.

A global music object was created to adjust the panning to all sounds within the Flash project. I created the music object this way to avoid any confusion. If you would like the sound controls to affect a certain Movie Clip's sounds, then declare the Sound object within that Movie Clip.

The onPress, onRelease, and onRleaseOutside handlers have all been used to flag the rest of the program when the user presses or releases the mouse button.

Even most of the juicy stuff within the onMouseMove has been retained from the last demo. All of the if structures that restrict movement and the slider positioning code do the same as in the last example. The main difference in this code is the last command, the setPan method of the Sound object.

```
_root.music.setPan(Math.floor(((this._x-this.minX)/(this.maxX-this.minX)*200)-100));
```

The setPan method accepts values from –100 (meaning the left speaker only produces sound) to 100 (where sound only comes out of the right speaker), with 0 being dead center. Of course, when 0 is passed on to the setPan method, sound comes out of both speakers equally. Anything in between these main values causes one speaker to produce more sound than the other, allowing your ears to pick up one side more prominently than the other. This is the beauty of stereo sound.

I'll show you how I used the values of this Movie Clip to determine the value to pass on to setPan. Just like in the last example, I calculated how far along the slider I was. I then divided this by how long the slider actually is. I then multiplied this value by 200 so I could have enough space to subtract another number that can yield a range from –100 to 100. This is why I then subtracted 100 from that value.

Let's say this slider bar was 200 pixels long. Our slider is positioned at 50. When dividing 50 by 200 we get 0.25. When this value is multiplied by 200, it yields 50. When 100 is subtracted from this, you get –50. This will cause the pan to steer the sounds to the left speaker and leave only some sound on the right.

Transforming Sounds

Flash allows you to create some very interesting effects with your sounds. A setTransform method exists that accepts a generic object as its only parameter. This method allows you to play some of the right channel information in your left speaker and some of your left channel information on your right speaker—heck, you can even flip the channels.

Using this technique you can program the sound so that when, in your action-adventure game, your character enters a cave, fires at a target, and misses, the bullet's "ricochet" can be heard. The cool thing about this is that you can have your program select what speakers and volume percentages output the sound depending on where (on the screen) your player's projectile ricocheted from.

I have written up demo GDA_PROG10.6.fla to demonstrate some of the things I'll discuss in this section. When you test the movie, it makes a sound that says "left" in the left speaker and then moves on to say "right" in the right speaker.

> **TIP**
>
> A stereo sound will be converted to mono if you use Flash's default settings. Adjust the settings by right-clicking (or Control-clicking for Macs) the sound on the Library window and selecting Raw from Export Settings then unchecking Convert to Mono.

When the Channel Swap button is clicked, "left" is spoken out the right speaker and "right" is spoken out of the left speaker. You can return this to normal by clicking the Reset button. How does this work? Check out the following listing.

```
// Game Development with ActionScript
// By Lewis Moronta (c) 2003
// In this demo you are shown
// how to create a sound object
// so you can control sounds
// from within ActionScript.

// Create the new Sound object
mySound = new Sound();

// Attach a sound to play from the library
mySound.attachSound("LeftRight");

// Play the sound starting at 0 pos
// looping for 9,999 times.
mySound.start(0, 9999);

// Define the transform objects
ChannelSwap = { ll: 0, rr: 0, lr: 100, rl: 100};
Reset = { ll: 100, rr: 100, lr: 0, rl: 0};
```

The generic object that is passed on to setTransform is an object with the following properties:

```
MyObject.ll
MyObject.rr
MyObject.lr
MyObject.rl
```

These properties can contain values that range from 0 to 100. The ll and rr properties act like individual volumes for the left and right speakers, respectively. In other words, when ll is 50 and rr is 100, this would mean that the left speaker is at 50 percent and the right speaker is at 100 percent.

The lr and rl properties represent how much leakage there is from one speaker to the other. The lr represents how much of the right channel comes out of the left speaker, and rl represents how much of the left channel comes out of the right speaker.

What if you want to reverse the channels? Use these settings:

```
MyObject.ll = 0;
MyObject.rr = 0;
MyObject.lr = 100;
MyObject.rl = 100;
```

If `MyObject` were to be passed onto `setTransform`, it would mute the `ll` and `rr` channels while blasting whatever is on the right channel through the left speaker and whatever is on the left channel through the right speaker.

So back to the listing. Besides declaring, attaching, and playing the sound from the `Sound` object, I also declared two generic objects with the properties described above:

```
ChannelSwap = { ll: 0, rr: 0, lr: 100, rl: 100};
Reset = { ll: 100, rr: 100, lr: 0, rl: 0};
```

The object `ChannelSwap` reverses the channels just as I explained. It doesn't do so by itself, though—the object has to be passed on to `setTransform`. You'll see how soon.

The `Reset` object actually mutes the channel swapping and sets the left and right channels back up to 100 percent.

Let's check out the button code—this is where the channel transformations are taking place.

Look at the actions in the Channel Swap button. You should see something like the following:

```
on (release) {
  mySound.setTransform(ChannelSwap);
}
```

Once this command is called with the object, the channels are adjusted immediately. I'm sure you already have a good idea of what the Reset button does:

```
on (release) {
  mySound.setTransform(Reset);
}
```

Just as you guessed, it passes on the `Reset` object to the `setTransform` method of the `mySound` object. Everything goes back to normal after the execution of this command. How nice.

Sound Monitoring

The `Sound` object has two very useful properties that tell you how far along a file is when playing the sound and how long the file is. These properties are `sound.position` and `sound.duration`.

Remember when I told you that if you divide the portion into the whole it would yield a percent amount if multiplied by 100? Well, if you divide `position` by `duration`

TIP

If at any time you think that your file is making your movie too heavy, try adjusting its compression settings. If worse comes to worst, just make it a mono file—who needs stereo when your whole movie is bogged down? To make your file a mono file, right-click it in your Library window and adjust the Export settings.

while the sound is playing, you can find out what percent the sound has played while it's playing

GDA_PROG10.7.fla is another demo I created for this chapter. It plays a long sound while displaying what percentage of the sound has been played. Let's jump into the listing to understand how it works.

```
// Game Development with ActionScript
// By Lewis Moronta (c) 2003
// In this demo you are shown
// how to create a sound object
// so you can control sounds
// from within ActionScript.

// Create the new Sound object
mySound = new Sound();

// Attach a sound to play from the library
mySound.attachSound("LongSound");

// Play the sound
mySound.start();

onEnterFrame = function() {

    // Calculate what percent of the file has been already played.
    var percent = (mySound.position/mySound.duration)*100;

    display = Math.floor(percent)+"%"; // Display to a text box.
};
```

The listing starts out with the usual: a Sound object is created, sound is then attached, and finally, the sound is played.

I have also prepared an onEnterFrame handler so that I can check the status of the sound that's playing during every frame. In the first line within this handler I decided to calculate the percentage of what has been already played. I used the following formula:

```
var percent = (mySound.position/mySound.duration)*100;
```

I divided the part into the whole then scaled the result by 100 to get the percent. Simple enough, so let's move on.

I then rounded down on the result of percent and then concatenated a percent symbol, as the value is being prepared for display and will be converted to a string value.

display is merely the variable that was attached to a textbox that is currently on stage.

Another way that you can detect if a sound has finished playing is by using the onSoundComplete callback function. This event handler alerts you when a sound is done playing. This works great for loops. For instance, if you had a loop going for 30 spins, it would be tedious tracking them with the sound's position and duration. With onSoundComplete, you can just wait until the functions called for you. Demo GDA_PROG10.8.fla shows you just that.

Observe the following listing. It allows the program to play the sound and then alerts the listener when it's done. This demo is pretty useless for practical purposes, but it's very handy when synchronizing data.

```
// Game Development with ActionScript
// By Lewis Moronta (c) 2003
// In this demo you are shown
// how to create a sound object
// so you can control sounds
// from within ActionScript.

// Create the new Sound object
mySound = new Sound();

// Attach a sound to play from the library
mySound.attachSound("LongSound");

// Play the sound
mySound.start();

// Setup Display
display = "Sound Playing...";

// Detect when it's done playing
mySound.onSoundComplete = function () {
  display = "Sound Complete!";
};
```

Besides creating and attaching and then playing the sound, the code calls the onSoundComplete function as soon as mySound finishes playing the sound. As a sign that it has finished, I set it to display a message on a textbox on the stage. The attached variable is called display.

Summary

Now you can hear your monster move, creep, and crawl—how about it? With nothing more than a little practice, you have learned most of the sound commands, along with some tricks and techniques along the way.

You learned how to import sounds into your library and even how to link them so you can use them from your code. Besides attaching sounds dynamically, you also learned how to construct a volume slider that actually adjusts the movie's volume.

From there, you learned how to create a similar slider that pans the movie's sound. You then learned how to swap channels and flip what you hear from what is coming from your speakers.

And adding to all that knowledge, you learned how to monitor your sounds. You learned to keep track of them and even check when they are done playing. You are on your way to mastery!

Question & Answer

Q. Is there a way to load and play a sound from disk?

A. Yes. You can use the method `sound.loadSound` to load MP3 audio. Just type the name of the file within the method's parentheses and you're set. If you would like more information on it, feel free to look it up on the Flash Help file.

Exercises

1. Load your favorite song into Flash and set up a file that can play it. Add volume and panning sliders. There's one catch—make the volume slider vertical.

2. Create a scaling bar that can visually display the status of a currently playing sound. This is a tough one, so plan well.

PART FOUR

THE MATH

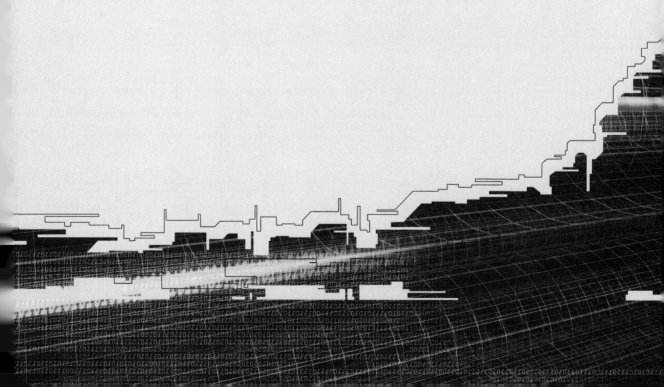

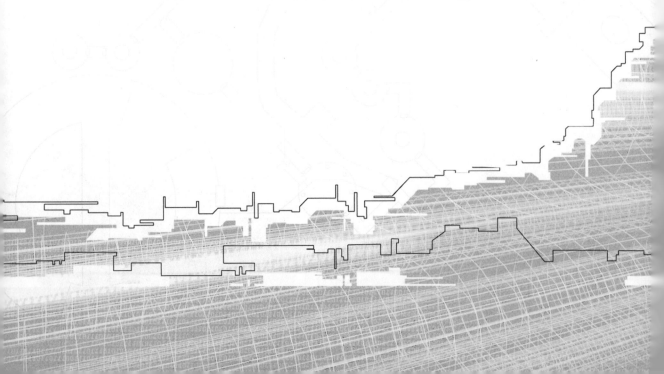

CHAPTER 11

TRIGONOMETRY MADE EASY

Your experience with Trigonometry probably starts in high school, but do you really remember it? The real question might be: Why would you *want* to remember it? Well, you want to program games, don't you? Having this knowledge will allow you to create cool effects in your games—such as having a tank move in whatever direction you desire. Without some knowledge of Trigonometry, this can't be done. The following list shows you what topics I'll cover in this chapter:

- The unit circle
- Radians
- Periods, domains, and ranges
- Trigonometric functions

The Unit Circle

Circles are found everywhere in the world around us, but to the trigonometry student, few are more important than the unit circle. This is a special case of a circle that has its center on the origin of a Cartesian plane. The unit circle's radius is exactly 1 unit long. This circle is used to define the trigonometric functions that you'll learn later. First, take a look at Figure 11.1, which shows what a unit circle looks like.

A *Cartesian plane* is a graph of a plane that contains two major axes. Usually they are labeled X and Y and where they intersect is the origin, or (0, 0). If you take a look at Figure 11.2, you can see that the two axes are perpendicular to each other and that this plane contains four quadrants. Moving counter-clockwise, they are Quadrant I, Quadrant II, Quadrant III, and Quadrant IV. The computer screen is like the first quadrant but with an inverted Y axis. In other words, the screen's Y axis gets larger as you move down the screen—unlike the Y axis on a Cartesian plane.

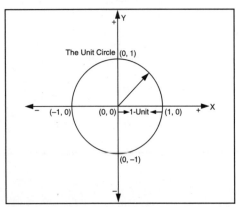

Figure 11.1

Presenting the unit circle

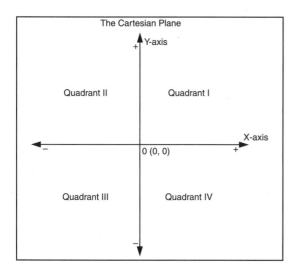

Figure 11.2

The Cartesian plane

TIP

If you wanted to graph this circle, the geography way, you could use the equation $x^2 + y^2 = 1$ to solve for each point on the circle.

Pretty soon we're going to go over trigonometric functions and their graphs. For the purposes of this demo, I briefly introduce sine and cosine but don't worry about them too much so that you can focus on how the program creates the circle you will see when you run the program. Sine and cosine can be used to solve for the x and y points around the circumference of a circle, allowing you to draw a circle at any scale. And guess what? This is exactly what I demonstrate in the following listing—also see Figure 11.3.

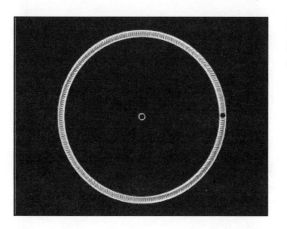

Figure 11.3

Drawing a circle with trigonometry

Feel free to look into the file GDA_PROG11.1.fla on the CD. You'll see how I set up the file so that I can produce the circle, using trig, which I wanted to produce. The following listing was written up in the "Circle" Movie Clip. In the file, you can double-click on the blue rectangle and look into the following actions in its timeline.

```
// Game Development with ActionScript
// By Lewis Moronta (c) 2003
// This program uses trig functions
// to draw a circle in ActionScript.

for (var i = 0; i < 360; i++) {

  radians = Math.PI/180 * i;

  // Solve for y
  var y = Math.sin(radians);

  // Solve for x
  var x = Math.cos(radians);

  // Scale the results for display
  x *= 100;
  y *= 100;

  // Plot the dot =D
  plot_dot(x, y, i);
}

function plot_dot(x, y, dotNum) {

  // Create a dot instance
  attachMovie("dot", "dot"+dotNum, dotNum);

  // Assign their positions...
  this["dot"+dotNum]._x = x;
  this["dot"+dotNum]._y = y;
}
```

The first thing I did when planning this demo was to decide where my origin would be. Then I decided how I was going to plot the points. I decided to use a small Movie Clip just big enough to represent a dot.

```
function plot_dot(x, y, dotNum) {

  // Create a dot instance
  attachMovie("dot", "dot"+dotNum, dotNum);
```

```
    // Assign their positions...
    this["dot"+dotNum]._x = x;
    this["dot"+dotNum]._y = y;
}
```

As you can see, this function is a generic function that creates an instance of the "dot" Movie Clip and assigns it to a new position. How does it do this? Well to start off, it has three parameters. One passes the x value, the other passes the y value, and the last passes the instance number that is used in creating the instance (in attachMovie).

The clip that is being created is referenced dynamically—you know how to do that already:

```
    this["dot"+dotNum]._x = x;
    this["dot"+dotNum]._y = y;
```

The "dot" string is added to dotNum to create a string that represents the instance name—this string is then passed on to the this keyword that resolves the Movie Clip instance. This then allows you to use the Movie Clip's methods and properties. I referenced the position properties in this case in order to place the Movie Clip in its new location.

The main code block loops 360 times—one iteration for every degree in a circle. It then uses the Math.sin and Math.cos functions to resolve the x and y values around the circumference. It then scales the coordinate points up to make the circle big enough to be viewed. Right after the positions are resolved, all of these values are passed on to the plot_dot function to actually draw something on the stage.

```
for (var i = 0; i < 360; i++) {

  radians = Math.PI/180 * i;

  // Solve for y
  var y = Math.sin(radians);

  // Solve for x
  var x = Math.cos(radians);

  // Scale the results for display
  x *= 100;
  y *= 100;

  // Plot the dot =D
  plot_dot(x, y, i);
}
```

> **NOTE**
>
> I scaled the x and y values because sine and cosine only return values from 0 to 1. If the circle were to be plotted that way, you wouldn't notice the circle on the stage because the pixels would be so tight.

So now that you've seen some trigonometry in action,—take a look at Figure 11.4 for an explanation of what `Math.sin` and `Math.cos` are doing.

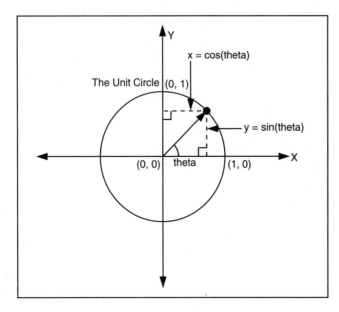

Figure 11.4

The values retuned by `Math.sin` *and* `Math.cos`

As you can see from Figure 11.4, `Math.cos` returns the x value of the point that lies on the circle. `Math.sin` returns the y value of where the point is on the circle. By plugging in different values, you can get all the points on the unit circle. Where do you get these values?

What Are Radians?

If you were to measure a circle along its circumference, the unit measure you would use would be a radian. In other words, a radian is the unit measure along the circumference of a circle, the unit measure of an arc. Radians are also the unit values that the trigonometric functions in ActionScript accept. Any positive degree from 0 to 359 can represent an individual point on the circumference. See Figure 11.5.

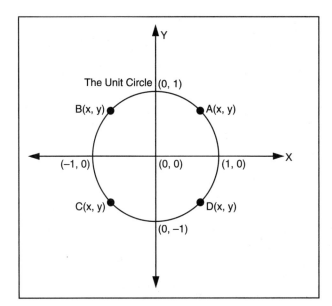

Figure 11.5

Points, in radians, along the circumference

Most of us were raised to think of a circle as 360 degrees, which makes working with radians seem counter-intuitive. Fortunately, there is a way to work entirely with degrees while still passing ActionScript's trig functions their parameters in the form of radians. To do this, all we need to do is *convert* our degree values to radians just before calling these functions. How do you convert a degree to a radian? Check out the following formula:

radians = Pi/180 * degrees

Pi is that magical number that keeps popping up in all places; it can be rounded to ~3.1415 as an accurate measure.

I've written a program that converts degrees to radians for you. You can find it on the CD as GDA_PROG11.2.fla. Figure 11.6 shows this demo.

> **TIP**
>
> **If the objects are grouped on the stage, you can ungroup them using the Modify menu. You can also double-click on the group to edit it. You can always go back to the Timeline by pressing on the stage controls.**

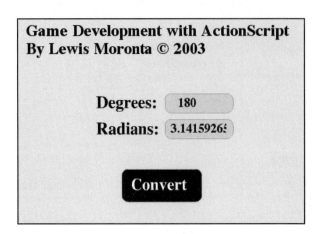

Figure 11.6

Converting degrees to radians

Open the FLA file and notice the properties, in the Properties panel, for the first textbox. Check out Figure 11.7 and see what options I selected.

Figure 11.7

Adjusting input textbox properties

You can see that I have selected Input Text from the drop-down menu and assigned degrees in the input box labeled Var:. This causes the degrees variable to update itself with the contents of the textbox—especially when the user types something in.

The textbox over the button on the stage is a normal dynamic box with a variable attached. The rest of the script lies within the button—check out the following listing.

```
// Game Development with ActionScript
// By Lewis Moronta (c) 2003
// This program converts degrees
// to radians.

on (release) {

    // Convert to Integer
    intDeg = parseInt(degrees);

    // Get the value of one radian
    oneRad = Math.PI/180;

    // Finally convert one radian to how many degrees
    radians = oneRad * intDeg;
}
```

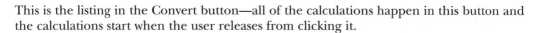

This is the listing in the Convert button—all of the calculations happen in this button and the calculations start when the user releases from clicking it.

```
on (release) {
```

As degrees is the variable attached to the input box, its content is in string format. As I need this value in a formula, I need to convert the value to a number so I can actually operate on it. This is where parseInt comes in. This command converts a string to its numerical equivalent.

```
    intDeg = parseInt(degrees);
```

In order to get the value of one radian, you have to divide the same amount of radians by the equivalent value in degrees to get 1 radian. I used Pi and 180 degrees to get my value.

```
    // Get the value of one radian
    oneRad = Math.PI/180;
```

According to the formula above, if you multiply onRad by intDeg, you should get the value of radians that you want. This is exactly what I did:

```
    // Finally convert one radian to how many degrees
    radians = oneRad * intDeg;
```

And that's what it takes to convert degrees to radians in Flash.

Periods, Domains, and Ranges

All the functions discussed so far fall into the periodic function category. What this means is that sine and cosine will forever repeat their values after a period, no matter what value is fed to them. The horizontal interval that function values take to repeat is called the *period* of the function. This period is 2Pi for both sine and cosine.

TIP

If you convert 2Pi to degrees you get 360 degrees. There goes that circle again. Try rearranging the radian formula so you can solve for degrees.

Figure 11.8 shows an example of an ongoing function period.

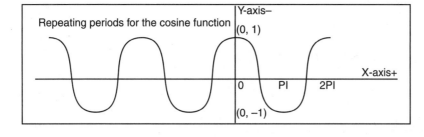

Figure 11.8

Repeating periods

Figure 11.8 shows what happens when you feed different values to a cosine curve. The curve was graphed for three periods—that would be its domain. A function's domain is the starting point to the ending point of the graph. As I said, sine and cosine usually have 0–2PI for their domains. Sine and cosine domains are exactly one period long.

The range of a function is a bit different. The range of a function is the vertical limits of that function. This means that when you sketch out a sine wave, the vertical limits of the wave are usually –1 to 1. You can always scale these as I did in previous demos in this chapter.

Trigonometric Functions

You probably learned some trigonometric functions in high school. The functions that you will see here are probably the most useful and common ones, and you may be familiar with them already. Remember that this won't be another boring math lesson but a cool way to put these once seemingly useless functions to good use.

The Sine

The sine of an angle is calculated as the opposite side of the angle divided into the hypotenuse of the right triangle. See Figure 11.9 for the visual.

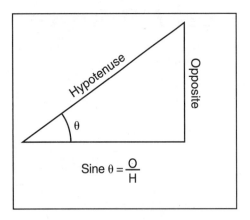

Figure 11.9

Defining the sine of an angle

You also might have learned other ways to represent the sine's values. Have you seen sine graphed as in Figure 11.10?

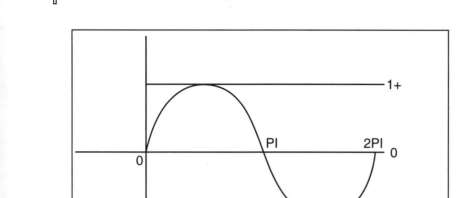

Figure 11.10

The sine graph

Looks a little bit more interesting doesn't it? Did you know that sine is used in many games, and that I just happened to write up an example of how it can be used? Before we go on, notice how its values only output from –1 to 1; this allows you to scale these values to get whatever other values you want.

Check out demo GDA_PROG11.3.fla and see how I made the projectile just move as if the sine gods had ordered it so. Figure 11.11 shows the projectile that I used for this motion.

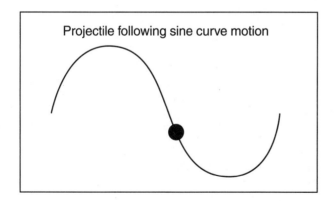

Figure 11.11

A sine projectile

Check out the SWF and then take a look at the listing.

```
// Game Development with ActionScript
// Lewis Moronta (c) 2003
// This program demonstrates how
// to use Math.sin methods.

degrees = 0;

onEnterFrame = function () {

  // Manipulate degrees
  degrees+=10;

  // Make sure it doesn't go overboard
  if (degrees > 360)
    degrees = 0;

  // Convert to radians
  var radians = Math.PI/180 * degrees;

  // This stores -1 to 1
  var sineY = Math.sin(radians);

  // Move the projectile from 100 to 300
  thing._y = sineY * 100 + 200

  // Now that we got him moving up and down
  // according to the power of the sine,
  // let's move him across the screen =)

  thing._x += 10;

  if (thing._x > 550)
    thing._x = 0;
};
```

If the sine function didn't exist, you could probably pull the same thing with a few more `if` statements, but to tell you the truth, it wouldn't be as smooth. The sine function actually has really cool slow ins and outs at its peaks.

The first global variable that I set up was `degrees`. I used this variable to increment itself to 359 then loop back to 0. Most of the code is in the `onEnterFrame` handler that I needed, so I can move the object on every frame entry.

```
degrees = 0;

onEnterFrame = function () {
```

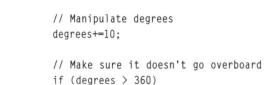

```
// Manipulate degrees
degrees+=10;
```

```
// Make sure it doesn't go overboard
if (degrees > 360)
  degrees = 0;
```

In the previous section you learned how to convert degrees to radians because radians are the only values that sine accepts. This is why I used this formula again:

```
// Convert to radians
var radians = Math.PI/180 * degrees;
```

For easier storage, and for convenience, I wrote the following line, one of the most important in this demo:

```
// This stores -1 to 1
var sineY = Math.sin(radians);
```

Once I acquired my value from the function, I know that I have an almost-predictable value that's between –1 and 1, so what I did was scale this range to something that the human eye can see. I scaled it to move from 100 to 300 on the Y-axis.

> **NOTE**
>
> This works because when sine is –1 (and multiplied by 100) it will yield –100, so by adding 200 to it, the result will yield 100 (our y value). When sine is 1 (and multiplied by 100) it will yield 100, so by adding 200 to it, it will make our y value 300.

```
// Move the projectile from 100 to 300
  thing._y = sineY * 100 + 200
```

As this will happen on every frame, you will have a ball smoothly bouncing up and down. I wanted the Movie Clip to scroll so you can visually see the sine within this picture so I added the following line.

```
thing._x += 10;
```

And of course, I made it loop so you can continue to be mesmerized by the mathematical visual.

```
if (thing._x > 550)
    thing._x = 0;
```

Is it just me, or does that projectile look like a good enemy for that game you're planning?

The Cosine

The next trig function we're going to discuss is similar to sine, and has an aptly similar name—cosine. See Figure 11.12 for a visual explanation of how cosine is defined.

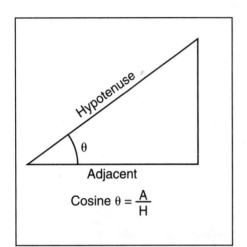

Figure 11.12

The cosine of an angle

Figure 11.12 tells you that the cosine of an angle is the adjacent side divided by the hypotenuse. How would this look graphically? See Figure 11.13.

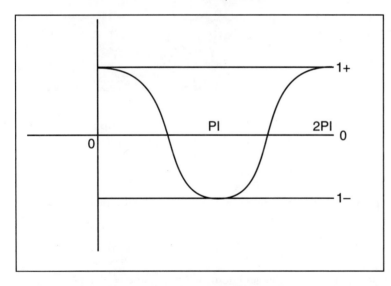

Figure 11.13

The cosine graph

As you examine the cosine graph, you'll note that it's very similar to the sine graph except that it's shifted to the right by 90 degrees (or Pi/2 for you math freaks). If you were to examine GDA_PROG11.4.fla, you would notice that the only difference from the sine version of the demo is that the projectile is receiving its values from the cosine function instead of the sine function. This causes the curve to start at a different point, but the curve itself is identical.

Let's check out the quick changes I made within this program.

```
// Game Development with ActionScript
// Lewis Moronta (c) 2003
// This program demonstrates how
// to use Math.sin methods.

degrees = 0;

onEnterFrame = function () {

  // Manipulate degrees
  degrees+=10;

  // Make sure it doesn't go overboard
  if (degrees > 360)
    degrees = 0;

  // Convert to radians
  var radians = Math.PI/180 * degrees;

  // This stores -1 to 1
  var cosineY = Math.cos(radians);

  // Move the projectile from 100 to 300
  thing._y = cosineY * 100 + 200

  // Now that we got him moving up and down
  // according to the power of the sine,
  // let's move him across the screen =)

  thing._x += 10;

  if (thing._x > 550)
    thing._x = 0;
};
```

If you play the SWF movie, you'll notice that not much has changed except that the code makes the projectile move on a different (shifted) curve. All I did was change this function from sine to cosine.

NOTE

This is a very basic introduction to the trigonometric functions. If you feel you need more, see the Math section in your local bookstore. To be honest with you, you already are equipped enough to build cool demos if you sit down with what you have. Don't let this information hold you back from learning more, though. Ask André LaMothe—he'll tell you that you can't ever intake too much math.

The Tangent

The tangent function is a combination of the last two. The tangent of an angle is the sine of that angle divided by the cosine of that same angle. What does this mean? It means that the tangent of an angle can also be the opposite side of that angle divided by its adjacent side.

See Figure 11.14 for a mathematical definition of tangent.

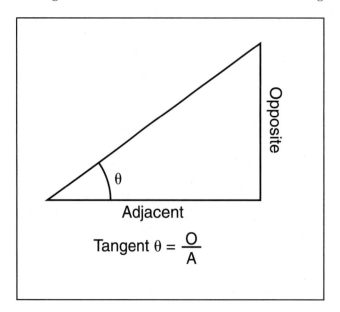

Figure 11.14

The tangent of an angle

The graph of tangent has many asymptotes, and it would be useless for me to show you the graph without telling you what an asymptote is. For definition purposes, an *asymptote* is a point on a graph where there is an unattainable value. The value can either be negative or positive, and the graph bends towards that direction. Observe Figure 11.15.

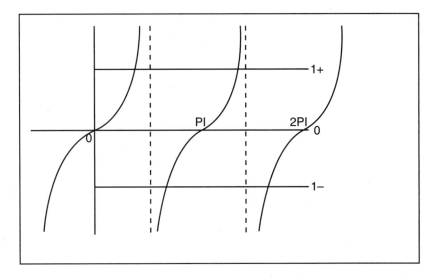

Figure 11.15

The tangent graph

See the dashed lines? As the curve gets closer to the dashed lines, it also gets closer to an unattainable position—every vertical line in this graph is an asymptote.

The Tank Demo

Ever wonder how to make your character move in any direction, not just the screen's up, down, left, and right directions? Well, now you can.

The following listing was taken from demo GDA_PROG11.5.fla; it allows you to move a little tank all over the screen. I bet you didn't realize it took some math to move a tank, eh? Check out the following listing.

```
// Game Development with ActionScript
// By Lewis Moronta (c) 2003
// This program demonstrates
// how to use the sine and cosine
// trig functions to allow the user
// to rotate the main player and
// move in which ever direction he
// wants. Feel free to modify.

// Setup old faithful...
onClipEvent(enterFrame) {

    // Initialize our velocity variables
    var yv = 0;
    var xv = 0;
```

```
// Check if the user wants to go left
if (Key.isDown(Key.LEFT)) {
  // Rotate counter-clockwise
    _rotation -= 10;
}


// If we are going rotate, we rotate that way
if (Key.isDown(Key.RIGHT)) {
  _rotation += 10;
}


// When the player is ready to move foward
// calculate which way is forward and then
// finally move that way... with the help
// of trigonometry...
if (Key.isDown(Key.UP)) {

    // Calculate the angle we are facing...
    var angle = this._rotation * (Math.PI/180);

    // Calculate the X coordinate for our next
    // position in our velocity map
    xv += Math.sin(angle)*10;

    // Caclulate the Y coordinate for our next position
    yv -= Math.cos(angle)*10;
}

// Finally move the player along...
_y += yv;
_x += xv;
}
```

Just in case you couldn't find the code in the timeline: I embedded it within the tank Movie Clip.

One of the first things I did in this code was set up our old event handler onClipEvent(enterFrame).

```
// Setup old faithful...
onClipEvent(enterFrame) {
```

As part of the movement mechanism, I have set up two velocity variables that will store the next position to which the tank can jump. You'll see how soon.

```
// Initialize our velocity variables
  var yv = 0;
  var xv = 0;
```

The next thing I did was check whether the user pressed the left arrow key—if it was pressed, then the object is rotated counter-clockwise 10 degrees.

```
if (Key.isDown(Key.LEFT)) {
    // Rotate counter-clockwise
        _rotation -= 10;
}
```

I did something similar with the right key, but this time it rotates clockwise 10 degrees.

```
if (Key.isDown(Key.RIGHT)) {
    _rotation += 10;
}
```

It would be kind of hard to detect when the user wants the tank to go forward without the code, so I set up a similar `if` structure. The only difference is that this one is more complicated.

```
if (Key.isDown(Key.UP)) {
```

The first thing I did was calculate the angle, in radians, of the position we were in.

```
var angle = this._rotation * (Math.PI/180);
```

After figuring this out, I went ahead and figured out that the projected point is 10 pixels away. I used sine and cosine for that.

```
    // Calculate the X coordinate for our next
    // position in our velocity map
    xv += Math.sin(angle)*10;

    // Caclulate the Y coordinate for our next position
    yv -= Math.cos(angle)*10;
```

Notice that the yv value is being subtracted—this is because your monitor's coordinates have y starting at (0, 0) from the upper left. The cosine function graph is on a Cartesian plane, which has y getting higher as you go up. On a monitor, y goes higher when you go down, thus the negative sign.

The next thing I did was very important—if this wasn't in the code, you wouldn't see any locomotion:

```
// Finally move the player along...
    _y += yv;
    _x += xv;
```

As new yv and xv values are being calculated on every frame, it's easy to rotate and move the tank to another rotation by calculating new values for them. Cool, right?

Summary

You learned all about radians in this chapter. The unit circle was introduced, and you also learned how to solve for any point on that circle given any angle.

Enhancing your knowledge of trigonometric graphs, you also learned about periods, domains, and ranges. Periods are all the non-repeating values within a domain of a graph. A domain is the range of values that the curve is graphed. And the range is the vertical limits that the graph is being graphed upon.

You also learned how to control an object's position with your sine and cosine values. You pretty much got the hang of it all, so enjoy your new knowledge.

Question & Answer

Q. Since you can find the sine and cosine values from a given angle, can you find the angle with the given sine and cosine values?

A. Yes you can. You can use the secant, cosecant, and arc tangent functions to get these values. The ActionScript equivalent would be `Math.asin`, `Math.acos`, and `Math.atan` functions. You can look them up in the Help file for more information.

Exercise

1. Draw up representations of our solar system's nine planets; set them up where they all move in orbit at different speeds. Have fun!

CHAPTER 12

THE PHYSICS:
MAKING IT
FEEL REAL

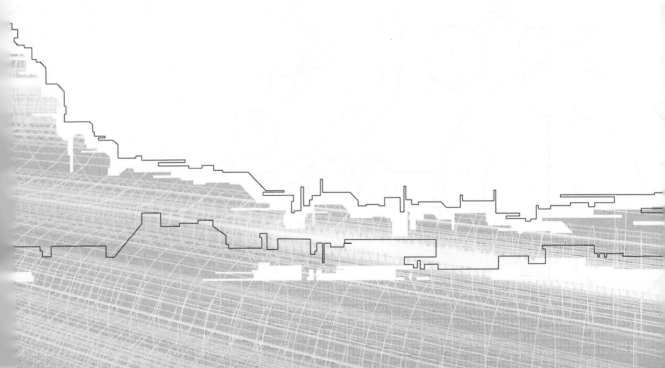

Physics is the science of energy and matter and the interaction of the two. Physics has become an extremely important factor in today's games. It's human nature to want objects in a game to respond realistically to the laws of physics—this is why a nice, solid physics foundation is required if you want to keep up with today's ever-changing game market.

Check out what you'll learn in this chapter:

- Vector and scalar values
- Speed, velocity, and acceleration
- Gravity
- Wind
- Friction

Vector and Scalar Values

Physics is all about math, so it shouldn't come as a surprise that the application of physics to a game involves many mathematical structures. We'll be discussing two of these structures in this section—scalars and vectors. If you're not a math guru, don't worry—the names may be intimidating, but they represent concepts that any programmer is familiar with, whether they know it or not. A *scalar* is basically a single value, like 10, 159, or 2.47. For those of you that are a bit rusty with math on a theoretical level, a scalar is analogous to a single variable in ActionScript. Defining a variable like x can only hold a single value, such as the ones listed above. The same goes for scalars.

A vector, on the other hand, represents multiple values, called *components*. The number of components a given vector represents is referred to as its "dimensions." For example, a 2-dimensional (or *2D*) vector represents two components; a 3D vector represents three components, and so on. Because of this, a scalar can also be referred to as a 1D vector, since both terms refer to the representation of a single value. The two components of a 2D vector are often thought of as *magnitude* and *direction*, which allow such a vector to extend from the origin of a 2D coordinate system to any distance (based on its magnitude), in any direction. See Figure 12.1.

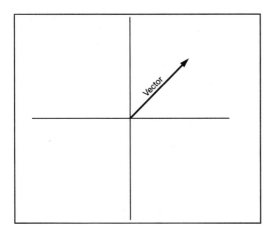

Figure 12.1

The visual representation of a vector

Vector values are very handy when working with more complicated physics. You can add them, subtract them, and even scale them. This can help you figure out things such as the physics involved in a simple game of pool. Let's say you were programming a game of pool, and you needed to know in which direction the ball should react after it collides with another ball. Vectors can help you determine the physics involved in two billiard balls colliding—without the use of vectors, your pool game could end up looking quite unrealistic.

Speed

Speed is a scalar value that represents the rate at which an object moves relative to some defined reference point. That sounds a bit geeky, so I'll restate it: Speed is the rate of change from point A to point B.

Speed is measured in meters per second (m/s). In a video game, you would have to measure speed in pixels per frame or something else that you could use to imitate the metric system. See Figure 12.2 an example.

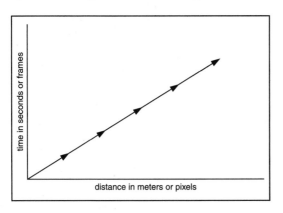

Figure 12.2

Measuring speed

Velocity

Velocity is a vector value that can be represented by a direction and the scalar value speed. Once you combine speed and a direction, you'll have a velocity value that is also measured in meters per second.

It is possible to plan out a direction path with vectors—this means that you can even store how fast an object would be going on each vector segment. See Figure 12.3.

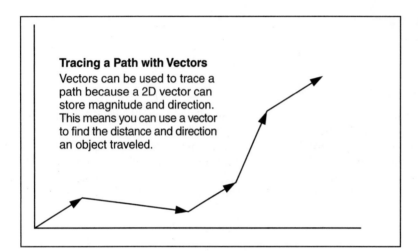

Tracing a Path with Vectors
Vectors can be used to trace a path because a 2D vector can store magnitude and direction. This means you can use a vector to find the distance and direction an object traveled.

Figure 12.3

Tracing a vector path

I have prepared a simple demo that is very easy to understand. But this time, I want you to look at a demo with different eyes. Check out the following listing, which was extracted from GDA_PROG12.1.fla.

```
// Game Development with ActionScript
// By Lewis Moronta (c) 2003

// Set up the preset velocity
onClipEvent(load) {
   xv = 10;
}

// Setup ol' faithful
onClipEvent(enterFrame) {

   // Add the even velocity on every frame
   _x += xv;


   // Reverse velocities if
   // we hit boundaries we don't like
```

```
if (_x > 550)
    xv = -xv;

if (_x < 0)
    xv = -xv;
}
```

There are two things that I want you to notice about this listing. One is that you can find the code within the Movie Clip, and two is that I reversed the velocities in this program just like I did in the bouncing ball demo a while back. I want you to think in terms of vectors, so check out Figure 12.4.

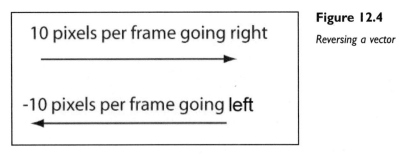

Figure 12.4

Reversing a vector

As you can note from Figure 12.4, reversing a vector that is going either left or right, or east or west, is as simple as inverting its magnitude, or negating its magnitude. If your object is moving 10 pixels/frame to the right and you want it to go left, just reverse its direction by negating its velocity variable—it will then be moving at -10 pixels/frame. The same rule applies for a vector moving vertically. Just remember that when dealing with horizontal or vertical, the sign of the magnitude will determine the vector's direction.

Acceleration

Acceleration is another vector quantity, but it's a bit deeper and harder to understand. It's the rate of change of velocity. This is why it's measured in meters per second squared (m/s/s).

Why should I even cover acceleration? Simply because nothing on this earth moves from point A to point B without speeding up or slowing down. If you can grasp and incorporate this concept in your games, you will achieve a new level of realism.

Take a look at Figure 12.5 see how the graph of a moving object is affected by accelera-tion—one is moving with no acceleration and the other is moving with acceleration.

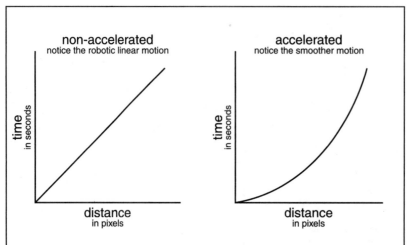

Figure 12.5

Graphed acceleration

GDA_PROG12.2.fla shows you the difference between a generic object with acceleration and another without. Each of the objects has its own code—the one with the acceleration was extracted to the following listing.

```
// Game Development with ActionScript
// By Lewis Moronta (c) 2003

onClipEvent(load) {

   // Setup the acceleration
   xa = 1;

   // Initialize the velocity with xa
   xv = xa;
}

// Setup ol' faithful
onClipEvent(enterFrame) {

   // Always add the velocity
   _x += xv;

   // Increase the change in velocity
   xv += xa;

   // Make sure we don't go overboard
   if (xv > 20)
      xv = 20;
```

```
    // Reset
    if (_x > 550) {
        x = 0;
        xv = 0;
    }
}
```

The first object glides along slowly then accelerates rapidly, and then it repeats this routine. The object at the bottom of the screen moves along at a boring, steady pace. Check out the acceleration code:

```
onClipEvent(load) {

    // Setup the acceleration
    xa = 1;

    // Initialize the velocity with xa
    xv = xa;
}
```

I set up two variables, one for the acceleration and the other for velocity. As acceleration is the change in velocity, I initialized the velocity variable with the change in velocity (acceleration).

I wrote up the code to move the object in the same way I always do—by adding the velocity to the current position to move the position:

```
    // Always add the velocity
    _x += xv;
```

As acceleration is the change of velocity, I changed the velocity with this line:

```
    // Increase the change in velocity
    xv += xa;
```

This causesd the velocity to increase, thus making the object move fast.

To prevent any crazy speeds on the part of the object, I restricted and capped the max speed to 20 pixels per second:

```
    // Make sure we don't go overboard
    if (xv > 20)
        xv = 20;
```

And finally, when the object goes off the side of the screen, I wanted it to repeat the whole accelerating motion, so I reset it with the following lines:

```
    if (_x > 550) {
        x = 0;
        xv = 0;
    }
```

You can now see how you can get creative and create a slow down. Mess around with this program and see what interesting results you can achieve.

> **NOTE**
>
> I won't throw any complicated physics math at you because you most likely won't use it in your game programming ventures when you're just starting out. When you master the simple concepts I'm showing you here, I do suggest you find a good game development physics book.

Working with Gravity

Gravity is a downward-accelerating force of 9.8 m/s/s. There is no need to program at this rate if your game world is not measured on the same scale as the Earth's gravitational pull. So what should you do? You eyeball it. You can only model so much within a game.

To make things more interesting, projectiles move in a trajectory. The reason this happens is because projectiles on earth are constantly affected by gravitational pull, which causes trajectories to be *parabolic arcs*, meaning they follow the general shape of a parabola as they travel up and back down. If this wasn't so, they would fly in a linear path and never come back down. These trajectories can be accurately replicated with complicated formulas, but they can also be replicated with some slick programming techniques.

See Figure 12.6 to see how the projectile in the next demo moves on a path.

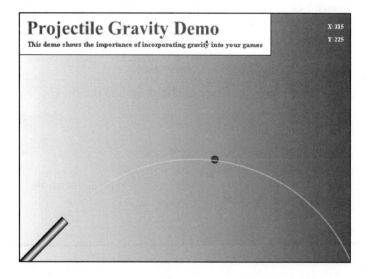

Figure 12.6

A trajectory path

If you open up GDA_PROG12.3.fla, you'll notice a small cannon on the left side of the screen. If you test the movie, you'll see that the cannon fires a projectile across the screen. When the projectile lands, the cannon fires again. One might think that a lot of difficult math went into this, but there's nothing difficult about it. Check out the code that I embedded into that projectile:

```
// Game Development with ActionScript
// By Lewis Moronta (c) 2003

// This program demonstrates the
// use of gravity in a game.

onClipEvent(load) {

  // Initialize some properties
  xv =  10;
  yv = -10;
  gravity = .5;
}


onClipEvent(enterFrame) {

  // Add some motion
  _x += xv;
  _y += yv;

  // Add some gravity
  yv += gravity;

  // Reset if off the screen
  if (_y > 400) {
    _x = 65;
    _y = 324;
    yv = -10;
  }
}
```

The first thing I did when the Movie Clip loaded was to create a few new properties. These properties will control the projectile's flow through the air.

```
onClipEvent(load) {

  // Initialize some properties
  xv =  10;
  yv = -10;
  gravity = .5;
}
```

I initialized two velocity variables. They lead the projectile up and to the right. The `gravity` variable will be used to pull the projectile down—it will directly affect the `yv` velocity variable. Let's see how in the next part of the code.

Besides creating an `onClipEvent(enterFrame)` handler, I also set up the program so velocity is *always* being applied to the projectile, even when it is at rest.

```
onClipEvent(enterFrame) {

    // Add some motion
    _x += xv;
    _y += yv;
```

As we have a y velocity variable, which is vertical, gravity should affect the variable if you want realistic-looking results. This is why I affect the velocity variable on every frame that passes with the following line:

```
// Add some gravity
    yv += gravity;
```

I finally took the liberty of performing a reset on all of the program variables once the ball was off the screen. This will cause the cannon to repeat and fire.

```
// Reset if off the screen
    if (_y > 400) {
        _x = 65;
        _y = 324;
        yv = -10;
    }
```

And you thought you were going to learn about boring theories without applications.

Working with Wind

When I discussed particle systems I touched briefly on wind; this time, you will see wind in different light. I have prepared a demo for this chapter that allows you to play God and adjust the wind on-the-fly with a slider. You will see all of the falling particles move in the direction you push the slider, and in the amount you push it as well.

Figure 12.7 shows the GDA_PROG12.4.fla demo, and how I set up the controls that enable you to control the program's wind factor.

NOTE

I'm going to start combining concepts that I've taught you because at this point you should be comfortable enough with them. This is why the demos may seem more complicated. Inspect them and make sure you know how they work, and you will be able to make even cooler effects in your games.

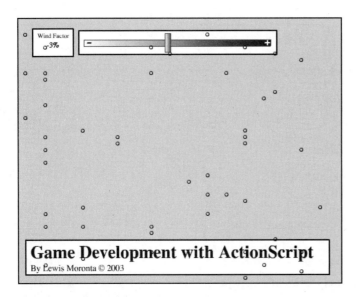

Figure 12.7

Adjusting the wind factor

I have embedded some of the code in the main Timeline and the rest of it within the slider Movie Clip. See the following listing for the code within the main Timeline.

```
// Game Development with ActionScript
// By Lewis Moronta (c) 2003
// This code segment shows you how
// to setup particles that can
// have an external force
// affect them.

onLoad = function () {

    // Setup a new property
    wind = 0;

    // Create 50 new particles and place them randomly
    for (var i = 0; i < 50; i++) {

        // Create another one
        attachMovie("circle", "circle"+i, i);

        // Store the new Movie Clip temporarily
        // to avoid any typos within the code
        var mc = _root["circle"+i];

        // Use the new alias to assign a pos
```

```
        mc._x = Math.random()*550;
        mc._y = Math.random()*400;
    }
};


onEnterFrame = function() {

  // Loop through all of them
  for (var i = 0; i < 50; i++) {

        // Access the current Movie Clip
        var mc = _root["circle"+i];

        // Move the Movie Clip
        mc._y += 10;
        mc._x += wind;

        //** Constrain the Movie Clip **//

        // Loop it around the top
        if (mc._y > 400)
          mc._y = 0;

        // Loop it around the right
        if (mc._x > 500)
          mc._x = 0;

        // Loop it around the left
        if (mc._x < 0)
          mc._x = 500;

  }
};
```

Besides setting up an onLoad function, I also set up a wind variable. This will hold the direction that the wind should flow.

```
onLoad = function () {

  // Setup a new property
  wind = 0;
```

To get the particles on the stage, I need to link one of the symbols with the library and just duplicate the particles on the stage in different positions. I used the following loop for this effect:

```
  // Create 50 new particles and place them randomly
  for (var i = 0; i < 50; i++) {
```

```
    // Create another one
    attachMovie("circle", "circle"+i, i);

    // Store the new Movie Clip temporarily
    // to avoid any typos within the code
    var mc = _root["circle"+i];

    // Use the new alias to assign a pos
    mc._x = Math.random()*550;
    mc._y = Math.random()*400;
}
```

Besides creating animation on each frame, I also had to loop through all the pieces on the stage, so I added a `for` loop for my `onEnterFrame` handler:

```
onEnterFrame = function() {

  // Loop through all of them
  for (var i = 0; i < 50; i++) {
```

For sake of clarity, I stored the current Movie Clip being accessed into a small variable—this will allow me to skip writing out the whole reference during other parts of the code:

```
    // Access the current Movie Clip
    var mc = _root["circle"+i];
```

Once that was prepared, I had each particle falling at a constant 10 pixels per second, and I also added the wind factor—this value depends on where the slider is. It all will come together soon.

```
    // Move the Movie Clip
    mc._y += 10;
    mc._x += wind;
```

I then made sure that if the particles go off the bottom of the stage that they loop around to the top of the stage.

```
    // Loop it around the top
    if (mc._y > 400)
      mc._y = 0;
```

I added the following two `if` statements because of the wind mechanism in the program. These statements will avoid any glitches and errors when the user goes crazy adjusting wind factors.

```
    // Loop it around the right
    if (mc._x > 500)
      mc._x = 0;
```

```
        // Loop it around the left
    if (mc._x < 0)
        mc._x = 500;
```

Now that you know how I created all the particles and how to have wind affect them, let's see how the user gets to control all this stuff. The following listing was extracted from the slider Movie Clip.

```
// Game Development with ActionScript
// By Lewis Moronta (c) 2003

// This clip contains slider code

onClipEvent(load) {

  // Setup min and max constraints
  min = 100;
  max = 400;

  // Make sure it's not being clicked
  active = false;

  // Calculate how far along the slider
  _root.display = "0%";

  // Flag the program that the user released
  onRelease = function () {
    active = false;
  };

  // Flag the program the user released outside
  onReleaseOutside = function () {
    active = false;
  };

  // Flag the program the user clicked
  onPress = function () {
    active = true;
  };

  Mouse.addListener(this);

  // Adjust the slider...
  onMouseMove = function() {

    // Only do this if this clip is pressed
    if (active) {
```

```
        // Follow the mouse on the x-axis
        _x = _root._xmouse;

        // Constrain motion
        if (_x < min)
          _x = min;

        if (_x > max)
          _x = max;

        // More calculations =)
        _root.wind = Math.round((_x-min)/(max-min)*60)-30;
        _root.display = _root.wind+"%";
      }
    };
}
```

What I wrote here can be intimidating at first because all the code is contained within the onClipEvent(load) handler.

In the beginning, I confidently set up two min and max variables that will act as my visual constrain positions. I also set up a flag variable that tells the program whether the user is dragging the slider or not. I also put a value into a dynamic text box that is on the _root.

```
// Setup min and max constraints
  min = 100;
  max = 400;

  // Make sure it's not being clicked
  active = false;

  // Calculate how far along the slider
  _root.display = "0%";
```

Then, I flagged to see whether the user released the slider:

```
  // Flag the program that the user released
  onRelease = function () {
    active = false;
  };
```

There was also the possibility of the user releasing outside the slider button, so I covered that, too.

```
  onReleaseOutside = function () {
    active = false;
  };
```

I flagged the rest of the program for when the user presses and drags the slider.

```
onPress = function () {
   active = true;
};
```

The next thing I did was add a mouse listener to this Movie Clip so that I can use the onMouseMove callback function:

```
Mouse.addListener(this);
```

Once in the onMouseMove function, I decided not to do anything if the slider wasn't active or being dragged, so I tested for that state:

```
onMouseMove = function() {

   // Only do this if this clip is pressed
   if (active) {
```

You of course have to follow the cursor position; that's why I added the following line:

```
// Follow the mouse on the x-axis
      _x = _root._xmouse;
```

In order to allow the user to only move the slider within certain parts of the stage, you must set up constraints, so that's exactly what I did:

```
// Constrain motion
      if (_x < min)
         _x = min;

      if (_x > max)
         _x = max;
```

The following line is the juiciest part of this code. It calculates the position of the slider and, from this, evaluates the strength and direction of the wind (there's a vector value for ya).

```
_root.wind = Math.round((_x-min)/(max-min)*60)-30;
```

This works because I divided the portion (the number of pixels along the slider) by the whole (the total length of the slider) to get a percentage amount in decimals. I multiplied by 60 to scale the value to a range of 0 to 60. I then subtracted 30 to get a new range of –30 to 30. In other words, when the slider is all the way to the left, it will yield –30. When the slider is all the way to the right, the max it can go is 30. When the slider is in the center, it will be 0.

And finally, for display purposes, I update the dynamic textbox that exists in the main Timeline.

```
_root.display = _root.wind+"%";
```

How do you like the interactivity now?

Working with Friction

Friction is a force created when objects act in opposition to one another. It may not be obvious, but friction can be caused by air particles and other objects. If there were no friction, you would be able to literally throw a ball around the world. How crazy is that? To show you how realistic a main character can look with a little friction and a few other forces added, I have written up a demo. Open up GDA_PROG12.5.fla.

Figure 12.8 shows what you are about to experience. The demo starts off with a small aircraft in the center of the screen. The first thing you notice is generating ammo that appears on the screen right under the ship. There is also a bouncing enemy that annoys you—shoot at it in order to gain points.

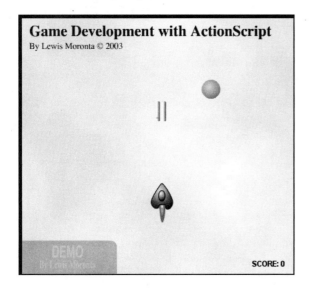

Figure 12.8

A physics demo

You can move the ship in two ways: You can use the arrow keys or you can drag it with the mouse. You can then shoot at the enemy with the spacebar. Move the ship around with the keyboard and experience all the forces you've learned about.

Let's start by dissecting all the code on the main Timeline; then we'll go into the buttons and Movie Clips. The following listing shows the code on the first frame of this movie.

```
stop();

onLoad = function () {

        attachMovie("ammo", "beam", 3);
        beam.x = 0;
        beam.y = 0;
        beam.status = "passive";
```

```
        attachMovie("enemy", "badguy", 2);
        badguy.status = "alive";
        badguy._y = Math.random()*(400-badguy._height);
        badguy._x = Math.random()*(440-badguy._width);
        badguy.dir_x = 10;
        badguy.dir_y = 10;
        unDieCount = 0;

        // Make them invisible for the first frame
        beam._visible = false;
        badguy._visible = false;
};

onUnload = function () {

        beam.removeMovieClip();
        badguy.removeMovieClip();
};

onEnterFrame = function () {

        // Compute the ammo
        if (beam.status == "passive") {
                beam.x = player._x-9;
                beam.y = player._y-20;
        }

        if (beam.status == "fired!") {
                beam.y -= beam._height;

                if (beam.y < -beam._height) {
                        beam.status = "passive";
                        beam.gotoAndPlay("fadein");
                }
        }

        beam._x = beam.x;
        beam._y = beam.y;

        // Compute the bad guy
        if (badguy.status == "alive") {

                badguy._x += badguy.dir_x;
                badguy._y += badguy.dir_y;

                if (badguy._x > (439-badguy._width))
```

```
                       badguy.dir_x = -badguy.dir_x;
              if (badguy._x < 0)
                       badguy.dir_x = -badguy.dir_x;

              if (badguy._y > (399-badguy._height))
                       badguy.dir_y = -badguy.dir_y;
              if (badguy._y < 0)
                       badguy.dir_y = -badguy.dir_y;

              if (badguy.hitTest(beam)) {

                       if (beam.status == "fired!") {
                                player.score += 10;
                                beam.status = "passive";
                                badguy.status = "dead";
                                badguy._alpha = 30;

                       }

              }

      } else if (++unDieCount > 12) {
              unDieCount = 0;
              badguy.status = "alive";
              badguy._alpha = 100;

      }
};
```

The first thing I did in this onLoad function was create the beam instance. I also created
some new properties within; they will help me track the aircraft later on. The status property will help me figure out if the beam has been fired or not.

```
attachMovie("ammo", "beam", 3);
beam.x = 0;
beam.y = 0;
beam.status = "passive";
```

The next thing I set up was our enemy, badguy. This guy has a lot of properties—take a
look:

```
attachMovie("enemy", "badguy", 2);
badguy.status = "alive";
badguy._y = Math.random()*(400-badguy._height);
badguy._x = Math.random()*(440-badguy._width);
badguy.dir_x = 10;
badguy.dir_y = 10;


unDieCount = 0;
```

The unDieCount variable helps me freeze the enemy in a dead state long enough for the user to see that the program is reacting to a hit.

As the demo doesn't start till the second frame, I've decided to hide the ammo and the bad guy until the user presses the button.

```
beam._visible = false;
badguy._visible = false;
```

The next snippet is from the onEnterFrame function that makes the ammo follow the ship if it's not being fired.

```
if (beam.status == "passive") {
        beam.x = player._x-9;
        beam.y = player._y-20;
}
```

And if the ammo has been fired, go ahead and move it up.

```
if (beam.status == "fired!") {
        beam.y -= beam._height;
```

When the missile hits the end of the screen, it is reset. Once I set the missile to passive, the code I went over previously will make the ammo follow the aircraft again.

```
if (beam.y < -beam._height) {
        beam.status = "passive";
        beam.gotoAndPlay("fadein");
}
```

Right after the properties are updated in the ammo Movie Clip, I start to check what's up with the enemy. If he's not alive, we move him.

```
if (badguy.status == "alive") {

        badguy._x += badguy.dir_x;
        badguy._y += badguy.dir_y;
```

To make the enemy bounce off the sides of the walls, I had to reverse the velocities once I detected a hit.

```
if (badguy._x > (439-badguy._width))
        badguy.dir_x = -badguy.dir_x;
if (badguy._x < 0)
        badguy.dir_x = -badguy.dir_x;
```

I also had to test the top and bottom walls.

```
if (badguy._y > (399-badguy._height))
        badguy.dir_y = -badguy.dir_y;
if (badguy._y < 0)
        badguy.dir_y = -badguy.dir_y;
```

If the ammo is fired and it collides with the enemy, then I add to the score and reset everything.

```
if (badguy.hitTest(beam)) {

    if (beam.status == "fired!") {
        player.score += 10;
        beam.status = "passive";
        badguy.status = "dead";
        badguy._alpha = 30;
    }

}
```

The reason I'm testing to see if the beam status is fired is because I don't want the beam to hit the enemy when it's still on the ship. If all these tests result to true, everything is reset and the bad guy dies. Cool, eh?

So what happens when the enemy is dead? Take a look at the code:

```
} else if (++unDieCount > 12) {
        unDieCount = 0;
        badguy.status = "alive";
        badguy._alpha = 100;
}
```

When the bad guy status is dead, the bad guy is dimmed. It will stay dimmed for at least 12 frames until this last condition is true. Once unDieCount is over 12, it resets itself and the bad guy is brought back to life.

Now that we know how the other stuff is controlled, let's see how the bad guy and the beam become visible once you go to the next frame. The following is the code found in the button:

```
on (release) {

  beam._visible = true;
  badguy._visible = true;

  nextFrame();
}
```

Let's jump into the code that I stored within the aircraft's Movie Clip.

```
// Game Development with ActionScript
// By Lewis Moronta (c) 2003
// This demo demonstrates how to
// incorporate physics within your game.

onClipEvent(load) {
```

```
        // Setup some properties
        score = 0;

        vel_x = 0;
        vel_y = 0

        acel_x = 4;
        acel_y = 4;
}

onClipEvent(enterFrame) {

        // Move the ship
        _x += vel_x;
        _y += vel_y;

        // Check boundaries
        if (_x < 0)
                _x = 0;
        if (_x > (440-_width))
                _x = 440-_width;

        if (_y < 0)
                _y = 0;
        if (_y > (400-_height))
                _y = 400-_height;

        // Slow down the ship
        // by simulating friction
        if (vel_x > 0)
                vel_x--;
        if (vel_x < 0)
                vel_x++;

        if (vel_y > 0)
                vel_y--;
        if (vel_y < 0)
                vel_y++;

        // CONTROLS //////////
        if (Key.isDown(Key.LEFT)) {

                vel_x -= acel_x;

                if (acel_x < -16)
                        acel_x = -16;
```

```
                }

        if (Key.isDown(Key.RIGHT)) {

                vel_x += acel_x;

                if (acel_x > 16)
                        acel_x = 16;
        }

        if (Key.isDown(Key.UP)) {

                vel_y -= acel_y;

                if (acel_y < -16)
                        acel_y = -16;
        }

        if (Key.isDown(Key.DOWN)) {

                vel_y += acel_y;

                if (acel_y > 16)
                        acel_y = 16;
        }

        if (Key.isDown(Key.SPACE)) {
                _root.beem.status = "fired!";
        }

        _parent.scoreDisplay = "SCORE: "+score;
}

onClipEvent(mouseDown) {
        if (this.hitTest(_root._xmouse, _root._ymouse)) {
                this.startDrag();
                Mouse.hide();
        }
}

onClipEvent(mouseUp) {
        this.stopDrag();
        Mouse.show();
}
```

In the beginning, there was velocity and acceleration. There was also another property named score. These are the variables initialized when the clip is loaded.

In the `onEnterFrame` handler, I wrote code to add velocity to the aircraft's current position even if it's stationary.

```
_x += vel_x;
_y += vel_y;
```

One of the first things I did after this was check to make sure that our player doesn't move out of the stage's viewable area.

```
if (_x < 0)
        _x = 0;
if (_x > (440-_width))
        _x = 440-_width;

if (_y < 0)
        _y = 0;
if (_y > (400-_height))
        _y = 400-_height;
```

Here are the most important lines in this section—the friction code. How does friction behave? It basically slows down motion in most cases. How did I achieve this in this demo? I went against my velocities until it reached 0—check it out:

```
if (vel_x > 0)
        vel_x--;
if (vel_x < 0)
        vel_x++;
```

The friction code tries to subtract 1 from the velocity in the x-axis until the aircraft comes to a complete halt—this is exactly what I do to the y-axis velocities:

```
if (vel_y > 0)
        vel_y--;
if (vel_y < 0)
        vel_y++;
```

When the user presses the Left arrow key, the aircraft accelerates in a west direction. The acceleration is capped at -16 pixels per frame. If the user were to just release the key, you'd see friction take over.

```
if (Key.isDown(Key.LEFT)) {

    vel_x -= acel_x;

    if (acel_x < -16)
            acel_x = -16;

}
```

I did something similar to the right motion but this time I add the acceleration and capped it at 16 ppf (pixels per frame):

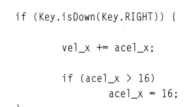

```
if (Key.isDown(Key.RIGHT)) {

        vel_x += acel_x;

        if (acel_x > 16)
                acel_x = 16;
}
```

The Up and Down arrow key responses and code are very similar so I'll be brief in my explanation:

```
if (Key.isDown(Key.UP)) {

        vel_y -= acel_y;

        if (acel_y < -16)
                acel_y = -16;
}

if (Key.isDown(Key.DOWN)) {

        vel_y += acel_y;

        if (acel_y > 16)
                acel_y = 16;
}
```

When the Up key is pressed, the aircraft is moved up and is capped at –16 ppf. When the Down key is pressed, the airplane is moved down and it's capped at 16 ppf.

In order to trigger the conditional structures that fire the projectile on the main Timeline, we must flag them that the user wants to fire (the spacebar is pressed).

```
if (Key.isDown(Key.SPACE)) {
        _root.beem.status = "fired!";
}
```

As the last thing in this handler, I wrote up this line to update the display:

```
_parent.scoreDisplay = "SCORE: "+score;
```

That concludes the friction code.

The following two functions allow the user to drag and drop the aircraft:

```
onClipEvent(mouseDown) {
        if (this.hitTest(_root._xmouse, _root._ymouse)) {
                this.startDrag();
                Mouse.hide();
        }
}
```

The `mouseDown` function checks to see if the mouse is being pressed—if it is, it starts to drag while hiding the mouse.

```
onClipEvent(mouseUp) {
        this.stopDrag();
        Mouse.show();
}
```

The `mouseUp` handler detects to see when the user stops dragging the aircraft, thus stopping the drag and showing the cursor.

All it required to create a semi-realistic game engine was a little physics!

Summary

Understanding physics is a nice way to start appreciating the natural world around us. Once you start observing and imitating your surroundings, your games will be more organic and believable. This is why I introduced vector and scalars values to you. One of the first scalar values that you already knew about was speed. You've been using the vector value velocity all this time, but now you understand it more in depth. Acceleration is the change in velocity, and you experienced some cool demos while learning all about it. You then touched upon gravity without getting into the highly complicated math that can go behind it. Then wind was introduced in a way that you were able to better understand it as a vector entity. And finally, you learned about friction, the force that opposes all other forces—this was also coupled with a cool demo.

Questions & Answers

Q. Does physics get any harder than this? This chapter was very easy.

A. Yes it does. You can get as deep into physics as you want. Remember one thing, though—you are reading this book to learn how to program games, and that's why these topics were discussed in a simplified manner.

Q. Collision detection is a big part of physics, why didn't you cover it in detail?

A. There are plenty of other books that cover this subject in detail. Try *Macromedia Flash MX Game Programming*, published by Premier Press.

Exercise

1. Set up two cannons, one on each side of the screen. Have them shoot cannon balls at each other. If their cannon balls collide, make a sound go off—if one hits the opponent, give the other opponent a point. Make sure that each cannon ball is launched with different physics factors. This will make each round different.

PART FIVE

Advanced Topics

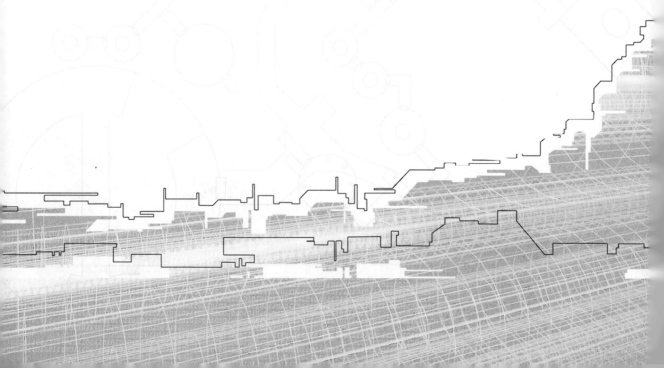

CHAPTER 13

SERVER AND CG1 COMMUNICATIONS

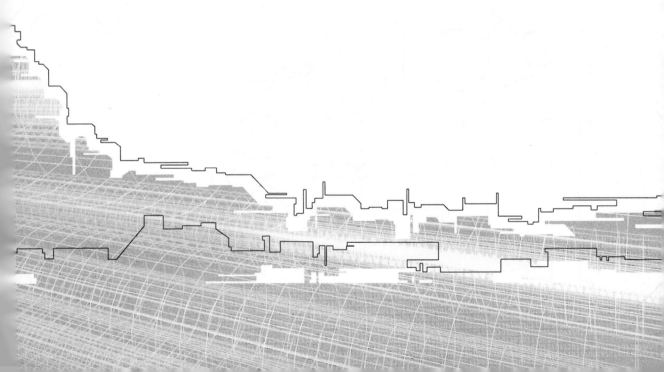

The World Wide Web is the foundation for communicating with the rest of the world over the Internet. Most of the Web is made up of HTML pages with other technologies, such as Flash movies, embedded in them. These Flash movies can communicate with the server where the page is being hosted, just like HTML can, to achieve very interesting effects. Thanks to the Web your Flash games can communicate with server programs to do many things such as saving high scores and other records.

Following is the list of topics I'll cover in this chapter:

- Exporting HTML
- Browser communication
- CGI scripts
- Sending info to the server

Exporting HTML

As you may know, HTML stands for *Hyper Text Markup Language*. As you may also know, HTML is a language that consists of many tags that format text, pictures, and other content. These tags are what most Web pages are composed of. Some of these tags allow your Web browser to load and play Flash movies.

It's not necessary for a Flash game developer to learn HTML just so that his audience can preview his game on the Web. Flash is actually nice enough to include a feature that outputs an HTML file for the game you're currently working on. This streamlines the process by letting you upload to your Web server as soon as you're done with your game.

To export a file, go to File, Publish Settings, click on the Formats tab, and make sure HTML is checked. Take a look at Figure 13.1; you will see exactly what I'm referring to.

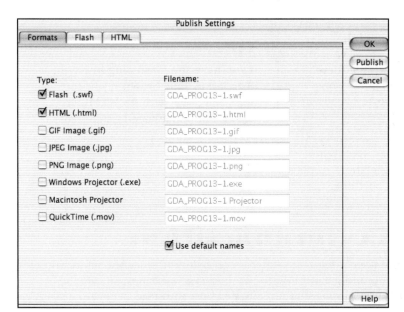

Figure 13.1

Exporting an HTML file

If you would like to change the name of the HTML file you will be exporting, uncheck the default names check box at the bottom.

Now click on the HTML tab. You can see the options that are available before you publish the file in Figure 13.2.

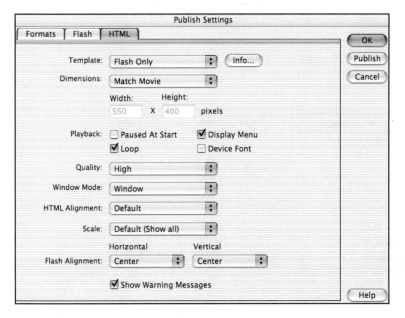

Figure 13.2

Changing options before publishing

Once you are done adjusting these settings, you can go ahead and click Publish under the OK button. If you go to where your file is stored, you'll find an HTML file there. Open it in your browser and guess what you'll see? You'll see your movie playing in your browser—in HTML!

The default settings are fine for your HTML export. If you'd like to learn what all these trivial settings are for, don't be afraid to play with them—you can't break anything.

TIP

If you have the Flash plug-in installed in your browser, you can open the SWF with no HTML. It works, but you'll have less control over the settings.

Browser Communication

I thought it might be a good idea to explain what goes on behind the scenes before you jump into any scripting. If you understand how the Web works, you can work *with* the Web—not against it. If you know all this stuff already, just bear with me.

When you type in a Web address, it is resolved through a Domain Name Server (DNS) at your Internet Service Provider (ISP). An initial response called "header information" is sent back to the browser on your computer—and is followed by HTML that formats the contents on your screen. Once the HTML contents are loaded, your page can then load Web forms and Flash movies. These forms and movies can communicate with the server where the Web site is stored. This is exactly what we are going to focus on. See Figure 13.3 so you can get a better idea of how you are connected to the Internet.

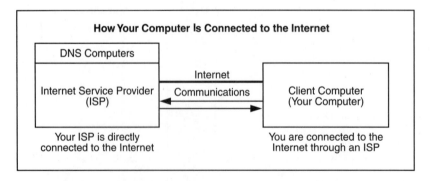

How Your Computer Is Connected to the Internet

DNS Computers

Internet Service Provider (ISP)

Internet Communications

Client Computer (Your Computer)

Your ISP is directly connected to the Internet

You are connected to the Internet through an ISP

Figure 13.3

You're connected to the Internet through an ISP.

The communication part is difficult to understand, but there are common protocols that the Internet uses to communicate. By learning a few rules, you can easily use these protocols. There is a standard called CGI, or *Common Gateway Interface*, which is a set of rules of how communication is transferred from client (your computer) to the host (Web server). This standard is what we will be using in this chapter.

All Web forms have Send buttons (sometimes referred to as Submit buttons) and when someone presses the button on a Web form, the information stored in the form is sent back to a script that is stored on the server. This script runs on the server and manipulates the data that was sent. The script has the capability to spit back another HTML file to show the results. The script can even access a database as big as Amazon.com and output a list from a database search, amongst other things. See Figure 13.4 for a visual of what happens when the average Web surfer clicks on a Send button.

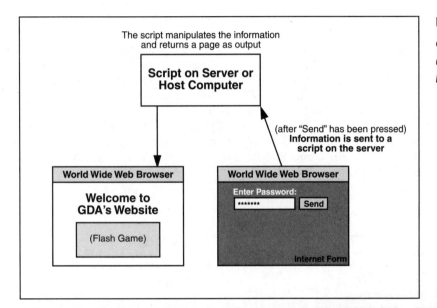

Figure 13.4

Communication after a user clicks on the Send button

> **NOTE**
>
> Due to space and time limitations, this chapter will not cover how to program CGI scripts. There are an abundance of books on this subject that can help you test your Flash movies. The reason this chapter is included is because when working in a team, the Flash developer must know how to work with the other Web programmers.

CGI Scripts

CGI scripts can be written in almost any language; what language they are written in depends on the programmer, and on and the server that's being used. A popular language used to program these types of scripts is Perl. Perl is an interpreted language much like ActionScript—it requires the Perl interpreter to run the script. This means that before you write up your script and put it on your server, make sure you have Perl installed somewhere up there.

Perl used to be a general-purpose scripting language for the UNIX platform, and now it's among the most popular CGI scripting languages on earth. If that doesn't motivate you to pick up some Perl later on, I don't know what will. Lucky for you, you won't have to write much of the utilities you would normally want to write. Why? Because most of these wheels have been invented already. You can find royalty-free scripts all over the Net—just do a quick search.

When data is submitted to the CGI script, it can be transferred in two ways: through a GET method or through a POST method—these are part of the HTTP protocol and have to do with where in the HTTP request the data is stored, and in what format. The GET method allows all of the information to be passed on as environment variables that the CGI script can just load and move on. The only downfall to GET is that it's not the most secure method. POST does something similar but in a more secure way—to top that, POST allows you to send an unlimited amount of data, whereas the GET method allows you to send only a limited amount. The GET method is less secure than POST because the GET method transfers data as part of the Web address and POST transfers data through environment variables that can be seen by the Web surfer.

Take a look at Figure 13.5. It will help you understand how the GET and POST methods transfer information.

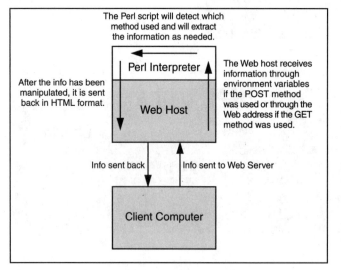

Figure 13.5

Understanding GET and POST methods

How Info Is Stored

Once information from a form is on the server side, the CGI script can pretty much do anything it wants with it, including leaving the information just as it was sent and saving into a text file on the server. Let's check out an example of information stored in this manner:

```
name=Lewis%2CJudy%2CJulie&score=321%2C213%2C465
```

What in the world is that? It's encrypted, but once I let you in on the secret it's not so bad. Allow me to break it down—there are two *key-value pairs* here, which are pairings of a *key* (the name of a value) and a *value* (the value itself). Our two variables (keys) are `name` and `score`; let's see what their values are.

But before we do that, let me quickly explain that when sending data over the Internet, spaces and commas and a few other characters are not allowed; special codes have been invented to represent these characters. The character combination %2C represents a comma. Don't worry though; you won't have to memorize all these codes because there's an object in ActionScript that converts them for you. Take a look at the line again—this time with no %2Cs, only commas.

```
name=Lewis,Judy,Julie&score=321,213,465
```

Ah, seems clearer. Now let's divide the valued pairs. This is what I ended up with:

```
name=Lewis,Judy,Julie
```

And

```
score=321,213,465
```

Let's say you had some information, such as a high score list, stored away on the server; you can have Flash load this information into the program and access these pairs. If Flash loads pairs like these in, they will be in string form. In order to access the individual values within these properties, you could use the `split` command to store them in an array. This will give you full access to Lewis, Judy, and Julie and also to their scores. How cool is that?

The LoadVars Object

I have taken the information that I explained in the last section and saved it into a text file named GDA_TXT13.1.txt; it's under the Chapter 13 folder on the CD.

You will be using the `LoadVars` object to read in this information and manipulate it. Check out Figure 13.6 and see how this demo loads in the variables from this external file.

| Lewis,Judy,Julie |
| 321,213,465 |

Figure 13.6

Loading variables from an external file

Demo GDA_PROG13.2.fla does just that—take a look at the listing.

```
// Game Development with ActionScript
// By Lewis Moronta (c) 2003
// This program demos how to use
// the LoadVars object to load
// info from a small database

// Create the object
webData = new LoadVars();

// Load the properties of the file
// NOTE: It has to be in the same
// domain unless you are running
// this program from your computer.
webData.load("GDA_TXT13.1.txt");

// Setup the LoadVars callback function.
// It is executed when the data is
// finished loading.
webData.onLoad = function (success) {

    // Do something with the info...
    if (success) {
      // Verify the info
          nameDisplay = webData.name;
          scoreDisplay = webData.score;

    } else {
      trace("Error!");
    }
};
```

Assuming that the CGI program already created the database with that file name, this program can be easily modified to achieve an endless number of results. The first thing you do in order to load variables from an external file is create a LoadVars object, like this:

```
// Create the object
webData = new LoadVars();
```

The next thing to do is load the information. The information must be encrypted, just as I explained before. An HTML form does this encryption automatically when the information is sent to the CGI script. However, when the information is loaded into Flash, it is parsed into understandable data.

```
// Load the properties of the file
// NOTE: It has to be in the same
// domain unless you are running
```

```
// this program from your computer.
webData.load("GDA_TXT13.1.txt");
```

As information is not immediately loaded (because it takes so long to download), you must check to see when all the information is done loading. If you do not do this, you will end up with undefined variables. To avoid ending up with a bunch of undefined variables, you can use a callback function that is called just as soon as all the variables are loaded.

```
webData.onLoad = function (success) {
```

As you can see, there is one parameter that is sent to the function. It is a Boolean success value. If everything went well (success == true), a true value means everything was loaded; if the loading didn't go well then the success value will be false and the program won't parse the data.

In this program, I set the code to display the information in two textboxes on the screen. The information variables become properties within this object, as you can see here:

```
// Do something with the info...
if (success) {
  // Verify the info
      nameDisplay = webData.name;
      scoreDisplay = webData.score;

} else {
  trace("Error!");
}
```

Just in case you were wondering, nameDisplay and scoreDisplay are the variables attached to the two textboxes on the stage.

Notice one thing—the data is still in string format and the information is still divided by commas. You can't use it like that, so what can you do? You have to use the split command to divide the information into arrays. This will allow you to use 1 index to access both of the pieces of information, including the name and the score of each individual. Let's see how in the following listing.

```
// Game Development with ActionScript
// By Lewis Moronta (c) 2003
// This program demos how to use
// the LoadVars object to load
// info from a small database

// Create the object
webData = new LoadVars();

// Load the properties of the file
// NOTE: It has to be in the same
// domain unless you are running
```

```
// this program from your computer.
webData.load("GDA_TXT13.1.txt");


// Setup the LoadVars callback function.
// It is executed when the data is
// finished loading.
webData.onLoad = function (success) {
  // Do something with the info...
  if (success) {
    displayData();
  } else {
    trace("Error!");
  }
};

function displayData() {

  // Divide the information up
  namesArray = webData.name.split(",");
  scoresArray = webData.score.split(",");

  // Store the information in a viewable format
  name1Display = namesArray[0];
  score1Display = scoresArray[0];

  name2Display = namesArray[1];
  score2Display = scoresArray[1];

  name3Display = namesArray[2];
  score3Display = scoresArray[2];
}
```

If you look at Figure 13.7, you'll see how I neatly organized the information into six different boxes.

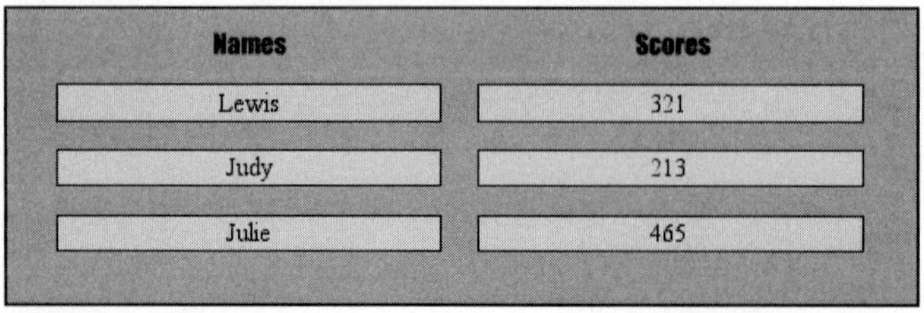

Names	Scores
Lewis	321
Judy	213
Julie	465

Figure 13.7

Manipulating individual pieces of data

In this program, I created the object then loaded and parsed the information, like this:

```
// Create the object

webData = new LoadVars();

// Load and parse...
webData.load("GDA_TXT13.1.txt");
```

After that, I decided to set up the object's `onLoad` function so that it can call another function if everything is successful. The other function is `displayData`.

```
webData.onLoad = function (success) {

    // Do something with the info...

    if (success) {

        displayData();

    } else {

        trace("Error!");

    }

}
```

I declared `displayData` with no parameters—it's a generic function name too.

```
function displayData() {
```

The first thing I did in this function was to divide the information up into elements of an array. I did this using the `split` method of a string.

```
    // Divide the information up

    namesArray = webData.name.split(",");

    scoresArray = webData.score.split(",");
```

Now that all the info is set into elements of an array, all I have to do is access each pair with one index—how cool is that?

In order to display the information, all I did was access the current name and score for each index.

> **TIP**
>
> As you're now dealing with arrays, you can use all the sorting and manipulation functions and methods that you learned before. This is great when you want to output lists and other things, like a high score screen perhaps.

```
    // Store the information in a viewable format

    name1Display = namesArray[0];

    score1Display = scoresArray[0];
```

The rest of the information was populated in much the same way.

```
name2Display = namesArray[1];
score2Display = scoresArray[1];


name3Display = namesArray[2];
score3Display = scoresArray[2];
```

And that's how to retrieve and organize information from the server.

Sending Info to the Server

Now that you know how to download information into your program, you can learn how to send information to the server. You can send your information to a CGI script that will then do something with it. In order for the CGI script to work, it must be installed somewhere that can run these scripts. You can install CGI scripts locally only if your computer is set up as a server.

I'll be using the following Perl script for the purposes of this chapter. I called the script saveData and listed the code in the following listing.

```
#!/usr/local/bin/perl

print "Content-type: text/html\n\n";
read (STDIN, $QUERY, $ENV{CONTENT_LENGTH});
open (FILE, ">data.txt");
print FILE "$QUERY";
close(FILE);
print "Data saved!";
```

As I'm not going to teach you how to program in Perl, I'm going to be brief about what each line does.

The first line is called the "shebang" line. This tells the UNIX system where to find the Perl interpreter.

```
#!/usr/local/bin/perl
```

On my Web server, the interpreter is installed under that path—yours might be different.

The following line tells the browser what type of information it is about to send. In this case, I will be sending HTML data.

```
print "Content-type: text/html\n\n";
```

Once I have this ready, I'm ready to read the key-value pairs from the system's environment variables—they are stored with the GET method of transferring data.

```
read (STDIN, $QUERY, $ENV{CONTENT_LENGTH});
```

The environment variables are in the encoded format we went through before. All we have to do now is set up a file and write the information into it.

```
open (FILE, ">data.txt");
print FILE "$QUERY";
close(FILE);
```

For confirmation purposes, I decided to output a one-liner to the HTML spit-back page.

```
print "Data saved!";
```

Go ahead and install the saveData program on your server. Once you're ready, come back and I'll show you how to send data to this program that will create the text file that you need to read in at a later time.

> **CAUTION**
>
> I have saveData installed on my server, but you cannot use it because Flash won't let you send data to a script on another computer. This is why you have to set it up on your server along with your SWF file.

I have written up GDA_PROG13.4.fla to show you how easy it is to send information to this script. Just click the button and you're set.

Check out the following listing to see what's in that magical button.

```
// Game Development with ActionScript
// By Lewis Moronta (c) 2003
// This program demos how to use
// the LoadVars object to send
// info to a CGI script


on (release) {
  // Create the object
  webData = new LoadVars();

  // Populate the object
  webData.name = "Lewis,Judy,Julie";
  webData.score = "123,456,987";

  // Send it to the CGI script and output it within this HTML page
  webData.send("cgi-bin/saveData", "_self");
}
```

First I created a new LoadVars object for when the user releases the button. I then created the properties in a format that I can later parse. I then used the send method to send the info to the CGI script.

```
// Send it to the CGI script and output it within this HTML page
  webData.send("cgi-bin/saveData", "_self");
```

The first parameter is the URL where the scripts are stored—remember that it must be on the same computer as the SWF. The second parameter tells the browser where to send the CGI script's response. When _self is used, the current Flash page is replaced with the output of the script.

Because this information was sent, a data.txt file was written with the following information:

```
score=123%2C456%2C987&name=Lewis%2CJudy%2CJulie
```

This information can now be parsed and loaded just like we did before.

Saving Game States

New programmers always wonder how to save their game. In Flash, you can only save your game on the Internet because Flash cannot write out information to individual files that can be stored locally; instead, Flash has to send information to a script that can then, in turn, write and save the information that Flash sent to it in an external file. It's not as difficult as it seems once you start to break down what your game really consists of.

Think about it—what's one thing your game can't function without? That's right, *information.* And where is this information stored? Yes, in variables. If you grab and organize all the variables in your game, you can easily put them in a small database and retrieve them at a later time. This would, thus, save the game state.

> **NOTE**
>
> There isn't a demo for this section because *you* are going to write the code. How does it feel to be let loose?

Let's say you had a side-scrolling game. What are some of the variables that you would constantly be updating to keep track of the game? Here is my list. You can add to it if you wish.

- Player score
- Player energy
- Player level
- Player weapons
- Enemies alive

If the player decides to save the game at any point in time, these variables should be recorded. When they're retrieved, the game should continue from where he left off. Figure 13.8 shows what I'm talking about.

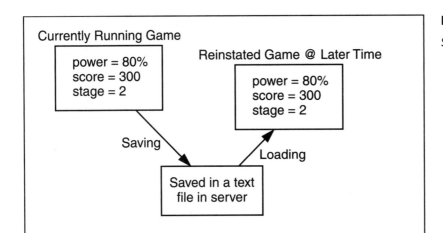

Figure 13.8

Saving game states

Summary

This chapter brought your game development skills online by bridging the gap between offline and internet-based programming. You learned the very basics of dealing with your server without learning any other programming languages. You even learned how to output HTML pages. You also learned how to deal with all aspects of the Web including sending and receiving data, and you can even detect when the data was sent or downloaded.

Questions & Answers

Q. I'm still not sure how to install a CGI Perl script on my server; where can I get more information?

A. Ask your host or ISP—their technicians can tell you how to set things up in their servers.

Q. I would like to learn how to program in Perl—is it much different from ActionScript?

A. Perl has many similar structures, but it can be cryptic in some parts. Like any language, it takes time to learn, but as you are already used to thinking like a computer you should have no problem adapting to some Perl after a short period of time.

Q. Is it possible to have the server-side script return information without jumping to an HTML page—in other words, without leaving my Flash movie?

A. Yes. Use the `sendAndLoad` method of the `LoadVars` object. Before moving on with your movie, you should use the `onLoad` callback function to make sure everything was reloaded into the properties or else you will have undefined variables in your way.

CHAPTER 14

Memory and Web Management

On the Internet, everybody is connected to one another at different speeds using differ-ent computers. The hardest part of communicating through the Internet is making sure that information, such as your games, reaches everyone intact. Another thing that you should keep in mind is that not everybody can stream animation at the same pace; this is why I teach you how to pre-load your games. These techniques and other secrets will be explored in this chapter. Take a look at the list of topics I'll cover:

- Designing a loader screen
- Using the bandwidth profiler
- Issues with linked objects

Designing a Loader Screen

If a would-be player of your game is downloading your huge file through a fast broadband connection, his computer, most likely, won't have a problem streaming the file frame by frame. As he doesn't have the issue of the animation stopping in the middle of execution to download more information, he won't ever notice a stutter.

What about when the player is on a 56k modem, downloading at a significantly slower speed? The beautiful animation that is supposed to move at 24 frames per second may be moving as slow as 1 frame per second if the animation is heavy enough. Or even worse, the animation can play chunks at a time.

A smart thing to do to prevent the second scenario is to preload all of the information before playing it. This way, all the information in the frames is downloaded into your client's computer and can be played locally from his RAM instead of from the Internet.

Flash offers more methods for determining how much of your movie has loaded—it also offers a method for determining how big a movie is. You can use this information to wait until the whole movie is downloaded before it's played. The following two methods return this information to you:

```
movieClip.getBytesLoaded()
```

and

```
movieClip.getBytesTotal()
```

As you can already guess, getBytesLoaded returns the number of bytes that have been already downloaded, and getBytesTotal returns the size of the whole SWF file.

So, if you think about it, when these two values are equal, they should be ready to play the movie with no problem, because the whole SWF would be on the client's computer.

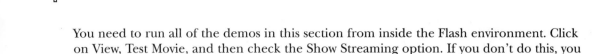

You need to run all of the demos in this section from inside the Flash environment. Click on View, Test Movie, and then check the Show Streaming option. If you don't do this, you won't experience the downloading effect that we are trying to achieve here.

Open GDA_PROG14.1.fla in Flash and test the movie. What you will see here is a bar animation that grows continuously until the movie is loaded—and then a huge sounds plays. If this were a slow connection without the loader code, the sound would play in bits and pieces with some major annoying breakups—no one wants this.

The animation plays from Frame 1 to Frame 12. I put the code in Frame 12, which makes it loop (to Frame 1) until the information is loaded completely. Check it out.

```
// Game Development with ActionScript
// By Lewis Moronta (c) 2003
// This demo shows you how to
// add a simple progress bar to
// your movie.


// Compare the amount of bytes loaded against the
// overall file size. When they are equal, we are
// ready to play our movie. If not, we keep playing
// our loadbar animation.
if (_root.getBytesLoaded() == _root.getBytesTotal()) {
        nextFrame();
} else {
        gotoAndPlay(1);
}
```

> **NOTE**
>
> The default include directory is usually X:\VSDirectory\VC\Include where **X** is the drive and VSDirectory is the directory where you installed Visual C++. All the C++ built-in headers are in that directory.

Every time Frame 12 is played, this condition is tested to see if getBytesLoaded is equal to getBytesTotal. If it is, the movie goes on to the next frame. If they are not equal, the movie returns to Frame 1, and will play again until Frame 12, where the condition is retested.

Now, if you remember how to get a percent amount from a part divided into a whole and then scale this value up by 100, then you're on the right track. My next demo, GDA_PROG14.2.fla, shows you how to incorporate this value into the display—and this can help calm a viewer's nerves.

Figure 14.1 shows how I set up the visuals for the file.

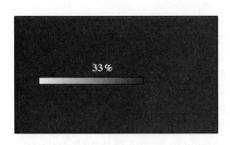

Figure 14.1

*Displaying the
percentage of the
movie that has loaded*

I have set up a textbox in the middle of the stage with a variable attached to it. This way, I can send the percent amount to be displayed. Take a look at the following listing to see the improvements.

```
// Game Development with ActionScript
// By Lewis Moronta (c) 2003
// This demo shows you how to
// add a simple progress bar to
// your movie.

// Display the percent amount of what's loaded
loadDisplay = Math.round(_root.getBytesLoaded()/_root.getBytesTotal()*100);

loadDisplay += "%";

// Compare the amount of bytes loaded against the
// overall file size. When they are equal, we are
// ready to play our movie. If not, we keep playing
// our loadbar animation.
if (_root.getBytesLoaded() == _root.getBytesTotal()) {
        nextFrame();
} else {
        gotoAndPlay(1);
}
```

Right off you can see that I started to calculate how much has been downloaded. I'll break down this formula:

```
// Display the percent amount of what's loaded
loadDisplay = Math.round(_root.getBytesLoaded()/_root.getBytesTotal()*100);
```

When I divide the value returned by getBytesLoaded by the value returned by getBytesTotal, I get a decimal value that can be scaled up by 100 to yield a percent amount. This percent amount is the amount of the movie that has been downloaded. As there was a division, there is a big possibility that I don't have a whole number; this is why I rounded this figure.

For display purposes, I concatenated the percent symbol to the display.

```
loadDisplay += "%";
```

I then compared how much was downloaded with the size of the file—if the amounts are equal, the movie proceeds to the next frame.

```
if (_root.getBytesLoaded() == _root.getBytesTotal()) {
      nextFrame();
}
```

If they're not equal, the movie loops back to the first frame.

```
else {
      gotoAndPlay(1);
}
```

Wouldn't it be cool if you could have a bar visually representing the percent amount along with the numerical value? This requires some setup, but it can be done.

> **TIP**
>
> You can change your streaming download speed when testing your movie by selecting your speed from the Debug menu.

Take a look at Figure 14.2 to see how much more visually appealing this load bar is.

Figure 14.2

The load bar

> **TIP**
>
> You can take the loader Movie Clip from **GDA_PROG14.3.fla** and just paste it into the first frame of your movie and it will work. All the code is embedded into the clip, so you won't have to worry about moving separate pieces of it.

Open up GDA_PROG14.3.fla and test the movie in streaming mode. Don't you like it better this way?

Let's see how it's done. Double-click the loader Movie Clip on the first frame. The first thing you should notice is that this clip is comprised of four layers; Display, Border, Bar, and Background. The Display layer has a dynamic textbox with a variable attached. The code uses this box to display the percent amount later on. The Border and Background are there only for decoration. The Bar layer, however, contains a Movie Clip. This is the Movie Clip that contains the code that I'll discuss here.

> **NOTE**
>
> Note that the Bar Movie Clip was drawn from 0, 0. In other words, all the graph-
> ics in the clip are to the right of its origin. This will allow us to scale the bar to
> one side—if it were drawn from the middle, the bar would scale symmetrically
> on both sides. This way, it will only scale to the right.

If you look into the Bar Movie Clip, you will find the following code:

```
// Game Develop with ActionScript
// By Lewis Moronta (c) 2003
// This code allows us to use
// a bar to visually tell us
// what percent the movie has
// loaded...


// Setup this code to execute all the time
onClipEvent (enterFrame) {

  // Calculate percent amount for display purposes
  percentLoaded = Math.round(_root.getBytesLoaded()/_root.getBytesTotal()*100);

  // Scale the bar with this amount
  _xscale = percentLoaded;

  // Add the percent sign and display it
  _parent.loadDisplay = percentLoaded+"%";

  // If we are ready, let's move on
  if (_root.getBytesLoaded() == _root.getBytesTotal()) {
    _root.nextFrame();
  }
}
```

As I want to check up on the loading process constantly, I set up the following:

```
// Setup this code to execute all the time
onClipEvent (enterFrame) {
```

Here I did the usual by calculating the percent amount for the display:

```
  // Calculate percent amount for display purposes
  percentLoaded = Math.round(_root.getBytesLoaded()/_root.getBytesTotal()*100);
```

I then scaled the bar to the current percent amount. This amount directly reflects how much of the movie has been downloaded. I have drawn the bar to the right of its registration point so that it can only scale to the right, not symmetrically on both sides. This completes the effect, but we're not done with the loader yet.

I then shoved the value into the textbox variable along with a percent sign:

```
// Add the percent sign and display it
_parent.loadDisplay = percentLoaded+"%";
```

After that, I tested to see if the movie was finished downloading—if it is, then it moves on to the next frame on the main Timeline.

```
// If we are ready, let's move on
  if (_root.getBytesLoaded() == _root.getBytesTotal()) {
    _root.nextFrame();
  }
```

Not so hard, was it?

Using the Bandwidth Profiler

The Bandwidth Profiler is a powerful tool—especially when you need your movie to play as smoothly as possible. Sometimes, your game might contain chunks of information that are too much to handle on your user's computer—you do not want this. This would then be a case when you would use the Bandwidth Profiler to smooth the streaming of your movie. The Profiler allows you to monitor download speeds and congestion through the movie. It even neatly charts where the bulk of the data lies within the file. Take a look at Figure 14.3, which shows you a sample screen when using the Profiler.

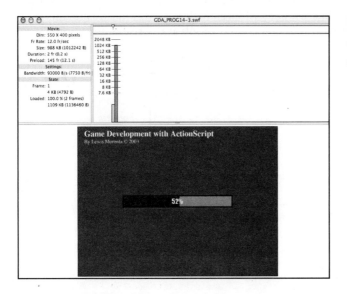

Figure 14.3

Using the Bandwidth Profiler

You can access the Profiler through the View menu when testing your movie. You can also press Ctrl+B or Command+B (if you're on a Mac). You will be using the Profiler when you start publishing your movies to the Web so don't forget it's there.

Issues with Linked Objects

> **TIP**
>
> **You can move to whatever frame you want once you're in the Profiler. Just push the little indicator to the frame you want—the indicator is over the size chart on the upper right.**

When you adjust the linkage properties for a symbol that is not in the movie (and that will be later attached) you must make sure the symbol is exported with the movie. Check the Export in First Frame option to ensure that the symbol is exported.

Setting up linkage properties means that even before your movie's playhead gets to the first frame, it loads in *all* of the linked objects. This is a big issue if the file is huge. For instance, if you have a 3MB file that is linked in, the whole file will load before moving on to the first frame. This will cause a huge delay on slow connections and it will be well nigh impossible for even slower connections.

The best thing to do is restructure your movie. You should try to set up your movie in a way that you do not need to link objects. Another idea would be to link your object but not export it in the first frame—make sure the Export in First Frame option is not checked. There is one problem with this method though: Flash won't export if you do not include the object in the scene. What you have to do is include the object strategically in another scene or within frames away from the action so it can be exported with the movie.

I have set up GDA_PROG14.4.fla just like GDA_PROG14.3.fla, except that I have linked the huge sound file and it exports in the first frame. As I already discussed, what this means is that it will be exporting before the first frame plays. Take a look at the streaming shot I took of the bandwidth profiler in Figure 14.4.

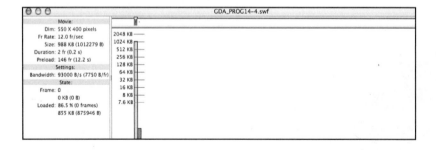

Figure 14.4

Examining linked objects

Notice that the movie is blank while it's loading. The Bandwidth Profiler has a huge bar in the first frame indicating that it stored the sound file there. This is how you can test your movie to make sure everything is running smoothly. Uncheck Export in First Frame from the sound's linkage properties to fix the problem of the sound loading prematurely.

Summary

You learned quite a few techniques in this short chapter. You learned and built upon knowledge of how to preload the whole movie before playing it. You even got advanced enough to have Flash represent the loading process with a progress bar—very cool. None of that could be done without the getBytesLoaded and getBytesTotal methods of your Movie Clip.

You even learned how to work with the Bandwidth Profiler and got a few tips on how to organize your movie when exporting objects by adjusting the linkage properties.

Question & Answer

Q. Can I set up a load bar for when I load a sound?

A. Yes. The sound object also has the getBytesLoaded and getBytesTotal methods.

Exercise

1. See if you can incorporate one of these loaders into your future projects. Be creative—instead of using a load bar, use sine and cosine to design a loader that looks like a clock or dial. Make the hand go clockwise while it's loading. Once it makes a 360-degree rotation, the whole file should be loaded.

CHAPTER 15

Advanced Interaction with Components

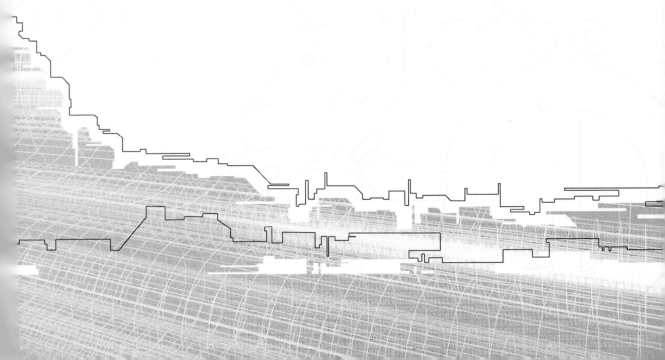

There comes a time when you need to collect information from the client, such as when you need him to adjust certain settings in your game, and you'll need a list of controls to do it. These controls can be designed from scratch or you can use Flash's built-in library of controls called Components. Either way, you should learn how to manage both hand-written and built-in controls in order to effectively manage your movie.

In this chapter, you'll learn about the following Components:

- PushButton
- CheckBox
- RadioButton
- ListBox
- ComboBox
- ScrollBar
- ScrollPane

Meet the Components

If you go to your Window menu and select Components to make sure your Components pane is visible, you'll notice a few icons within the pane. These icons represent really complicated Movie Clip controls that have been pre-programmed for you. It is possible to program your own controls, but teaching you to do so would fill up another entire book, at least. Take a look at Figure 15.1 to see what these Component icons look like.

Figure 15.1

The Flash Components

The PushButton

The PushButton Component is one of the simplest of all. It's a button that you can program in a similar way to how you can program a regular Flash button symbol. To use it requires but a few steps:

1. Drag the Component to the stage.

2. Name the instance.

3. In the Properties panel or in the Component Parameters panel, assign a label and a Click Handler.

4. Write the Click Handler—use one parameter that will hold the name of the instance that was clicked. All you'll have to do is check to see if this is the instance that was clicked.

Open up file GDA_PROG15.1.fla and notice that I followed the steps above. I dragged the PushButton to the stage to create an instance, and then named the instance clickme. I then changed the label to Click Me! and the Click Handler function to clickmeHandler. This handler detects whether clickme was the instance clicked before it does anything. Check out the following listing. This code was written in the main timeline—all Components require their handlers to be written on the same Timeline their instance is on.

> **TIP**
>
> **You have to check whether your instance was the one that was pressed because when there are many instances on the stage, they all receive a message when the mouse is down.**

```
// Game Development with ActionScript
// By Lewis Moronta (c) 2003
// This function is attached to the
// PushButton Component on stage.
// It also detects to see if it was
// its instance that was clicked.

function clickmeHandler(buttonInstance) {

   if (buttonInstance == clickme) {
         trace("Yeah baby!!");
   }
}
```

The function that we define must have one parameter. This parameter will carry the name of the instance that was pressed. You can then use this information to figure out if this instance of the button was the last button that was pressed in order to execute whatever the button was designed to do.

What if you had multiple buttons on the stage? Take a look at GDA_PROG15.2.fla, and notice that I placed three buttons on the stage. These three buttons are sharing the same Click Handler. The Click Handler is written on the main Timeline in the first frame—it's also listed in the following listing.

```
// Game Development with ActionScript
// By Lewis Moronta (c) 2003
// This function is attached to the
// PushButton Component on stage.


function clickmeHandler(buttonInstance) {

  // Echo which button was recently pressed.
  trace("You pressed "+buttonInstance._name);


}
```

All this function does is tell you what button instance you pressed. You can easily write up a conditional structure that will route the code to a function that pertains to the last button that was pressed (see Figure 15.2). In other words, you can detect which button was pressed with this one handler and make it do something like saving your game.

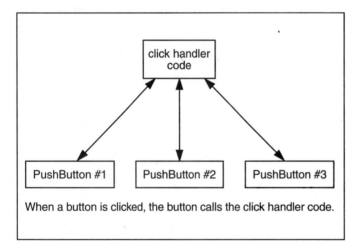

Figure 15.2

The relationship between buttons and a Click Handler

The CheckBox

The CheckBox Component is not much more difficult to use or program than the PushButton component—it just introduces a few differences. If you take a look at Figure 15.3, you'll see that there are a couple more parameters for the CheckBox.

Component		Label	Check Box #1
	<Instance Name>	Initial Value	false
		Label Placement	right
W: 100.0 X: 112.0		Change Handler	checkboxHandler
H: 13.0 Y: 126.5			Properties Parameters

Figure 15.3

Adjusting parameters for the CheckBox

Besides having a label parameter, you'll also catch an Initial Value parameter. This parameter is false by default, and all that means is that the CheckBox will be unchecked when the movie is started. If the Initial Value parameter is set to true, this means that the CheckBox is checked.

There's also a Label Placement parameter. This parameter allows you to place the text either on the left or right of the CheckBox.

The Change Handler parameter is similar to the button's Click Handler—it's a function that you write on the same timeline as the instance that will respond when the user clicks on the CheckBox.

GDA_PROG15.3.fla has two CheckBoxes on the stage. They were both dragged from the Components palette. When you drag the CheckBoxes to the stage, Flash creates a very organized component folder in your Library window. Check out Figure 15.4.

Figure 15.4

Neatly packed Components

The program doesn't do much but display the last CheckBox checked. Once you can detect which was the last CheckBox checked (and also know the current state) you can do anything you wish with the CheckBox. See the handler that I wrote in the main Timeline in the following listing.

```
// Game Development with ActionScript
// By Lewis Moronta (c) 2003



// This handler takes care of the CheckBox
// that was last clicked.
function checkboxHandler(boxInstance) {
```

```
    display = boxInstance._name;
}
```

The display variable is a variable that is attached to a textbox on the stage. This variable displays the name of the last box instance that was checked.

What if you wanted to check the current state of the box? See the screenshot of my next demo, GDA_PROG15.4.fla, in Figure 15.5, and check out the code.

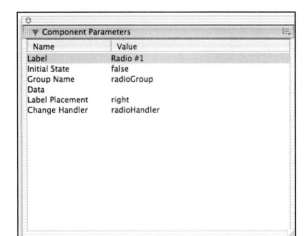

Figure 15.5

Displaying a CheckBox state

This demo isn't much different from what you have been learning so far; it's merely a combination of what I've gone over so far. You'll notice only one new command, getValue. This command returns the current state of the CheckBox component.

```
// Game Development with ActionScript
// By Lewis Moronta (c) 2003


// This handler takes care of the CheckBox
// that was last clicked.
function checkboxHandler(boxInstance) {

    display = boxInstance._name;
}

// This handler takes care of the PushButton
function pushbuttonHandler(buttonInstance) {

    if (getValueButton == buttonInstance) {
        display01 = check01.getValue();
        display02 = check02.getValue();
    }
}
```

The checkboxHandler only displays the name of the last instance that was checked. Simple enough.

The pushbuttonHandler goes a step further—it checks to make sure that the getValueButton instance was the last clicked. It then runs the getValue method on both CheckBox instances and then stores the values in two textboxes on the stage. Everything's neat and everybody's happy—let's move on.

The RadioButton

RadioButtons are a nice control to have built in to your movie. They allow the user to only select one option from a group. You can have as many groups of RadioButtons as you want.

Look at Figure 15.6 and notice all of the newly added properties. The panel that you see in the figure is the Component Properties panel, which can be accessed from the Window menu.

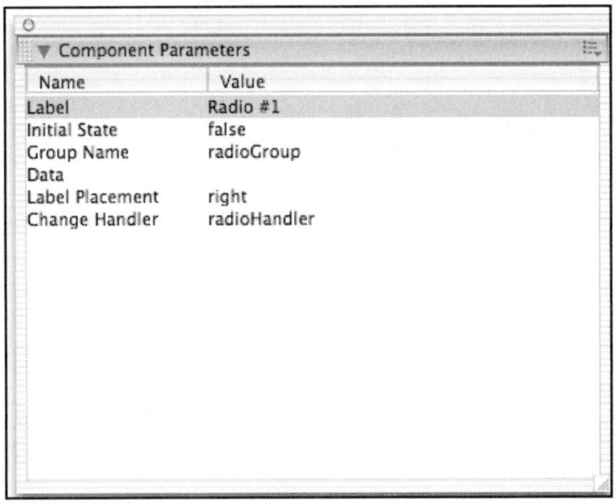

Name	Value
Label	Radio #1
Initial State	false
Group Name	radioGroup
Data	
Label Placement	right
Change Handler	radioHandler

Figure 15.6

The parameters for a RadioButton

One important difference between a RadioButton and a CheckBox is the group name. Different sets of RadioButtons should have different group names. These groups will be treated as separate entities.

In demo file GDA_PROG15.5.fla, I have set up a group of RadioButtons called radioGroup. This information can be verified from the Properties panel. I have attached a handler to this group that alerts us, through the Output Window, that the RadioButton's state has changed.

There is also a PushButton on the stage that outputs the state of this group. Check out The following listing to see how this works.

```
// Game Development with ActionScript
// By Lewis Moronta (c) 2003
// This small program demos how to
// use RadioButton Components.
```

```
// Let us know when something changed
function radioHandler(component) {

    trace("radioHandler was called");

}

// Let's find the one that is active
function buttonHandler(buttonInstance) {

    // Make sure this is the button
    if (button == buttonInstance) {

        // Display the state of each RadioButton
        trace(radioOne.getState());
        trace(radioTwo.getState());
        trace(radioThree.getState());
        trace(radioFour.getState());
    }
}
```

Before I start explaining this listing, you should know that I named the radioGroup RadioButtons radioOne, radioTwo, radioThree, and radioFour. I named the PushButton instance button.

The getState method of the RadioButton component returns a Boolean value indicating whether the radio button is selected or not.

The radioHandler function has one parameter—the object that was last clicked on is returned in this one. All the function does is shout out that a button from the group was pressed.

The buttonHandler also has one parameter. This is the button that was last clicked. As there is only one button on the stage, the conditional could be easily omitted. The button simply returns the current state of each RadioButton and outputs this information to the Output Window.

The ListBox

The ListBox is a great alternative to the previous two controls. It can vary the visual hierarchy of your controls and just make things look cool. A ListBox allows you to select multiple options at once, just like a CheckBox setup.

The ListBox has four parameters. Drag one to the stage from the Components panel or open GDA_PROG15.6.fla. Select the ListBox and take a look at the Properties panel. It should look like Figure 15.7.

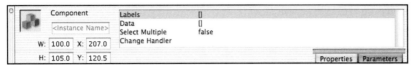

Figure 15.7

ListBox properties

The Select Multiple parameter will allow the user to select more than one option if set to true. When the parameter is set to true, the user can use the Shift, Control, or the Command key (if on a Mac) to select multiple options.

The Change Handler is, of course, the function that will be called once this box is clicked. It's up to you to write it.

One of the most important parameters here is the Labels parameter. It allows you to enter a list of values that will be displayed when the program is run. If you double-click the Labels parameter, you should get a dialog box similar to that in Figure 15.8.

Figure 15.8

Adding options to your ListBox

You can use the plus sign at the top of the dialog box to add more options. You can use the minus sign to delete the entries, and you can use the Up and Down arrows to rearrange them.

TIP

If you're paying close attention you have noticed that I am overlooking the Data parameter. This is because this is an optional parameter that you can use to store extra data. It can come in handy one day so don't forget it's there. You can use the getValue method to retrieve information from an internal Data variable—the getData method only works with RadioButton.

Check out the following listing. It'll show you how to retrieve values for a box that was set up for multiple selections.

```
// Game Development with ActionScript
// By Lewis Moronta (c) 2003
// This demo shows you how to install
// and use the Component ListBox

function buttonHandler(component) {
  if (button == component) {

        // Since we have Select Multiple ON, we use "getSelectedItems".
        // This returns an array object with everything selected.
        // If Select Multiple was OFF, you have to use "getSelectedItem"
        var selectedChoices = choices.getSelectedItems();

        // Since we don't know how many objects were selected, we
        // loop for the length of the array. This is an array of
        // objects that have two properties: label and data. Since
        // we didn't put anything in the data parameter, we will
        // only be looking in the label section.
        for (var i = 0; i < selectedChoices.length; i++)
          trace("You have selected: "+selectedChoices[i].label);
  }
}
```

This ListBox Component returns an array of objects—*if* you have your Select Multiple option selected. If the Select Multiple option is off, then use `getSelectedItems` to retrieve the selections.

It's simple to get the information that the user input. As an array of objects is returned, it's best to assign the array to a local variable. Once the array is assigned, you have to find out how many options are selected in order to store them all. Loop for the length of the array to find out the number of selected options. Each object can use the `iteration` variable to access its properties. Each object returned has a `label` and a `data` property. As you didn't assign any data, you won't reference that property.

TIP

The ListBox is very complicated internally and has a lot of methods. If you're interested in finding out more about these methods, look up ListBox in your Flash Help file.

The ComboBox

The ComboBox is another great Component. You can use it to add a drop-down box that allows users to select from a list, and if you, the programmer, adjust its parameters, even type their own values.

The Component parameters for the ComboBox are shown in Figure 15.9.

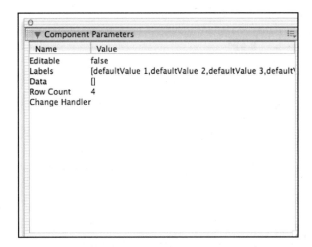

Figure 15.9

ComboBox parameters

Demo GDA_PROG15.7.fla contains a ComboBox and a PushButton that repeats the information selected in the ComboBox. The information in the ComboBox was added in much the same way the information was added for the ListBox in the last section—all you have to do is double-click on the Labels property and add or delete entries.

The Data entry can be left blank as usual. It can come in handy when you want to include values with your labels, but ignore it for now.

The Row Count parameter allows you to change the amount of rows that are displayed when the drop-down box is open. If there are more options than there are rows, then a scrollbar will appear.

The Editable option is a new one. This option, if true, allows the user to type their value into the box. If the value is false, the user can only choose from the list.

Let's check out the code that was put in the button's handler.

```
// Game Development with ActionScript
// By Lewis Moronta (c) 2003
// This demo shows you how to install
// and use the Component ListBox

function buttonHandler(component) {
  if (button == component) {
    trace(combo.getValue());
  }
}
```

Easy to decrypt, it's plain, simple, and neat. The ComboBox instance in the stage was named combo—this is the instance name that I used to execute the getValue method.

When the user clicks on the button, the value of the ComboBox is output.

The ScrollBar

If you ask me, the ScrollBar Component is the easiest Component to use. You can just drag it to a dynamic text field and it installs itself. See GDA_PROG15.8.fla and play with the settings. You don't even have to adjust the Component properties to make it a vertical or horizontal ScrollBar—just drag it to the side or bottom and you're set.

> **TIP**
>
> It's a great idea to name your dynamic textbox instance before dragging the ScrollBar to it. If you don't, your instance name will be chosen at random. It's also a great idea to set the text box to Multiline. If you don't do this, you may not get a working scroll bar.

The ScrollPane

The ScrollPane is a combination of a lot of the other objects. You use it to allow the user to scroll around and view a graphic on the screen. When you drag out an instance of the ScrollPane, it should look like the one in Figure 15.10, except it should have no graphics in it yet. Check out the file GDA_FIG15.9.fla for the complete story.

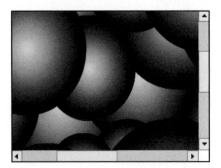

Figure 15.10

The ScrollPane at work

There is no code associated with this file except some adjusted parameters. See Figure 15.11 so we can go over what was done.

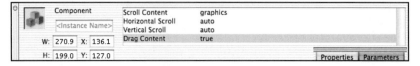

Figure 15.11

ScrollPane parameters

The first parameter, Scroll Content, takes the linkage export name of a Movie Clip. In this file, I created a graphic and gave it a generic linkage name. I then passed on this name to the ScrollPane. The horizontal and vertical parameters for the scroll bars are set to auto—this disables the scrolling if the graphic is small enough to be within the pane. Drag

Content was set to true—this allows the user to move the graphic around by dragging it with the mouse.

Designing an Options Screen

Almost every game you create will contain an Options screen. This Options screen should be well varied and diverse. For instance, if you programmed and designed a racing game, an ideal Options screen for it should contain an option for how many laps you want your user to race, how many other vehicles you want racing with your user, the difficulty level and so on. You can base the rest of your program on these options, but to do this you have to be neat and organized because you need to keep track of variables that are affected by these options and will affect your game—even more importantly, you have to know your Components.

Now that you're at a stage where your program can require many scenes, you should start creating new scenes for them. How? Go to the Modify menu and select the Scenes item from the GDA_PROG15.10.fla file. See Figure 15.12.

Figure 15.12

Creating new scenes

Creating new scenes allows you to create multiple timelines that help you stay organized. Each timeline is independent and you can easily jump to another scene with a `gotoAndPlay` or `gotoAndStop` command.

To create a new scene, just click on the plus sign at the bottom of the Scene pane. To delete a scene, just highlight it in the list and click on the garbage can. You can rename a scene by double-clicking on its current name on the list and typing in the new name.

Now that we got that out of the way, let me show you how I organized GDA_PROG15.10.fla. I set up two scenes. The first one is a generic splash screen of a game. It contains a button that takes you to the Options screen. Take a look at Figure 15.13.

Figure 15.13

A generic game splash screen

Once the user clicks on that button, the following code executes:

```
on (release) {
  gotoAndStop("Options", 1);
}
```

Looks a bit different, doesn't it? This version of the function allows you to input the name of the scene you want to jump to as the first parameter and the frame number of that scene as the second parameter.

Go to the Scene panel and select the Options scene from the pane. You'll instantly see the Timeline change to this scene. You should see something similar to Figure 15.14.

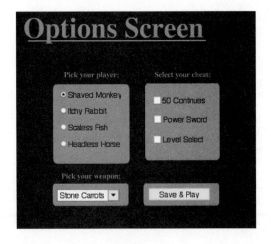

Figure 15.14

An Options screen layout

I have only one RadioButton group on the stage, radioGroup. Each group instance is named radio1, radio2, radio3, and radio4 respectively. You'll see why when we get to the code.

I also have three CheckBoxes on there, named check1, check2, and check3, respectively.

A drop-down combo box was also added to the scene. Its instance name is weapon.

And finally, I have a button that is, allegedly, saving all of this info. In reality it's merely outputting it to the screen. The button instance is called save and the saveHandler was attached to it.

Now that you are familiar with the setup, I think you're ready for the code in saveHandler. It's nothing new but the practice is worth it.

```
// Game Development with ActionScript
// By Lewis Moronta (c) 2003
// Demos how to put together a form
// for a game's option screen.

function saveHandler(component) {
  if (save == component) {

        // Check which player he chose.

        // Loop through all possible radio buttons
        // in the group and then find which one is on.
        for (var i = 1; i <= 4; i++) {

          // Once we find which one is selected
          // we retrieve its value and display it.
          if (_root["radio"+i].getState()) {

                trace("Your player is " + _root["radio"+i].getValue() + "...");
          }
        }

        // Check what weapon he chose.
        trace("...and you're fighting with the " + weapon.getValue() + " weapon.");

        // Check to see what cheats he wanted.
        if (check1.getValue())
          trace("The 50 Continues Cheat is Activated.");

        if (check2.getValue())
          trace("The Power Sword Cheat is Activated.");

        if (check3.getValue())
```

```
                trace("The Level Select Cheat is Activated.");
    }
}
```

When the user clicks the Save button, I want all this information to be saved and displayed. The toughest, yet simplest, part of all was extracting which RadioButton was clicked and what value it contained.

The first step I took in this logic was create a loop that can loop through all four instances in that group. As I named them similar names in sequential order, I can easily reference the instances on-the-fly.

```
// Loop through all possible radio buttons
// in the group and then find which one is on.
for (var i = 1; i <= 4; i++) {
```

As I'm in a loop now, I can reference each instance with some slick ActionScripting. At the same time, I'll be checking to see if that button is the one that's checked.

```
// Once we find which one is selected
// we retrieve its value and display it.
if (_root["radio"+i].getState()) {
```

Once I found which one is the one that is selected, I output its value by using the following line:

```
    trace("Your player is " + _root["radio"+i].getValue() + "...");
```

I then decided to check what value was in the ComboBox under the RadioButton group. I did this by using this line:

```
// Check what weapon he chose.
trace("...and you're fighting with the " + weapon.getValue() + " weapon.");
```

To finish off, I used conditional statements for the CheckBoxes. These statements output only if the box was checked—if it wasn't, the code ignores the option.

```
// Check to see what cheats he wanted.
if (check1.getValue())
    trace("The 50 Continues Cheat is Activated.");

if (check2.getValue())
    trace("The Power Sword Cheat is Activated.");

if (check3.getValue())
    trace("The Level Select Cheat is Activated.");
```

Does it get any easier than this?

Summary

Now you can produce a nice Options screen. You met the PushButton and everything that came along with it. It's the simplest of Components yet one of the most used. After that, it got a little tougher with the CheckBox Component. A few more parameters didn't stop you from mastering it, though. The RadioButton was the next one at bat—what a home run that was.

Once you mastered the basic controls, you picked up something called the ListBox. This nice structure allows the user to select from one to multiple values all in one neat place. The ComboBox was next. This box allows users to enter their own values in the line and even select from a list—might as well feed them, too. The ScrollBar and ScrollPane are very easy to use as well, you learned, because they require no ActionScripting. Most of the setup is included within the dragging part of installing them. The rest lies within the parameters.

Questions & Answer

Q. Some of these Components are really generic and lame; is there a way I can modify their appearance?

A. Yes. You can change their "skin" to anything you want. To get more information on this subject, please look up "Customizing Component Skins" in the Flash Help file. You can also adjust Component styles—look in the Flash Help file for that one, too. Before you go on and conquer the world, make sure you've mastered what you learned in this chapter first.

Exercise

1. Set up an Options screen that can send the option information to a Web server. Then set up another scene that can retrieve and populate the form. It's okay to use input text boxes—they are all part of the interactivity factor that's part of Flash. Isn't it great?

CHAPTER 16

Debugging and Avoiding Common Programming Pitfalls

If you ask John Carmack, he'll tell you that every bit of code can be improved. You can get close to perfection by avoiding certain programming pitfalls that won't allow you to optimize unless you rewrite the whole program. Then again, in the world of programming, most code is rewritten with a positive outlook every day, so why not join the club?

Either way, here are a few things you will learn in this chapter:

- How to avoid pitfalls involving cursor positions
- How to avoid pitfalls involving Movie Clips and button scope
- How to avoid pitfalls involving block structures
- How to use the Flash Debugger

Common Pitfalls

When you're just learning to program, and even when you're learning how to program in a new language, you will encounter many pitfalls. By *pitfalls*, I'm referring to those times when you get stuck and have to figure out why. Sometimes, only exposure to these pitfalls can teach you to avoid them. One mistake might mean that none of your code will work, so in this chapter, I'll spend some time showing you some of the common ActionScript pitfalls.

Cursor Position within a Clip

When writing code within a Movie Clip, you might decide that you need to track the cursor position by using the _xmouse and _ymouse properties.

An example of this is the slider code that you played with in earlier chapters. It uses the cursor's x position and follows it (within certain constraints). Sometimes, you might write this script in such a way that you will have your program misbehaving. Below, I have intelligently written a bug into the program in such a way that everything looks nice and smooth, yet, the program doesn't behave properly.

Check out GDA_PROG16.1.fla and try to find out what's wrong. I have listed the code here.

```
// The onClipEvent(load) handler
// initializes all other handlers
// in this Movie Clip.
onClipEvent(load) {
```

```
// These properties
// are used and can be
// adjusted to where you
// want your slider min
// and max to be on the
// x axis.
this.minX = 100;
this.maxX = 300;

// This handler is declared
// and executed for when the
// mouse clicks on the mc--
// it then flags its variable
this.onPress = function() {
  this.active = true;
}

// This flags the rest of the
// handlers that the mouse was
// released.
this.onRelease = function() {
  this.active = false;
}

// This function was also declared
// for when the user releases the
// mouse outside of the clip.
this.onReleaseOutside = function() {
  this.active = false;
}

// This is the heart of it all--
// It is executed when the mouse is
// moved and if pressed.
this.onMouseMove = function() {

  // This only executes if the mouse
  // is being pressed (and flagged)
  if (this.active) {

        // Follow the _xmouse to
        // simulate dragging.
        this._x = _xmouse;

        // Constrain this position to
        // the max property that we set.
```

```
      if (this._x > this.maxX) {
   this._x = this.maxX;
 }


   // Also constrain our position
   // to the min property we set.
   if (this._x < this.minX) {
   this._x = this.minX;
 }
 }
 }
}
```

The code looks neat, but try to run the program and see if it works correctly. When you test the program, you can see that every time you try to drag the slider button, it jumps to random parts of the slider and it also tends to dock itself to the far left. What's the deal? See Figure 16.1.

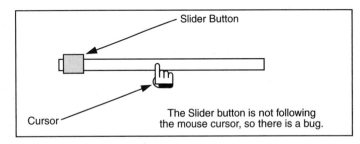

Slider Button

Cursor

The Slider button is not following the mouse cursor, so there is a bug.

Figure 16.1

A slider that doesn't behave!

Before I explain, compare the previous listing with this one (that's the working code within GDA_PROG16.2.fla).

```
// The onClipEvent(load) handler
// initializes all other handlers
// in this Movie Clip.
onClipEvent(load) {

   // These properties
   // are used and can be
   // adjusted to where you
   // want your slider min
   // and max to be on the
   // x axis.
   this.minX = 100;
   this.maxX = 300;

   // This handler is declared
   // and executed for when the
```

```
// mouse clicks on the mc--
// it then flags its variable
this.onPress = function() {
  this.active = true;
}


// This flags the rest of the
// handlers that the mouse was
// released.
this.onRelease = function() {
  this.active = false;
}


// This function was also declared
// for when the user releases the
// mouse outside of the clip.
this.onReleaseOutside = function() {
  this.active = false;
}


// This is the heart of it all--
// It is executed when the mouse is
// moved and if pressed.
this.onMouseMove = function() {

  // This only executes if the mouse
  // is being pressed (and flagged)
  if (this.active) {

        // Follow the _xmouse to
        // simulate dragging.
        this._x = _root._xmouse;

        // Constrain this position to
        // the max property that we set.
        if (this._x > this.maxX) {
      this._x = this.maxX;
    }

        // Also constrain our position
        // to the min property we set.
        if (this._x < this.minX) {
      this._x = this.minX;
    }
  }
 }
 }
}
```

In case you haven't found the line that makes the program work, it is:

```
this._x = _root._xmouse;
```

In GDA_PROG16.1.fla, the line that caused the error is explained in the following paragraphs and the line was this:

```
this._x = _xmouse;
```

As you can see, there was no problem writing either but the logic can be easily overlooked. The way I first wrote it, which was the wrong way, could be easily rewritten, again wrongly, as:

```
this._x = this._xmouse;
```

This way, it will return the cursor position relative to the Movie Clip where you wrote the code. You do not want this—you want to reference the position of the cursor off the main stage from inside the Movie Clip, not the position of the cursor from inside the clip. The reason you got crazy values with the first line is because the Movie Clip was a lot smaller than the main movie—these small values made it dock left.

This is where you go, "Ahhhhhhhhh, I knew that."

From Buttons to Movie Clips to Timelines

Sometimes you may get confused about how to reference functions off the main Timeline when you want to call them from inside buttons or Movie Clips. Even if you already know how to do this, when you're in a rush to see something work you can easily get careless.

In GDA_PROG16.3.fla, I have embedded code within the main Timeline, in a button and a Movie Clip. There is a trace function called traceTest in the main Timeline; both the button and the Movie Clip will use this function.

The scope of a button is within the same scope as the code that was written in the same frame as that button. In other words, you won't have to use any dot syntax when referencing a function from the main timeline from within a button.

See the following listing for the function you will use to test these facts.

```
// Game Development with ActionScript
// By Lewis Moronta (c) 2003

function traceTest() {
  trace("traceTest was called!");
}
```

When calling this function from a button, it's okay to use the following:

```
on (release) {
  traceTest();
}
```

Even though you are never too safe to write:

```
on (release) {
  _parent.traceTest();
}
```

Movie Clips are quite different than buttons. As Movie Clips are objects themselves, they can also contain methods. This means that you have to be specific with the ActionScript if you want to call a function; nothing will happen if you don't call the function correctly.

The clip that I'm using within this demo contains the following code:

```
onClipEvent(load) {
  traceTest();
}
```

The code above doesn't work—why? Because there aren't any `traceTest` methods within this clip. But you already knew that—you're trying to call the one on the main Timeline. To fix things, you can either use _parent or _root as you are only one level up:

```
onClipEvent(load) {
  _parent.traceTest();
}
```

And everything works like a charm.

Working with Curly Brackets

Yes, I know you've been through this before but topics like these warrant revisiting. Many novice programmers seem to have a problem writing neat code, and it's easy to fall into bad habits. Luckily, the Actions panel has an Auto-Format button that can help you clean up your code. Personally, I believe you should use this button until you are ready to pick up your own style of coding.

Check out the following listing, that was extracted from GDA_PROG16.4.fla.

```
// Game Development with ActionScript
// By Lewis Moronta (c) 2003

var a = 30;
var b = 40;

if (a > b)
  trace("Do this then that...");
  trace("Do more stuff...");

for (; a > 20; a--)
  trace("Counting down - count #"+a);
```

If this program was doing something important, can you guess what can go wrong? See the if block below where it compares a with b? How many statements are in that block? If you said two, take a closer look.

```
if (a > b)
  trace("Do this then that...");
  trace("Do more stuff...");
```

Remember that when there are no brackets in a block, you can only have one statement in that block. This would be a bad thing if the statement is false, because it would execute the "second" trace statement without the condition being true (see below), and this can cause errors in your program.

```
  trace("Do more stuff...");
```

This would be a sample output:

```
Do more stuff...
Counting down - count #30
Counting down - count #29
Counting down - count #28
Counting down - count #27
Counting down - count #26
Counting down - count #25
Counting down - count #24
Counting down - count #23
Counting down - count #22
Counting down - count #21
```

As you can see, a statement from the block escaped and executed without consent of that if block. How do you fix this? Yes, you guessed right—you have to bring the curly brackets to the rescue. Check it out:

```
if (a > b)
{
  trace("Do this then that...");
  trace("Do more stuff...");
}
```

Now you can get the expected output:

```
Counting down - count #30
Counting down - count #29
Counting down - count #28
Counting down - count #27
Counting down - count #26
Counting down - count #25
Counting down - count #24
Counting down - count #23
Counting down - count #22
Counting down - count #21
```

Now, what would be the output if that conditional statement were true? Just to verify it, I have listed it here:

```
Do this then that...
Do more stuff...
Counting down - count #30
Counting down - count #29
Counting down - count #28
Counting down - count #27
Counting down - count #26
Counting down - count #25
Counting down - count #24
Counting down - count #23
Counting down - count #22
Counting down - count #21
```

It's great practice to verify all your code, no matter how simple it is, until you are absolutely sure how all the code works. This is how you achieve expert status.

The pitfalls discussed here are but a few to keep in mind. As you get more experienced, you will stack up your own list of "things-not-to-do." This will be a never-ending list that changes with times and technologies.

Using the Debugger

A debugger is a special tool that programmers use to pinpoint errors, or bugs, in their programs. The Flash Debugger, like any debugger, helps you keep track of things such as function calls and variable values. In addition to tracking your program status, you can also set *breakpoints*. When you set a breakpoint, it means that you are telling the debugger to pause at a specific line of code when the program executes. By doing this, you can literally pause execution and check the status of all your variables and make sure everything is working properly; if the program isn't working properly, you can take the opportunity to correct the code. Where you set your breakpoints is up to you and where you think the bug is originating from.

A bug can be the result of careless programming or of forgetting something as simple as a curly bracket. As you expose yourself to ActionScript, you will learn to pick out the most common bugs and errors yourself and you will learn how to fix them on the spot.

Most of the time, you can get away with sprinkling trace statements all over the place to pinpoint your errors by output debugging information, but the truth is that sometimes even using the trace statement will be difficult. This is when you whip out the Flash Debugger.

Take a look at Figure 16.2; it shows GDA_PROG16.5.fla in the Debugger. To access the Debugger, instead of doing the usual of testing the movie, go to the Control menu and select Debug the Movie. The Debugger will open.

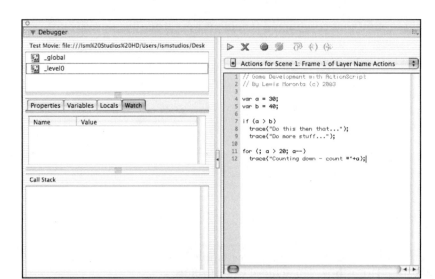

Figure 16.2

The invaluable Debugger

> **NOTE**
>
> Every time you run the Flash Debugger, it will generate an SWD file that is stored in the same directory where you created your project. The file cannot be edited and is for internal use only. Don't get freaked out when you keep seeing the file regenerate itself after you've deleted it. It's not a Macromedia virus!

The right side of the Debugger panel allows you to select the code that you want to debug and set breakpoints. A *breakpoint* is a point in a program at which you want it to stop its execution so that you can inspect all its properties and variables.

The red Stop button over the code sets or removes a breakpoint from whatever line number you are on. See Figure 16.3 below so you can see how the Debugger indicates that a breakpoint was set by a small red stop sign to the left of the line number.

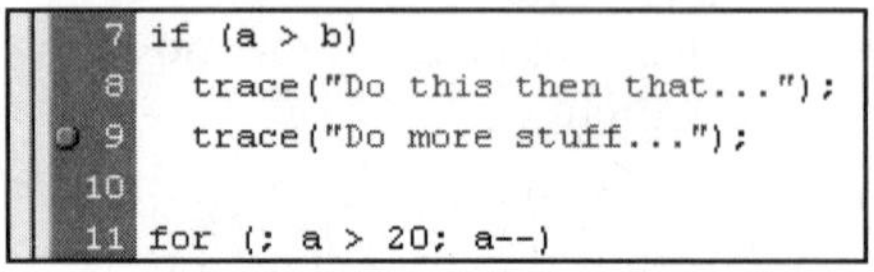

```
 7  if (a > b)
 8      trace("Do this then that...");
 9      trace("Do more stuff...");
10
11  for (; a > 20; a--)
```

Figure 16.3

Setting a breakpoint on the ninth line of code

You can use the X button to stop debugging and continue execution. Once you are ready to test the program, you can just press the green Play button.

Once the program hits a breakpoint, it stops. You can then step into, step over, or step out of the breakpoint. This allows you to see what is happening in slow motion, so that you can trap errors that have been plaguing you. Figure 16.4 shows how the Debugger behaves when it hits a breakpoint—it turns the breakpoint icon into a small stop sign with a yellow arrow within. At this point, execution has stopped and is waiting for you to allow the program to continue after you perform your inspection on the program.

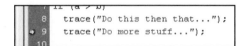

Figure 16.4

The yellow arrow indicates that the Debugger has hit a breakpoint.

The box on the upper-left of the Debugger panel neatly organizes all of the global variables and Movie Clips (in layers) so that you can easily select them and bring their properties up in the panels below.

The Stack pane helps you track what function the program is currently in—when a function calls another function, you will be able to see this in the pane. The reason this feature was put into this Debugger is because you can follow variable values as they are passed through functions while following your game's execution accurately.

Now that you are familiar with the options in the panel, experiment with GDA_PROG16.5.fla and make sure you know how to step through it. Set breakpoints and step into them, then inspect the variables and make sure everything is going the way you want it. This light introduction to the Debugger will benefit you many times—so don't forget you now have a new resource you can use.

> **TIP**
>
> If you pick up any good habit from this book, please make it the art of neat programming. I promise that if you make layers on your Timeline for your graphics, comment your code, and name and separate your scenes, you've already won 90% of the battle.

Summary

You have just put your guard up and will forever look out for common programming mistakes and pay extra attention to your code—even when speed-coding. You should now be aware and try to never forget your curly brackets, or how to reference your mouse position, or even how to reference functions from a Movie Clip. And if you do end up forgetting these things, you know how to find the Macromedia Flash Debugger. Have fun.

Questions & Answers

Q. How do I avoid holes in my code that can cause bugs to creep up later on?

A. You can carefully take care of all a possibilities on paper while testing every part of your program.

Q. Do I have to use the Debugger to find bugs?

A. No. You can use whatever you want—even your favorite command, `trace`. Do whatever it takes and most importantly, do whatever makes you feel comfortable.

CHAPTER 17

Matridia II: The Project

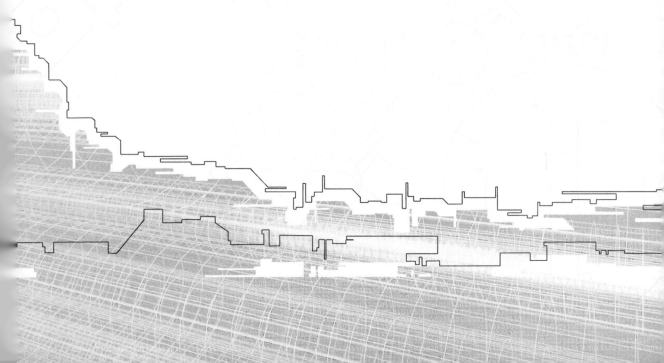

You've made it through the work, and now it's time to play—after all, what is all work and no play? In this final chapter, you will experience all that you learned in this book in one package; you will dissect a complete game called *Matridia II*. And during this dissection, you will revisit the following topics and experience how they interact together in a complete game:

- The idea
- The approach
- The setup
- The code
- The future

The Idea

You might be wondering why there is a sequel to a game that you've never heard of before. One of the first games I created for the DOS operating system was called *Matridia*. It was a top-view shooter with a cheesy story, but the real challenge was creating it from scratch. I took from the original idea for this chapter's project, and it led to the sequel.

Lucky for you, you won't have to write any video or sound card code because you already have drivers installed for those purposes. Instead, you will be dissecting the Flash version of *Matridia*, *Matridia II*; doing so will give you that extra push, allowing you to head off on your own into the world of Flash.

As for the game's ideas, I decided I wanted a scrolling star field. I wanted to imitate depth by using different levels of alpha. To improve the effect, I also planned on assigning different sizes and speeds to each star.

I wanted a lot of explosions, missiles and bombs, so I decided to create Movie Clips of all of these. They all have their linkage properties set up too.

In *Matridia II*, you can shoot the bad guys to gain some points when flying through space, but don't let them hit you, because you will lose power. If you make it through all the floating sine control enemies, you will make it to the Boss—this guy loves to spit tons of firepower, so watch out!

If he kills you, you will see a Game Over screen and you will be taken to the splash screen. If you win, you will be congratulated and then taken to the splash screen.

Check out Figure 17.1 for a shot of the splash screen.

Figure 17.1

The Matridia II splash screen

See Figure 17.2 for a look at the game in action.

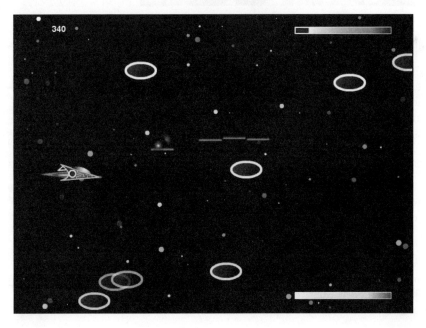

Figure 17.2

Matridia II in action

Figure 17.3 shows the player battling the Boss.

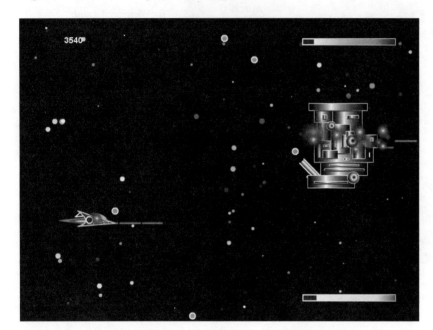

Figure 17.3

Save the universe!

The Approach

I decided to tackle this piece by piece. The first thing I decided to create was the star field. This star field needs to scroll to the left at all times while moving the stars with different speeds, sizes, and opacities. I accomplished this by using, from the library, one linked symbol that was nothing more than a white circle with no stroke. When I created the instances with `attachMovie`, I assigned new `_alpha`, scale and velocity values. To move all of them once they were created, all I did was loop through each instance within each frame while adding the velocities to their x values. This caused the simultaneous motion.

The player's ship was one of the easiest things to create. I first drew the ship with all the built-in animations I wanted (like the engine flame animation) and made it into a symbol that can be linked into the movie.

As far as motion goes, the player is restricted to moving the ship up and down with the respective keyboard arrows.

The player needed some missiles with which to attack, so I also created a symbol for the missiles. This symbol helped the program create a certain number of instances that can be active at one time. In other words, one variable controls how many missiles the player can shoot at once.

The enemies that I created for this game are very dumb. All they do is float to the left while moving in a sine motion. I created the enemies in much the same way I created the star particles—much of the difference is in the motion code.

After a few seconds of battle, I have the big Boss come out to kick some butt. The energy bar at the bottom of the screen is his, the one up top is the player's, and the battle is to the end. The Boss was created in much the same way the main character was created, except that the computer moves him up and down at all times. I wanted the Boss's bombs to launch at random. I also set them up the same way I did the star field and the main character's missiles—in such a way that only a certain number can be launched at once.

Once I had made decisions on all these factors and elements, I began setting up the source file.

The Setup

One of the first things I did to my FLA project was create scenes. This was my first step towards the organization of the game. See Figure 17.4 and check out all the scenes I created in this project.

Figure 17.4

Scenes set up for
Matridia II

The Splash scene is simply the screen that introduces the game and leads the player to either modify options or to play the game. The Game scene is where all the code is stored. There are three layers here that simply carry the code, a dynamic textbox, and an empty Movie Clip with more code—I'll go over this later.

The GameOver and Congrats scenes are very simple scenes that alert the player to some sort of resolution within the game; if he wins or loses, the program will play the respective scene.

If you take a look into the Library window, you will notice that there are many linked symbols. These symbols are used to create the instances you see within the game. All these symbols were drawn as Movie Clips and they therefore contain properties that can be managed from within ActionScript.

The Code

The code was written in a day's worth of work. It may look really complicated because there's lot of it, but focus on the smaller parts and how they unite as a whole. I approached the code writing just as I approached each idea in the game.

Once of the things you will notice when you look into the Game scene is that there is an empty Movie Clip in the middle of the screen. The purpose of the Movie Clip is to manage all the functions stored in the first frame with the onClipEvent handlers.

As you have already guessed, the game is run by two main onClipEvent functions. One of them initializes the game and the other helps animate all the frames. Go into the Game scene and click F9 after selecting the blank Movie Clip in the middle of the stage. See the following listing for the code within this clip. Without this code, nothing will happen and all the other functions will be ignored.

> **NOTE**
>
> You might be wondering why I didn't use the onEnterFrame and onLoad call-back functions on the main timeline instead of the onClipEvent functions from inside another Movie Clip. The reason is because when the onEnterFrame and onLoad functions are defined anywhere except the first frame of the first scene, they won't work. This is why I decided to use the similar functions built inside a regular Movie Clip.

```
// Game Development with ActionScript
// By Lewis Moronta (c) 2003

// Initialize the game
onClipEvent(load) {

    // Change this number to change
    // the amount of stars in the field
    _root.MAXSTARS = 100;

    // Change this value to adjust
    // the number of missles and bombs
    // that can be fired at once.
    _root.MAXMISSILES = 6;
    _root.MAXBOMBS = 10;

    // This variable will decide
    // if enemies or boss should attack
    _root.BOSSMODE = false;

    // This decides how many enemies
    // can exist at one time...
    _root.MAXENEMIES = 20;
```

```
    // Setup how many explosions
    // can explode at one time...
    _root.MAXEXPLOSIONS = 13;

    // Hide the cursor
    // Mouse.hide();

    // This plots stars all over the place
    _root.initializeStarField();

    // Create the ship
    _root.initializeShip();

    // Set up the enemies
    _root.initializeEnemies();

    // Set up the missiles
    _root.initializeMissiles();

    // Set up the explosions
    _root.initializeExplosions();

    // Setup the Boss
    _root.initializeBoss();

    // Now that everything is set up
    // let's keep track of the time...
    _root.startTime = getTimer();
}

// Let there be movement!
onClipEvent(enterFrame) {

    // Let's make sure the stars
    // move along and wrap around.
    _root.moveStarField();

    // Allow the player to move
    // the space ship
    _root.moveShip();

    // Attack...
    _root.moveEnemies();

    // Fire!!!
    _root.moveMissiles();
```

```
// Move the big daddy
_root.moveBoss();

if ((getTimer()-_root.startTime) > 30000) {
  _root.BOSSMODE = true;
}


  _root.scoreDisplay = _root.Player.score;
}
```

The onClipEvent(load) function performs a few interesting tasks. First, it initializes a few important variables called *constants* because they dictate a few important attributes to the game, and never change throughout the game.

```
// Change this number to change
// the amount of stars in the field
_root.MAXSTARS = 100;

// Change this value to adjust
// the number of missiles and bombs
// that can be fired at once.
_root.MAXMISSILES = 6;
_root.MAXBOMBS = 10;

// This variable will decide
// if enemies or BOSS should attack
_root.BOSSMODE = false;

// This decides how many enemies
// can exist at one time...
_root.MAXENEMIES = 20;

// Setup how many explosions
// can explode at one time...
_root.MAXEXPLOSIONS = 13;
```

You can change the value assigned to MAXSTARS to modify the number of stars in the universe, and you can also change the value assigned to MAXENEMIES to state how many enemies can be on the stage at one time. By changing the values assigned to MAXMISSILES and MAXBOMBS, you change the number of missiles that the player can fire at one time and how many bombs the Boss can spit out at once. MAXEXPLOSIONS is another variable that you can change to allow any number of explosions to explode on the stage at one time. BOSSMODE is a special game state variable that tells the game whether to produce more enemies or to allow the Boss to attack.

As instances had to be created based on these constants, I created initialization functions that do just that:

```
// This plots stars all over the place
_root.initializeStarField();

// Create the ship
_root.initializeShip();

// Set up the enemies
_root.initializeEnemies();

// Set up the missiles
_root.initializeMissiles();

// Set up the explosions
_root.initializeExplosions();

// Set up the Boss
_root.initializeBoss();

// Now that everything is setup
// let's keep track of the time...
_root.startTime = getTimer();
```

The `initializeStarField` function creates `MAXSTAR` number of stars. It assigns additional properties to each star, as you will soon see. The `initializeShip` creates an instance of the player's ship and restricts it to an axis. The `initializeEnemies`, `initializeExplosions` and `initializeMissiles` are very similar to one another—they all create a certain number of enemies, explosions, and missiles, and place them in their proper positions.

The `initializeBoss` function creates the Boss's instance hiding off the side of the screen until the game enters `BOSSMODE`.

The variable `startTime` records the time at which the game started. `getTimer` is used in this case, because it returns the number of milliseconds from the beginning of the movie. `startTime` will be used later to decide when `BOSSMODE` should be entered.

Now that I've finished initializing the game, I now enter the `onClipEvent(enterFrame)` function. This function starts off by moving the star field.

```
// Let's make sure the stars
// move along and wrap around.
_root.moveStarField();
```

After moving the star field, the player is moved by receiving input that the following function interprets:

```
// Allow the player to move
// the space ship
_root.moveShip();
```

I needed a function that could generate enemies at random, so I created the moveEnemies function which waits until an enemy dies to create a new one. It can also consider an enemy dead if it flies off the left side of the stage.

```
// Attack...
_root.moveEnemies();
```

In order to manage the firing missiles that are launched from the player's ship, I had to create a moveMissiles function.

```
// Fire!!!
_root.moveMissiles();
```

The last thing I wanted to move (and only if the game is in BOSSMODE) is the Boss. I wrote the following lines to do so:

```
// Move the big daddy
_root.moveBoss();
```

One of the things I needed was to shift the game into BOSSMODE after a certain period of time. I did this by checking to see whether 30 seconds had passed—if so, I then switched to BOSSMODE by setting the BOSSMODE variable to true.

All of the core functions that we've just gone over were written within the first frame of the Actions layer of the Game scene on the main timeline. I will discuss these functions in the following sections.

If you took a peek at how long the code on the main Timeline is, there probably is a defeated look on your face, but think of it this way: The code could have been much more complicated. I kept it simple because after all, this is a beginner book. You should be able to understand all of this code without a problem. Let's jump into the code.

The Star Field Functions

There are only two star field functions that create the effect of flying through the universe. The first function to explore is the initializeStarField function. Take a look at Figure 17.5 for a screen shot of some stars.

Figure 17.5

Take a look at the stars! All of them are instances of the same symbol.

```
function initializeStarField() {

   // Let's create MAXSTARS Movie Clips
   for (var i = 0; i < MAXSTARS; i++) {

           // Attach the movie from the linked symbol
           attachMovie("StarLayer", "star"+i, i);

           // Store the clip for easy reference
           var star = _root["star"+i];

           // Plot it at a random place
           star._x = Math.random()*640;
           star._y = Math.random()*480;

           // Adjust the alpha channel for
           // a depth effect...
           star._alpha = Math.random()*100;

           // Adjust the scale for a greater
           // depth effect...
           star._xscale = Math.random()*80;
           star._yscale = _root["star"+i]._xscale;

           // Make sure stars move from 2 to 22 pixels per frame
           star.velocity = -(Math.round(Math.random()*20)+2);
   }
}
```

The first thing you bump into within this code is a loop that is looping for MAXSTARS times. Every time the loop iterates, it attaches a new instance and stores the instance name in a simple variable for easy access.

```
           // Attach the movie from the linked symbol
           attachMovie("StarLayer", "star"+i, i);

           // Store the clip for easy reference
           var star = _root["star"+i];
```

After the instance has been created, the star instance is placed in a random position.

```
           // Plot it at a random place
           star._x = Math.random()*640;
           star._y = Math.random()*480;
```

As an added effect, I decided to modify the opacity of the white instance—this helps enhance the depth effect.

```
           star._alpha = Math.random()*100;
```

Just to vary things, I scaled each star at a random interval.

```
// Adjust the scale for a greater
// depth effect...
star._xscale = Math.random()*80;
star._yscale = _root["star"+i]._xscale;
```

And finally, to make the particles an even more interesting piece of the game, I decided to make them move at different speeds.

```
// Make sure stars move from 2 to 22 pixels per frame
star.velocity = -(Math.round(Math.random()*20)+2);
```

As each star is initialized with random values, this causes an interesting star field that becomes a big part of this game.

The next function we will check out will be moveStarField. This function starts off by looping through all of the stars available.

```
function moveStarField() {

  // Let's move ALL the star clips
  for (var i =  0; i < MAXSTARS; i++) {

      // Store for easy reference
      var star = _root["star"+i];

      // Move it along with its
      // own velocity property.
      star._x += star.velocity;

      // Wrap it around if
      // it's off the screen.
      if (star._x < -star._width)
        star._x = star._width+640;

  }
}
```

Within each loop, the symbol's velocity moves each star by adding its own velocity property that was initialized in the previous function.

The last thing the program does is check to see whether the star is off the left side of the screen. If it is, the star is forced to wrap around to the right side of the screen.

And this concludes the star field code. Remember that the stars are loaded and moved from within the empty Movie Clip I discussed in previous sections.

The Ship Functions

Now that you know exactly how the star field was created, you should have very little trouble figuring out how the player's ship was created and moved. Take a look at Figure 17.6 so you can see what the ship looks like.

Figure 17.6

Matridia II's main character

The following function is the `initializeShip` function that creates the player's instance:

```
function initializeShip() {

    // Let there be Player!
    attachMovie("Ship", "Player",8000);

    // Position him...
    Player._x = 100;
    Player._y = 240;

    // Y-Axis Velocity
    Player.yv = 0;

    // Y-Axis Acceleration
    Player.ya = 4;

    // Setup Score
    Player.score = 0;

    // Setup the Power Bar
    initPowerBar();
}
```

The ship was given a depth of 8000—it started out as an arbitrary number but as I wrote the game, the depth became a relative thing. What I mean by this is that I wanted the ship above its missiles, and explosives over the ship and missiles, and so on.

The ship was then given a position and velocity and acceleration properties. The score property was also assigned; this property will keep track of all the points the player earns.

You will also notice an `initPowerBar` function. This function creates and places an energy bar on the upper right of the screen. You'll see how it is adjusted later on.

The `moveShip` function is a bit long but simple. Let's jump right into it.

```
function moveShip() {
```

```
// Adjust the velocities
if (Key.isDown(Key.UP)) {
   Player.yv += -Player.ya;
}

if (Key.isDown(Key.DOWN)) {
   Player.yv += Player.ya;
}

var MAXVEL = 20;

// Cap Velocity
if (Player.yv > MAXVEL)
   Player.yv = MAXVEL;

if (Player.yv < -MAXVEL)
   Player.yv = -MAXVEL;

// Move the player
Player._y += Player.yv;

// Add Friction
if (Player.yv > 0)
   Player.yv--;
if (Player.yv < 0)
   Player.yv++;

// Set boundaries
if (Player._y < 0)
   Player._y = 0;

if (Player._y > (480-Player._height))
   Player._y = (480-Player._height);


/////////////////////////////////////////////
//// Check If Player Fired /////////////////////
/////////////////////////////////////////////
if (Key.isDown(Key.SPACE)) {

   for (var i = 0; i < MAXMISSILES; i++) {
      // Store for easy reference
      var missile = _root["missile"+i];

      // Find an inactive one and activate it.
      if (!missile.fired) {
```

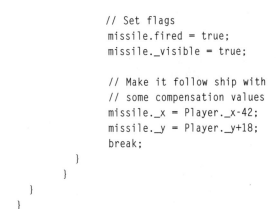

```
                    // Set flags
                    missile.fired = true;
                    missile._visible = true;

                    // Make it follow ship with
                    // some compensation values
                    missile._x = Player._x-42;
                    missile._y = Player._y+18;
                    break;
                }
            }
        }
    }
```

One of the first things the function is doing is detecting when the user presses either the Up or Down keys. These keys cause the acceleration to be added to its velocity value, which in turn causes the ship to move vertically either up or down.

I needed to cap this value so that the ship doesn't fly off the screen as a result of exaggerated values.

```
var MAXVEL = 20;

  // Cap Velocity
  if (Player.yv > MAXVEL)
    Player.yv = MAXVEL;

  if (Player.yv < -MAXVEL)
    Player.yv = -MAXVEL;
```

And finally, to make the ship move no matter what the velocity is, I made sure the velocity variable is added to its current y position.

```
  // Move the player
  Player._y += Player.yv;
```

There is very little friction in space, but I decided to break some rules and add a lot of it. All I did was subtract 1 from the velocity until the velocity is 0. It worked out perfectly.

```
// Add Friction
  if (Player.yv > 0)
    Player.yv--;
  if (Player.yv < 0)
    Player.yv++;
```

And of course, I had to add constraints to the ship. I didn't want the player to fly off the screen.

```
// Set boundaries
  if (Player._y < 0)
    Player._y = 0;
```

```
if (Player._y > (480-Player._height))
    Player._y = (480-Player._height);
```

The next section is quite a big section within this function. It's a segment of code that fires a missile if there is one available to fire. This is only done if the user presses or holds the spacebar.

```
if (Key.isDown(Key.SPACE)) {

    for (var i = 0; i < MAXMISSILES; i++) {
        // Store for easy reference
        var missile = _root["missile"+i];

        // Find an inactive one and activate it.
        if (!missile.fired) {
            // Set flags
            missile.fired = true;
            missile._visible = true;

            // Make it follow ship with
            // some compensation values
            missile._x = Player._x-42;
            missile._y = Player._y+18;
            break;
        }
    }
}
```

What I did here was loop through all the missiles looking for one that was not fired. If an unfired missile is found, I then set its status to "fired" and "visible." To finish the initialization, I set up a position that looks as if it is coming out of the ship's guns.

The moveMissiles function will detect the missiles whose status was switched to "fired" and move them.

The Missiles Functions

Let's jump right into the initializeMissiles function. Many of the familiar constructs are being used here.

```
function initializeMissiles() {
    for (var i = 0; i < MAXMISSILES; i++) {

        // Attach the movie from the linked symbol
        attachMovie("Ammo", "missile"+i, 7000+i);

        // Store the clip for easy reference
        var missile = _root["missile"+i];
```

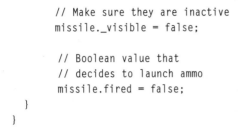

```
      // Make sure they are inactive
      missile._visible = false;

      // Boolean value that
      // decides to launch ammo
      missile.fired = false;
   }
}
```

The initialization function goes through the usual loop—it iterates for MAXMISSILES. It then attaches an instance and then stores this Movie Clip within a variable for easy access.

All of the missiles are made invisible until the player triggers them. They are also all set to "not fired" status. The "not fired" status will give them the passive state that we want.

The moveMissiles function needs to be dissected carefully for you to understand all the parts. Take a look at the function:

```
function moveMissiles() {
  for (var i = 0; i < MAXMISSILES; i++) {

    // Store for easy reference
    var missile = _root["missile"+i];

    if (missile.fired) {

      // Move it if it was fired
      missile._x += missile._width;

      // Kill it if it went off the screen
      if (missile._x > 640) {
        missile.fired = false;
        missile._visible = false;
      }

      for (var j = 0; j < MAXENEMIES; j++) {

        var badGuy = _root["Enemy"+j];

        if (missile.hitTest(badGuy)) {

          Player.score += 20;

          badGuy.alive = false;
          badGuy._visible = false;

                if (!BOSSMODE) {
```

```
                    badGuy._x = badGuy._width + 640;
                    badGuy._y = Math.round(Math.random()*480);

              } else {

                    // Draw it outside of the screen...
                    // this avoids any random explosions
                    // caused by the hitTest function
                    // testing to true...
                    badGuy._x = -badGuy._width;
                    badGuy._y = 0;
              }

              missile.fired = false;
              missile._visible = false;

            // Start and explosion
            for (var k = 0; k < MAXEXPLOSIONS; k++) {

             // Store the clip for easy reference
             var Explosion = _root["Explosion"+k];

             if (!Explosion.active) {
               Explosion._x = missile._x+(missile._width/2);
               Explosion._y = missile._y;
               Explosion.active = true;
               Explosion.gotoAndPlay(2);
               break;
             }
            } // End for k

       } // End if missile.hitTest
} // End for j

if (missile.hitTest(bigBoss)) {

    Player.score += 40;
    bossPower.Bar._xscale -= 0.5;

   // Game Over!
   if (bossPower.Bar._xscale < 0) {
     bossPower.Bar._xscale = 0;

     unLoadGame();
     gotoAndPlay("Congrats", 1);
   }
```

```
        // Start and explosion
        for (var j = 0; j < MAXEXPLOSIONS; j++) {

            // Store the clip for easy reference
            var Explosion = _root["Explosion"+j];

            if (!Explosion.active) {

                Explosion._x = missile._x+(missile._width/2);
                Explosion._y = missile._y;
                Explosion.active = true;
                Explosion.gotoAndPlay(2);
                break;
            }
        } // End for j
    }


    } // End if missile.fired
  } // End for i
} // End moveMissiles
```

Beyond the usual, the program checks to see whether the missile is fired before acting upon it. If it has been fired, the program then moves the missile along. If it has gone off the screen, the missile will be reset.

```
if (missile.fired) {

    // Move it if it was fired
    missile._x += missile._width;

    // Kill it if it went off the screen
    if (missile._x > 640) {
        missile.fired = false;
        missile._visible = false;
    }
}
```

The program then loops through all the enemies to see which ones have been hit. It then adds to the player score if there was a collision and kills the enemies that have been hit.

```
for (var j = 0; j < MAXENEMIES; j++) {

    var badGuy = _root["Enemy"+j];

    if (missile.hitTest(badGuy)) {

        Player.score += 20;
```

```
        badGuy.alive = false;
        badGuy._visible = false;
```

To clean up a little, the missile is also removed temporarily:

```
        missile.fired = false;
        missile._visible = false;
```

To add to the effect, I then looked for an inactive explosion to use, then set it off where the point of contact occurred.

```
    for (var j = 0; j < MAXEXPLOSIONS; j++) {

        // Store the clip for easy reference
        var Explosion = _root["Explosion"+j];

        if (!Explosion.active) {

            Explosion._x = missile._x+(missile._width/2);
            Explosion._y = missile._y;
            Explosion.active = true;
            Explosion.gotoAndPlay(2);
            break;
        }
    } // End for j
```

This code can be easily implemented in any game you create, so make sure you understand it.

The Enemy Functions

As I said before, the enemies are not programmed much differently from the rest of the game. They are initialized then moved. See Figure 17.7 for a screen shot of a bunch of the enemies in action.

Figure 17.7

Enemies in action

Examine the following initialization function:

```
function initializeEnemies() {
    for (var i = 0; i < MAXENEMIES; i++) {

        attachMovie("sineEnemy", "Enemy"+i, 9000+i);

        var badGuy = _root["Enemy"+i];
```

```
        badGuy._x = badGuy._width + 640;
        badGuy._y = Math.round(Math.random()*440+40);

        badGuy.xv = -Math.round(Math.random()*10+10);
        badGuy.yv = 0;

        badGuy.alive = false;
        badGuy._visible = false;

        badGuy.degrees = Math.round(Math.random()*360);
        badGuy.radians = Math.PI/180*badGuy.degrees;

        badGuy._alpha = Math.round(Math.random()*60+40);
    }
}
```

Each enemy was placed randomly on the stage. They were also given random velocities. To start off, they were made invisible and their alive status property was set to false.

In order to have them follow their own sine path on the y axis, I added two new properties, degrees and radians.

To make things more interesting, I also played with the enemies' alpha channels. They will be transparent from a level of 40 to 100 percent.

```
function moveEnemies() {

    // If the Boss steps on stage,
    // make sure no new enemies are spawned.
    if (!BOSSMODE) {
        for (var i = 0; i < MAXENEMIES; i++) {

            var badGuy = _root["Enemy"+i];

            // Spit out another enemy only if random()
            // returns 1 (or true) and the badGuy is not alive...
            if (!badGuy.alive && (Math.round(Math.random()*30) == 3)) {
                badGuy.alive = true;
                badGuy._visible = true;
                break;
            }

        }
    }

    for (var i = 0; i < MAXENEMIES; i++) {

        var badGuy = _root["Enemy"+i];
```

```
// If alive, move the enemy along...
if (badGuy.alive) {

  badGuy._x += badGuy.xv;

  if (badGuy.degrees++ > 360)
    badGuy.degrees = 0;

  badGuy.radians = Math.PI/180 * badGuy.degrees;
  badGuy.yv = Math.round(Math.sin(badGuy.radians)*2);
  badGuy._y += badGuy.yv;


  // If an enemy hits the Player,
  // dock the Player 2 percent...
  if (badGuy.hitTest(Player)) {
      Power.Bar._xscale -= 2;

        // Game Over!
        if (Power.Bar._xscale < 0) {
          Power.Bar._xscale = 0;

          unLoadGame();
          gotoAndPlay("GameOver", 1);
      }

    // Start and explosion
    for (var j = 0; j < MAXEXPLOSIONS; j++) {

      // Store the clip for easy reference
      var Explosion = _root["Explosion"+j];

      if (!Explosion.active) {
          Explosion._x = Player._x;
          Explosion._y = Player._y+12;
          Explosion.active = true;
          Explosion.gotoAndPlay(2);
          break;
      }
    }
  }

  // If off the left side, reset.
  if (badGuy._x < -badGuy._width) {
    badGuy.alive = false;
    badGuy._visible = false;
```

```
            badGuy._x = badGuy._width + 640;
            badGuy._y = Math.round(Math.random()*440+40);
        }
    }
  }
}
```

If the game is not in BOSSMODE, the game will keep generating enemies until it is.

```
if (!BOSSMODE) {
    for (var i = 0; i < MAXENEMIES; i++) {

        var badGuy = _root["Enemy"+i];

        // Spit out another enemy only if random()
        // returns 1 (or true) and the badGuy is not alive...
        if (!badGuy.alive && (Math.round(Math.random()*30) == 3)) {
          badGuy.alive = true;
          badGuy._visible = true;
          break;
        }

    }
  }
```

Once the function is finished spawning new enemies, it finds the enemies that are alive and moves them.

```
for (var i = 0; i < MAXENEMIES; i++) {

    var badGuy = _root["Enemy"+i];

    // If alive, move the enemy along...
    if (badGuy.alive) {

        badGuy._x += badGuy.xv;
```

Depending on the enemy's degrees value, the enemy will move along a sine curve—this makes each enemy look as if it is a lower life form.

If by chance the bad guy hits the player, the code will decrease the scale of the player's power bar. If the scale is below zero, the game will remove all of the Movie Clips and will play the Game Over screen.

```
        if (badGuy.hitTest(Player)) {
            Power.Bar._xscale -= 2;

            // Game Over!
            if (Power.Bar._xscale < 0) {
              Power.Bar._xscale = 0;
```

```
        unLoadGame();
        gotoAndPlay("GameOver", 1);
    }
```

What the code then does is set off an explosion. This is, of course, is relative to where the impact occurred.

```
    for (var j = 0; j < MAXEXPLOSIONS; j++) {

        // Store the clip for easy reference
        var Explosion = _root["Explosion"+j];

        if (!Explosion.active) {
            Explosion._x = Player._x;
            Explosion._y = Player._y+12;
            Explosion.active = true;
            Explosion.gotoAndPlay(2);
            break;
        }
    }
```

The final piece of code in this function tests to see if the enemy is off the left side of the screen—if it is, it is killed.

```
    if (badGuy._x < -badGuy._width) {
      badGuy.alive = false;
      badGuy._visible = false;
      badGuy._x = badGuy._width + 640;
      badGuy._y = Math.round(Math.random()*440+40);
    }
```

The Explosions Function

The explosions themselves required more setup than the other objects because there is an animation to the explosion Movie Clip. When first triggered, this animation is stopped and blank on the first frame. When played, the animation would have to start playing from Frame 2 and the script on the last frame of the clip would make it jump and pause it again in Frame 1; this makes the explosion symbol reset ready for yet another animation.

As you understand the structure of the Movie Clip, just check out the code that I wrote for it. The function you'll see here is initializeExplosions. This is the only function that is needed to make any other part of the program ready to cause some explosions.

```
function initializeExplosions() {

  for (var i = 0; i < MAXEXPLOSIONS; i++) {
```

```
        // Attach the movie from the linked symbol
        attachMovie("Explosion", "Explosion"+i, 11000+i);

        // Store the clip for easy reference
        var Explosion = _root["Explosion"+i];

        Explosion.active = false;
    }
}
```

As you can see, this function is nothing different from what we have been doing before. The only thing that needs to be explained is that I assigned a new property, called active, to each new clip. This helps the program track which explosion is dormant so I can wake it up when I need to.

The Boss Functions

The big Boss functions complete the game and can easily be rewritten for a different boss AI. In order to have the Boss load up, I had to write up an initialization function called initializeBoss. You probably would have guessed that already.

```
function initializeBoss() {

    attachMovie("Boss", "bigBoss", 10000);

    bigBoss._x = 640+bigBoss._width;
    bigBoss._y = 240-(bigBoss._height/2);

    bigBoss.yv = 10;

    initBossPowerBar();
    initializeBombs();
}
```

As you can see, the Boss function sets up its own bombs and power bar. This leaves no worries for the rest of the game. I gave the Boss a vertical velocity and also placed him off the screen so that he can scroll in with the following code—the moveBoss code:

```
function moveBoss() {

    if (BOSSMODE) {
        bigBoss._x += -5;

        if (bigBoss._x < 430)
            bigBoss._x = 430;

        bigBoss._y += bigBoss.yv;
```

```
    if (bigBoss._y < 0)
      bigBoss.yv = -bigBoss.yv;
    if (bigBoss._y > (480-bigBoss._height))
      bigBoss.yv = -bigBoss.yv;

    moveBombs();
  }
}
```

If the game enters BOSSMODE, the Boss will start scrolling left until it hits a certain point on the screen. Thereafter, the Boss will start moving up and down according to this code. At the same time, the moveBombs code is called. You'll see what that does shortly.

The Bomb Functions

The bomb functions are the last functions I needed for this to be a complete game. Just like every other part of this game, I initialized these bombs with the following code:

```
function initializeBombs() {
  for (var i = 0; i < MAXBOMBS; i++) {
      attachMovie("Bomb", "Bomb"+i, 9500+i);

      var bossBomb = _root["Bomb"+i];

      bossBomb._x = bigBoss._x+2;
      bossBomb._y = bigBoss._y+96;
      bossBomb.fired = false;

      bossBomb.force = 2;
  }
}
```

One thing that you noticed here is that the bombs were placed all relative to the bigBoss. They start out as all dormant, and I also added a mysterious gravity-like force property to them. I thought the force made their motion interesting.

The moveBombs function became a little more exciting with all the action written within it. Check it out:

```
function moveBombs() {
  for (var i = 0; i < MAXBOMBS; i++) {

      var bossBomb = _root["Bomb"+i];

      // Decide when to fire...
      if (Math.round(Math.random()*30) == 3) {
        if (!bossBomb.fired) {
            bossBomb.fired = true;
```

```
            bossBomb._x = bigBoss._x+2;
            bossBomb._y = bigBoss._y+96;

            bossBomb.xv = -Math.round(Math.random()*10+10);
            bossBomb.yv = -20;
        }
    }

    if (bossBomb.fired) {
      bossBomb._x += bossBomb.xv;
      bossBomb._y += bossBomb.yv;

      bossBomb.yv += bossBomb.force;
    }

if (bossBomb._x < -bossBomb._width) {
  bossBomb.fired = false;
}

if (bossBomb._y > 480) {
  bossBomb.fired = false;
}

if (bossBomb.hitTest(Player)) {
  Power.Bar._xscale -= 2;

  // Game Over!
if (Power.Bar._xscale < 0) {
    Power.Bar._xscale = 0;

    unLoadGame();
    gotoAndPlay("GameOver", 1);
}

  // Start and explosion
  for (var j = 0; j < MAXEXPLOSIONS; j++) {

    // Store the clip for easy reference
    var Explosion = _root["Explosion"+j];

    if (!Explosion.active) {
      Explosion._x = Player._x;
      Explosion._y = Player._y+12;
      Explosion.active = true;
      Explosion.gotoAndPlay(2);
      break;
```

```
            }
          }
        }
      }
    }
```

After entering the loop and going through all the bombs available in the game, you'll see the code that decides when to fire another bomb.

```
if (Math.round(Math.random()*30) == 3) {
  if (!bossBomb.fired) {
      bossBomb.fired = true;

      bossBomb._x = bigBoss._x+2;
      bossBomb._y = bigBoss._y+96;

      bossBomb.xv = -Math.round(Math.random()*10+10);
      bossBomb.yv = -20;
  }
}
```

The code will only fire a new bomb if a random number from the range of 0 to 30 is 3. The chances of that are 1 out of 30. This causes the bombs to vary their behavior a bit. So if the bomb is not fired, it will position itself by the Boss's cannon and get itself ready to fire.

If the bomb has fired, the following block causes it to move in a projectile way.

```
if (bossBomb.fired) {
  bossBomb._x += bossBomb.xv;
  bossBomb._y += bossBomb.yv;

  bossBomb.yv += bossBomb.force;
}
```

If by chance the bomb doesn't hit the player and it goes off the side or bottom of the screen, the following code was written to disable it and reserve it for the next throw:

```
if (bossBomb._x < -bossBomb._width) {
  bossBomb.fired = false;
}

if (bossBomb._y > 480) {
  bossBomb.fired = false;
}
```

If the bomb hits the player, 2 percent is subtracted from the player's power bar.

```
if (bossBomb.hitTest(Player)) {
  Power.Bar._xscale -= 2;
```

```
    // Game Over!
    if (Power.Bar._xscale < 0) {
      Power.Bar._xscale = 0;

      unLoadGame();
      gotoAndPlay("GameOver", 1);
    }
```

And finally, if a hit was detected, the following code starts up some fire:

```
for (var j = 0; j < MAXEXPLOSIONS; j++) {

    // Store the clip for easy reference
    var Explosion = _root["Explosion"+j];

    if (!Explosion.active) {
      Explosion._x = Player._x;
      Explosion._y = Player._y+12;
      Explosion.active = true;
      Explosion.gotoAndPlay(2);
      break;
    }
}
```

The Future

If you dedicate any time to upgrading this game, you will bump into the bugs and frustra-
tions that are part of every programmer's life. What you can do is plan carefully before
adding anything to this program. Don't forget to use the Debugger, your friendly trace
command, and any other strategic algorithms that can get you out of a programmer's pit.

If you follow the same style *Matridia II* was written in, you should have no problems adding
more enemies, power-ups, power-shields, and explosives. Just remember one thing: the limitations of your viewer's computer. Not everybody has a power computer. Flash MX 2004 has
been improved and is at least 25% more speed-efficient than Flash MX, but the user's computer will forever affect your code.

Now that you have dissected a complete game, the next step would be to create your own.

Summary

You broke apart a complete game in this chapter. All the principles that you have learned
throughout the book were combined here in one chapter. You went through the idea,
setup, approach, and code that went into creating *Matridia II*. You learned how to install a
nice star field into a working game. You also learned how to create explosives, bombs, enemies, and even bosses that work together to make a complete game. Enjoy!

Questions & Answers

Q. How does the flame stay animated off the ship's back?

A. The animated flame is nothing more than a Movie Clip that is tweened with the same frame in the beginning and end of its Timeline. This causes the smooth transition.

Q. The enemies were coming out at random—is there a way I can write something more stable?

A. Yes. You can store a pattern in an array and have the game check it at a certain interval. This will cause the enemies to come out in a predictable manner.

Exercises

1. Add an option screen to this game that allows the user to modify the constants that were set in the initialization part of the game. HINT: Make them global.

2. Make the game have at least three levels and create three different bosses for each stage.

3. Give the player three lives—in other words, three chances to finish the game. Every time he loses a life, have the bar go back to 100%.

4. Create a nice animated ending that will only play if the player can get through the game without dying.

APPENDIX A

Keyboard Keys and Key Code Values

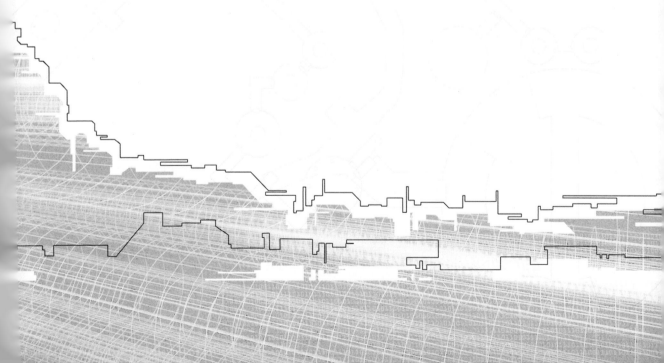

The following tables list all of the keys on a standard keyboard and the corresponding ASCII key code. To look up your ASCII code, just look for your character or key on the left side of the table and match it with its code on the right side.

This table should be used in conjunction with Chapter 8, along with the isDown method in ActionScript.

Table A.1 Letters A to Z and Standard Numbers 0 to 9

Letter or number key	Key code
A	65
B	66
C	67
D	68
E	69
F	70
G	71
H	72
I	73
J	74
K	75
L	76
M	77
N	78
O	79

Letter or number key	Key code
P	80
Q	81
R	82
S	83
T	84
U	85
V	86
W	87
X	88
Y	89
Z	90
0	48
1	49
2	50
3	51
4	52
5	53
6	54
7	55
8	56
9	57

Table A.2 Keys on the Numeric Keypad

Numeric keypad key	Key code
Numpad 0	96
Numpad 1	97
Numpad 2	98
Numpad 3	99
Numpad 4	100
Numpad 5	101
Numpad 6	102
Numpad 7	103
Numpad 8	104
Numpad 9	105
Multiply	106
Add	107
Enter	108
Subtract	109
Decimal	110
Divide	111

Table A.3 Function Keys

Function key	Key code
F1	112
F2	113
F3	114
F4	115
F5	116
F6	117
F7	118
F8	119
F9	120
F10	121
F11	122
F12	123
F13	124
F14	125
F15	126

Table A.4 Other Keys

Key	Key code
Backspace	8
Tab	9
Clear	12
Enter	13
Shift	16
Control	17
Alt	18
Caps Lock	20
Esc	27
Spacebar	32
Page Up	33
Page Down	34
End	35
Home	36
Left Arrow	37
Up Arrow	38
Right Arrow	39
Down Arrow	40
Insert	45
Delete	46
Help	47
Num Lock	144
;:	186

Key	Key code
= +	187
- _	189
/ ?	191
\Q ~	192
[{	219
\ |	220
] }	221
" '	222

Index

Gamedev.net

The most comprehensive game development resource

- The latest news in game development
- The most active forums and chatrooms anywhere, with insights and tips from experienced game developers
- Links to thousands of additional game development resources
- Thorough book and product reviews
- Over 1000 game development articles!
  Game design
  Graphics
  DirectX
  OpenGL
  AI
  Art
  Music
  Physics
  Source Code
  Sound
  Assembly
  And More!

 **Gamedev.net**

License Agreement/Notice of Limited Warranty

By opening the sealed disc container in this book, you agree to the following terms and conditions. If, upon reading the following license agreement and notice of limited warranty, you cannot agree to the terms and conditions set forth, return the unused book with unopened disc to the place where you purchased it for a refund.

License:
The enclosed software is copyrighted by the copyright holder(s) indicated on the software disc. You are licensed to copy the software onto a single computer for use by a single user and to a backup disc. You may not reproduce, make copies, or distribute copies or rent or lease the software in whole or in part, except with written permission of the copyright holder(s). You may transfer the enclosed disc only together with this license, and only if you destroy all other copies of the software and the transferee agrees to the terms of the license. You may not decompile, reverse assemble, or reverse engineer the software.

Notice of Limited Warranty:
The enclosed disc is warranted by Premier Press, Inc. to be free of physical defects in materials and workmanship for a period of sixty (60) days from end user's purchase of the book/disc combination. During the sixty-day term of the limited warranty, Premier Press will provide a replacement disc upon the return of a defective disc.

Limited Liability:
THE SOLE REMEDY FOR BREACH OF THIS LIMITED WARRANTY SHALL CONSIST ENTIRELY OF REPLACEMENT OF THE DEFECTIVE DISC. IN NO EVENT SHALL PREMIER PRESS OR THE AUTHORS BE LIABLE FOR ANY OTHER DAMAGES, INCLUDING LOSS OR CORRUPTION OF DATA, CHANGES IN THE FUNCTIONAL CHARACTERISTICS OF THE HARDWARE OR OPERATING SYSTEM, DELETERIOUS INTERACTION WITH OTHER SOFTWARE, OR ANY OTHER SPECIAL, INCIDENTAL, OR CONSEQUENTIAL DAMAGES THAT MAY ARISE, EVEN IF PREMIER AND/OR THE AUTHORS HAVE PREVIOUSLY BEEN NOTIFIED THAT THE POSSIBILITY OF SUCH DAMAGES EXISTS.

Disclaimer of Warranties:
PREMIER AND THE AUTHORS SPECIFICALLY DISCLAIM ANY AND ALL OTHER WARRANTIES, EITHER EXPRESS OR IMPLIED, INCLUDING WARRANTIES OF MERCHANTABILITY, SUITABILITY TO A PARTICULAR TASK OR PURPOSE, OR FREEDOM FROM ERRORS. SOME STATES DO NOT ALLOW FOR EXCLUSION OF IMPLIED WARRANTIES OR LIMITATION OF INCIDENTAL OR CONSEQUENTIAL DAMAGES, SO THESE LIMITATIONS MIGHT NOT APPLY TO YOU.

Other:
This Agreement is governed by the laws of the State of Indiana without regard to choice of law principles. The United Convention of Contracts for the International Sale of Goods is specifically disclaimed. This Agreement constitutes the entire agreement between you and Premier Press regarding use of the software.